THE REVELS PLAYS

Former general editors
Clifford Leech, F. David Hoeniger
and E. A. J. Honigmann

General editors
David Bevington, Richard Dutton, J. R. Mulryne
and Eugene M. Waith

THOMAS OF WOODSTOCK

THE REVELS PLAYS

THE REVELS PLAYS

THOMAS OF WOODSTOCK

or RICHARD THE SECOND, PART ONE

ANON.

edited by
Peter Corbin and Douglas Sedge

MANCHESTER
UNIVERSITY PRESS

Manchester and New York

Distributed exclusively in the USA by Palgrave

Introduction, critical apparatus, etc. copyright
© Peter Corbin and Douglas Sedge 2002

The right of Peter Corbin and Douglas Sedge to be identified as the editors
of this work has been asserted by them in accordance with the Copyright,
Designs and Patents Act 1988.

Published by Manchester University Press
Oxford Road, Manchester M13 9NR, UK
and Room 400, 175 Fifth Avenue, New York, NY 10010, USA
www.manchesteruniversitypress.co.uk

Distributed exclusively in the USA by
Palgrave, 175 Fifth Avenue, New York NY 10010, USA

Distributed exclusively in Canada by
UBC Press, University of British Columbia, 2029 West Mall,
Vancouver, BC, Canada V6T 1Z2

British Library Cataloguing-in-Publication Data
A catalogue record for this book is available from the British Library

Library of Congress Cataloging-in-Publication Data
A catalog record for this book is available from the Library of Congress

ISBN 13: 978 0 7190 8067 8

First published in hardback 2002 by Manchester University Press
This paperback edition first published 2009

Printed by Lightning Source

Contents

General Editors' Preface

Clifford Leech conceived of the Revels Plays as a series in the mid-1950s, modelling the project on the New Arden Shakespeare. The aim, as he wrote in 1958, was 'to apply to Shakespeare's predecessors, contemporaries and successors the methods that are now used in Shakespeare's editing'. The plays chosen were to include well-known works from the early Tudor period to about 1700, as well as others less familiar but of literary and theatrical merit: 'the plays included', Leech wrote, 'should be such as to deserve and indeed demand performance'. We owe it to Clifford Leech that the idea became reality. He set the high standards of the series, ensuring that editors of individual volumes produced work of lasting merit, equally useful for teachers and students, theatre directors and actors. Clifford Leech remained General Editor until 1971, and was succeeded by F. David Hoeniger, who retired in 1985.

Since 1985 the Revels Plays have been under the direction of four General Editors: initially David Bevington, E. A. J. Honigmann, J. R. Mulryne and E. M. Waith. E. A. J. Honigmann retired in 2000 and was succeeded by Richard Dutton. Published originally by Methuen, the series is now published by Manchester University Press, embodying essentially the same format, scholarly character and high editorial standards of the series as first conceived. The series concentrates on plays from the period 1558–1642, and includes a small number of non-dramatic works of interest to students of drama. Some slight changes have been made: for example, in editions from 1978, notes to the introduction are placed together at the end, not at the foot of the page. Collation and commentary notes continue, however, to appear on the relevant pages.

The text of each Revels play, in accordance with established practice in the series, is edited afresh from the original text of best authority (in a few instances, texts), but spelling and punctuation are modernised and speech headings are silently made consistent. Elisions in the original are also silently regularised, except where metre would be affected by the change; since 1968 the '-ed' form is used for non-syllabic terminations in past tenses and past participles ('-'d' earlier), and '-èd' for syllabic ('-ed' earlier). The editor emends, as distinct from modernises, the original only in instances where error is patent, or at least very probable, and correction persuasive. Act divisions are given only if they appear in the original or if the structure of the play clearly points to them. Those act and scene divisions not in the original are provided in small type. Square brackets are also used for any other additions to or changes in the stage directions of the original.

Revels Plays do not provide a variorum collation, but only those variants which require the critical attention of serious textual students. All departures of substance from 'copy-text' are listed, including any relineation and those changes in punctuation which involve to any degree a decision between alternative interpretations; but not such accidentals as turned letters, nor necessary additions to stage directions whose editorial nature is already made clear by the use of brackets. Press corrections in the 'copy-text' are likewise collated. Of later emendations of the text, only those are given which as alternative readings still deserve attention.

One of the hallmarks of the Revels Plays is the thoroughness of their annotations. Besides explaining the meaning of difficult words and passages, the editor provides comments on customs or usage, text or stage-business—indeed, on anything judged pertinent and helpful. Each volume contains an Index to the Commentary, in which particular attention is drawn to meanings for words not listed in *OED*, and (starting in 1996) an indexing of proper names and topics in the Introduction and Commentary.

The introduction to a Revels play assesses the authority of the 'copy-text' on which it is based, and discusses the editorial methods employed in dealing with it; the editor also considers the play's date and (where relevant) sources, together with its place in the work of the author and in the theatre of its time. Stage history is offered, and in the case of a play by an author not previously represented in the series a brief biography is given.

It is our hope that plays edited in this fashion will promote further scholarly and theatrical investigation of one of the richest periods in theatrical history.

DAVID BEVINGTON
RICHARD DUTTON
J. R. MULRYNE
E. M. WAITH

Preface

In editing this text we have taken due account of the perceptions of previous editors, but we have not been able to confirm all of their decisions—sometimes they have seen readings and inks which we have been unable to endorse. In facing such difficulties we must acknowledge the exemplary work of Wilhelmina Frijlinck, whose Malone Society edition remains essential for any edition of this play. A. P. Rossiter's 1946 edition convincingly argued for its quality and significance and, more recently, George Parfitt and Simon Shepherd have maintained scholarly interest in the play. Any edition of the play is indebted to these previous editors' work.

Further debts are owed to the staff of the British Library, for enabling us to make joint inspection of the manuscript, and to the staff of Exeter University Library for their willingness to assist. Thanks are also due to Leslie Thomson of the University of Toronto who provided us with information on stage directions in advance of the publication of *A Dictionary of Stage Directions* which she co-authored with Alan C. Dessen. We are especially grateful to Steve Sims and The Shakespeare Club of Crediton for their interest and enthusiasm for the play. A final debt is owed to Professor Ronnie Mulryne for his advice and discrimination and to John Banks for his invaluable help in preparing the typescript for publication.

A recent paper by Macd. P. Jackson, which argues that the text belongs to the early seventeenth century, unfortunately came too late for consideration in the preparation of this edition.

PETER CORBIN

DOUGLAS SEDGE

Abbreviations and References

All references to Shakespeare's plays are to *The Complete Works* (Oxford, 1988), eds Stanley Wells and Gary Taylor. *OED* and Onions are the basis of most glossarial notes; Partridge, Colman, Rubinstein and Williams have been consulted for bawdy meanings and word-play; Sugden for topographical references; Linthicum for costume. Tilley's reference number only is given in the case of most of the proverbial expressions in the play, though Dent has also been consulted.

EDITIONS

In the commentary and textual collation the following abbreviations have been used for the various editions and textual commentators:

Armstrong   *Woodstock* in *Elizabethan History Plays*, ed. W. A. Armstrong (Oxford, 1965).

Bullough   *Thomas of Woodstock* in *Narrative and Dramatic Sources of Shakespeare*, vol. III, ed. G. Bullough (London, 1960), extracts.

Carpenter   'Notes on the Anonymous *Richard II*', ed. W. I. Carpenter, *Journal of Germanic Philology* III (1900).

Everitt   *Woodstock* in *Six Early Plays Related to the Crown*, eds E. B. Everitt and R. L. Armstrong (Copenhagen, 1965).

Frijlinck   *The First Part of the Reign of King Richard II, or Thomas of Woodstock*, ed. W. P. Frijlinck (The Malone Society: Oxford, 1929).

Halliwell   *A Tragedy of King Richard the Second*, ed. J. O. Halliwell-Phillips (London, 1870).

Keller   '*Richard II. Erster Teil*', ed. W. Keller, *Shakespeare Jahrbuch* XXXV (1899).

MS   MS Egerton 1994 fols 161–185b (no title).

Parfitt   *Thomas of Woodstock*, eds George Parfitt and Simon Shepherd (Nottingham, 1977).

Rossiter   *Woodstock: a Moral History*, ed. A. P. Rossiter (London, 1946).

WORKS BY SHAKESPEARE

AYL   *As You Like It*

Contention   *The First Part of the Contention of the Two Famous Houses of York and Lancaster* (*2 Henry 6*)

Ham.   *Hamlet*

1H4   *The History of Henry the Fourth*

H5   *The Life of Henry the Fifth*

H8   *King Henry VIII* (*All Is True*)

JC   *Julius Caesar*

Lear (*History*)   *The History of King Lear*

Lear (*Tragedy*)   *The Tragedy of King Lear*
LLL   *Love's Labour's Lost*
Meas.   *Measure for Measure*
MerV.   *The Comical History of the Merchant of Venice*
R2   *The Tragedy of King Richard II*
R3   *The Tragedy of King Richard the Third*
R&J   *The Most Excellent and Lamentable Tragedy of Romeo and Juliet*
Temp.   *The Tempest*

PERIODICALS

EETS   *The Early English Text Society*
ELN   *English Language Notes*
MLR   *The Modern Language Review*
N&Q   *Notes and Queries*
PLMA   *Publications of the Modern Languge Association of America*
RenD   *Renaissance Drama*
ShS   *Shakespeare Survey*
SP   *Studies in Philology*
SQ   *Shakespeare Quarterly*

OTHER REFERENCES

Abbott   E. A. Abbott, *A Shakespearean Grammar* (London, 1888).
Barry   Lording Barry, *Ram Alley*, eds Peter Corbin and Douglas Sedge (Nottingham Drama Texts: Nottingham, 1981).
Bentley   G. E. Bentley, *The Jacobean and Caroline Stage*, 7 vols (Oxford, 1941–68).
Boorde   Andrew Boorde, *A Compendyous Regyment or a Dyetary of Helth*, ed. F. J. Furnivall, in *Andrew Boorde's Introduction and Dyetary* (*EETS*: London, 1870).
Chamberlain   John Chamberlain, *The Letters of John Chamberlain*, ed. N. E. McClure, 2 vols (Philadelphia, 1939).
Chambers, *ES*   E. K. Chambers, *The Elizabethan Stage*, 4 vols (Oxford, 1923).
Chambers, *MS*   E. K. Chambers, *The Medieval Stage*, 2 vols (Oxford, 1903).
Chambers, *WS*   E. K. Chambers, *William Shakespeare*, 2 vols (Oxford, 1930).
Chapman, *Bussy*   George Chapman, *Bussy D'Ambois*, ed. Nicholas Brooke (The Revels Plays: London, 1964).
Clare   Janet Clare, '*Art Made Tongue-tied by Authority*': *Elizabethan and Jacobean Dramatic Censorship* (The Revels Plays Companion Library: Manchester, 1990, 2nd edition, 1999).
Clemen   Wolfgang Clemen, *English Tragedy before Shakespeare* (London, 1961, repr. 1967).
Colman   E. A. M. Colman, *The Dramatic Use of Bawdy in Shakespeare* (London, 1974).
Curye on Inglysch   Anon., *Curye on Inglysch*, eds Constance B. Hieatt and Sharon Butler (*EETS*: Oxford, 1985).

Dekker, *Witch*   Thomas Dekker, John Ford and Samuel Rowley, etc., *The Witch of Edmonton*, eds Peter Corbin and Douglas Sedge in *Three Jacobean Witchcraft Plays* (The Revels Plays Companion Library: Manchester, 1986).

Dent   R. W. Dent, *Shakespeare's Proverbial Language: An Index* (Berkeley, 1981).

Dessen and Thomson   Alan C. Dessen and Leslie Thomson, *A Dictionary of Stage Directions in English Drama 1580–1642* (Cambridge, 1999).

DNB   *The Concise Dictionary of National Biography*, 3 vols (Oxford, 1992).

Dutton   Richard Dutton, *Mastering the Revels: The Regulation and Censorship of English Renaissance Drama* (London, 1991).

Edelman   Charles Edelman, *Brawl Ridiculous: Swordfighting in Shakespeare's Plays* (The Revels Plays Companion Library: Manchester, 1992).

Edward III   Anon., *Edward III*, ed. William A. Armstrong, in *Elizabethan History Plays* (London, 1965).

Everyman   Anon., *Everyman*, in *Everyman and Medieval Miracle Plays*, ed. A. C. Cawley (Everyman's Library: London, 1956).

Famous Victories   Anon., *The Famous Victories of Henry V*, eds Peter Corbin and Douglas Sedge, in *The Oldcastle Controversy* (The Revels Plays Companion Library: Manchester, 1991).

Grafton   Richard Grafton, *A Chronicle at Large, to the First Yere of Q. Elizabeth* (1568/9).

Hall   Edward Hall, *The Union of the two Noble and Illustre Famelies of Lancastre & Yorke . . .* (1550).

Hattaway   Michael Hattaway, *Elizabethan Popular Theatre* (London, 1982).

Hayward   John Hayward, *The First and Second Parts of John Hayward's The Life and Raigne of King Henry IIII*, ed. John J. Manning, Camden Fourth Series, vol. 41 (London, 1991).

Heinemann   Margot Heinemann, 'Political Drama', *The Cambridge Companion to English Renaissance Drama*, eds A. R. Braunmuller and Michael Hattaway (Cambridge, 1990), pp. 161–205.

Heywood   Thomas Heywood, *A Woman Killed with Kindness*, ed. R. W. Van Fossen (The Revels Plays: London, 1961).

Holinshed   Raphael Holinshed, *The Third Volume of Chronicles . . . Beginning at Duke William the Norman . . . First Compiled by Raphaell Holinshed, and by him Extended to the Yeare 1577. Now Newlie Recognised, Augmented and Continued . . . to the year 1586* (1587).

Howard-Hill   T. H. Howard-Hill, 'Marginal Markings: the Censor and the editing of Four English Promptbooks', *Studies in Bibliography* (1983), pp. 168–77.

Hunter *Seneca*   'Seneca and the Elizabethans', *ShS* 20 (Cambridge, 1967), pp. 17–26.

Hutchison   Harold F. Hutchison, *The Hollow Crown* (London, 1961).

Jack Straw   Anon., *The Life and Death of Jack Straw* (1595), eds Kenneth Muir and F. P. Wilson (The Malone Society: Oxford, 1957).

Jonson, *Devil*   Ben Jonson, *The Devil Is an Ass*, ed. Peter Happé (The Revels Plays: Manchester, 1994).

Jonson, *Every Man In*   Ben Jonson, *Every Man In His Humour*, ed. J. W. Lever (Regents Renaissance Drama Series: London, 1971).

Jonson, *Poems*   Ben Jonson, *The Complete Poems*, ed. George Parfitt (Harmondsworth, 1976).

King Leir   Anon., *The True Chronicle Historie of King Leir*, in *Narrative and Dramatic Sources of Shakespeare*, vol. VII, ed. G. Bullough (London, 1973), extracts.

Lake   D. J. Lake, 'Three Seventeenth-century Revisions: Thomas of Woodstock, The Jew of Malta, and Faustus B', *N&Q* (April 1983), pp. 133–43.

Linthicum   M. C. Linthicum, *Costume in the Drama of Shakespeare and his Contemporaries* (Oxford, 1936).

Lodge   Thomas Lodge, *Rosalynde*, in *Narrative and Dramatic Sources of Shakespeare*, vol. II, ed. Geoffrey Bullough (London, 1963).

Long, *Bed*   William B. Long, ' "A bed / for woodstock": a Warning for the Unwary', *Medieval & Renaissance Drama in England* 2 (1985), pp. 91–118.

Long, *Few*   William B. Long, ' "Precious few": English Manuscript Playbooks', in *A Companion to Shakespeare*, ed. David Scott Kastan (Oxford, 1999), pp. 414–33.

Manheim   M. Manheim, 'The Weak King History Play of the Early 1590s', *RenD*. n.s. II (1969), pp. 71–80.

Marlowe, *Edward*   Christopher Marlowe, *Edward II*, ed. Charles R. Forker (The Revels Plays: Manchester, 1994).

Marlowe, *Faustus*   Christopher Marlowe, *Dr Faustus*, eds David Bevington and Eric Rasmussen (The Revels Plays: Manchester, 1993).

Marlowe, *Jew*   Christopher Marlowe, *The Jew of Malta*, ed. N. W. Bawcutt (The Revels Plays: Manchester, 1978).

Marston   John Marston, *Sophonisba*, eds Peter Corbin and Douglas Sedge in *Three Jacobean Witchcraft Plays* (The Revels Plays Companion Library: Manchester, 1986).

Mathew   Gervase Mathew, *The Court of Richard II* (New York, 1968).

McKisak   May McKisak, *The Oxford History of England: Vol. V, The Fourteenth Century 1307–1399* (Oxford, 1959).

Melchiori   Giorgio Melchiori, 'The Corridors of History: Shakespeare the Re-maker', British Academy Lecture, 1986 (London, 1986).

Middleton   Thomas Middleton, *A Trick to Catch the Old One*, ed. C. J. Watson (The New Mermaids: London 1968).

Mirror   *The Mirror for Magistrates*, ed. Lily B. Campbell (New York, 1938).

Neale   J. E. Neale, *Queen Elizabeth I* (London, 1936, repr. 1960).

OED   *The Compact Oxford English Dictionary* (Oxford, 1989).

Onions   C. T. Onions, *A Shakespeare Glossary* (1911, enlarged and revised, Robert D. Eagleson, Oxford, 1986).

Partridge, *Bawdy*   Eric Partridge, *Shakespeare's Bawdy: a Literary and Psychological Essay and a Comprehensive Glossary* (London, 1947: revised and enlarged 1969).

Partridge, *Orthography*   A. C. Partridge, *Orthography in Shakespeare and Elizabethan Drama: a Study of Colloquial Contractions, Elision, Prosody and Punctuation* (Lincoln, Nebraska, 1964).

Preston   Thomas Preston, *Cambyses, King of Persia*, introduction by Ashley Thorndike, in *The Minor Elizabethan Drama*, 2 vols, vol. I, *Pre-Shakespearean Tragedies* (Everyman's Library: London, 1951).

Ralegh   Sir Walter Ralegh, *The Poems of Sir Walter Ralegh*, ed. Agnes Latham (London, 1951).

Rubinstein   Frankie Rubinstein, *A Dictionary of Shakespeare's Sexual Puns and their Significance* (London, 1984, 2nd ed., 1989).

Sass   Lorna Sass, *To the King's Taste: Richard II's Book of Feasts and Recipes* (London, 1976).

Saul   Nigel Saul, *Richard II* (New Haven, 1997).

Schoenbaum   S. Schoenbaum, '*Richard II* and the Realities of Power', in *Shakespeare and Others* (Washington and London, 1985).

Second Maiden   Anon., *The Second Maiden's Tragedy*, ed. Anne Lancashire (The Revels Plays: Manchester, 1978).

Skelton   John Skelton, *Magnificence*, ed. Paula Neuss (The Revels Plays: Manchester, 1980).

Somerset   Anne Somerset, *Unnatural Murder: Poison at the Court of James I* (London, 1997).

Stravopoulos   J. C. Stravopoulos, 'A masque is treason's license: the Design of Woodstock', *The Journal of the South Central Modern Language Association* (summer 1988), pp. 1–14.

Stone   Lawrence Stone, *The Crisis of the Aristocracy 1558–1641* (London, 1965).

Stow   John Stow, *The Chronicles of England, from Brute unto this Present Yeare 1580. Collected by John Stow Citizen of London* (1580).

Sugden   E. H. Sugden, *A Topographical Dictionary to the Works of Shakespeare and his Fellow Dramatists* (Manchester, 1925).

Tilley   M. P. Tilley, *A Dictionary of the Proverbs in England in the Sixteenth and Seventeenth Centuries* (Ann Arbor, 1950).

Tourneur   Cyril Tourneur, *The Revenger's Tragedy*, ed. R. A. Foakes (The Revels Plays: London, 1966).

Tudor Interludes   Anon., *Two Tudor Interludes: Youth and Hick Scorner*, ed. Ian Lancashire (The Revels Plays: Manchester, 1980).

Webster   John Webster, *The White Devil*, ed. John Russell Brown (The Revels Plays: London, 1960).

Wentersdorf   K. P. Wentersdorf, 'Shakespeare's *Richard II*: Gaunt's Part in Woodstock's Blood', *ELN* 18, no. 2 (1980), pp. 99–104.

Williams, *Dictionary*   Gordon Williams, *A Dictionary of Sexual Language and Imagery in Shakespearean and Stuart Literature*, 3 vols (London, 1994).

Williams, *Glossary*   Gordon Williams, *A Glossary of Shakespeare's Sexual Language* (London, 1997).

Introduction

The manuscript of *Thomas of Woodstock* is contained within a well-known collection of fifteen manuscript play-books (MS Egerton 1994), apparently assembled by the actor William Cartwright, a King's Revels actor in the Caroline period who became a bookseller and collector of plays during the Civil War. A meticulous account of the nature and characteristics of the manuscript, its various hands and inks, is given by Wilhelmina Frijlinck in her introduction to her Malone Society edition.[1] The manuscript is incomplete, lacking a title-page and, more seriously, a conclusion, probably contained on a final leaf now missing. It suffers further loss of text from the fraying of the edges of some of its sheets, and the problem for the editor in retrieving the text is exacerbated by the fact that the manuscript is badly worn or even torn in places: in particular, there are frequent ink-blots and the top and bottom lines and prose passages extending to the outer margin of the page have in some cases become obscured by dirt from frequent thumbing and turning in what may have been extensive use in the playhouse.

The status of the manuscript as a book-keeper's copy is confirmed by the intermittent marginal jottings which are of considerable interest in the evidence they provide of contemporary theatre practice. As with most of the other surviving theatre manuscripts of the period, the added playhouse notations are sparse and intermittent and do not amount to the systematic tidying-up or regularising of a play-text which might be associated with the more modern concept of a prompt-book.[2] The marginal notations, in a variety of hands, suggest a range of occasions and purposes and seem to belong to various stages in the life of the playhouse manuscript. Some appear to be the kind of jotting which a book-keeper might make as a reminder of the requirements for a performance,[3] such as noting the names of actors for minor parts (e.g. 'George' at 3.2.109, 'Toby' at 4.2.95) or of properties required for the action (e.g. 'Peticions' and 'Mace' immediately before the group entry in 2.2, 'Blankes' at 3.1.5 and 'A bed / for woodstock' before the beginning of the final act); others, such as 'Shrevs ready' at 4.2.217, might seem to indicate a prompter's note for an actual performance, but more probably belong to some theatre contingency now lost to us. In some cases, particularly with sound effects attendant on entrances or exits, the marginal additions appear to reinforce existing stage directions, perhaps indicating an anxiety that certain specific effects should not be missed; at other times, there is a suggestion of more ambitious effects being sought, perhaps at a more elaborately staged revival (e.g. the added directions, 'Anticke', 'fflorish Cornetts: Dance & musique: cornetts' for the opening of the Masque in 4.2).[4]

Of special interest is the marginal instruction 'out', which occurs on three occasions in the manuscript and which appears each time to indicate cuts to be made in the text. It is not clear whether this direction is playhouse in origin, either for artistic reasons or out of self-censorship, or whether it indicates the direct intervention by the censor, the Master of the Revels. A further complicating factor is the occurrence of a number of pencilled crosses, mostly in the left-hand margin of the manuscript but sometimes in the body of the text itself, which, it has been argued, are clear evidence of the interventions of the Jacobean censor, Sir George Buc.[5]

Frijlinck argues that the manuscript is clearly the work of a scribe (copying from an author's rough draft) not that of the author himself. Evidence supporting this view can be found: for example, at 1.2.113 the first half of the line is left blank, apparently because the scribe was unable to read the original, and another hand has subsequently provided the missing text. Further evidence to support Frijlinck's view is the fact that the speech prefixes have clearly in many (possibly all) cases been added after the text has been transcribed, a habit which appears to have facilitated the process of copying.[6] There are also occasions where stage directions have no relation to the immediate dramatic action (e.g. at 2.1.165–7 and 4.3.98–9) but appear to belong to scenes which have either been abandoned or rearranged. This may suggest a copyist working with the author's foul papers which had become obscured through alteration.

Rossiter takes issue with Frijlinck's view that the manuscript is clearly the work of a copyist rather than that of the author. He notes that there are 'a number of alterations of lines which suggest direct contact with an author, if not authorship'.[7] The matter is complicated by the existence in the manuscript of several other hands besides that of the main scribe. Commenting on this, William B. Long argues that it is more likely that revisions and adjustments to

the text in different hands indicate that the play was written colla-
boratively, a common enough practice at the time, rather than that
so many scribes were working over a single playwright's 'foul'
papers.[8] However, the credibility of the theory that the manuscript
is authorial in some form or other rests very much upon the assumption that the manuscript belongs to the period of the play's composition in the early 1590s.[9] Recent studies of its stylistic and
grammatical features do not support such a dating.

A. C. Partridge has argued persuasively that the manuscript of the
play contains a number of contracted forms, elisions and spellings
which are not found commonly in surviving written material until
after 1600. He concludes that 'the extant manuscript of *Woodstock*
is a good example of stratification, the final version being prepared
not earlier than about 1607'.[10] Partridge's findings are supported by
a more recent study by D. J. Lake which examines particular contractions used in the manuscript, concluding that these present 'a
typical pattern of contractions for a colloquial play of the period
1604–10'.[11] Such evidence, whilst not conclusive, is consistent with
the likelihood that the manuscript shows the intervention of the
Jacobean censor,[12] and adds weight to the probability that the manuscript is a Jacobean transcription of an earlier 1590s text, copied
for a revival of the play.

TITLE

The play is given no title in the manuscript; possibly the title originally appeared on a wrapper for the manuscript which has now been
lost. The play has been previously edited under a number of different titles: *Richard II*,[13] *A Tragedy of Richard II*,[14] *Richard II, Part 1*,[15]
The First Part of the Reign of Richard II or Thomas of Woodstock,[16] *Woodstock*,[17] *Woodstock: A Moral History*,[18] and *Thomas of Woodstock*.[19]
Richard II, Part 1 has considerable attractions as a title since it has
the merit of identifying the play with Richard's reign whilst distin-
guishing it from Shakespeare's better-known play; it also neatly indicates that the play deals with the earlier part of Richard's reign
immediately prior to the opening of Shakespeare's play. However,
as Rossiter points out, the play is not about the fall of Richard of
Bordeaux,[20] but presents the character and fortunes of 'Plain
Thomas' (another alternative title?) of Woodstock as the central
focus of the dramatic action throughout its five acts. It does so not
primarily as biography but as a means of representing and reflect-

ing upon the 'state' of England. Thus in the necessary invention of
a title by which to refer to the play it seems appropriate to give
prominence to Woodstock but to retain as an alternative the name
of the king whose troublesome reign it partly traces.[21]

AUTHORSHIP

As with the title, the manuscript leaves us in the dark as to the author
(or authors) of the play and any attempt at identification must
remain conjectural. Intriguingly, Shakespeare is perhaps the one
known dramatist in the 1590s whose dramatic style most closely
resembles that of *Thomas of Woodstock*. The 'Shakespearian' characteristics of the play may be summarised as follows: a sophisticated
handling of chronicle material; a careful and fruitful juxtaposition
of low-life scenes over and against court life; the sense of England
as a significant 'character' throughout the play; a sure handling of
dramatic technique as in the economical and engaging exposition;
the careful drawing of effective female characters (specifically Anne
o' Beame); Nimble's malapropisms, anticipating Costard, Dogberry
and Mrs Quickly; the dramatist's ability to manipulate audience
sympathy in a complex fashion towards Richard and to present
Woodstock as a figure of conscience in a manner which anticipates
Gaunt. Any ascription of the play to Shakespeare or any other
dramatist must, however, remain highly speculative; what is certain
is that the level of dramatic skill deployed suggests an author (or
authors) of considerable range and competence.

DATE AND LITERARY INFLUENCES

Thomas of Woodstock is usually dated between 1591 and 1595 on the
assumption that it was influenced by Shakespeare's *2 Henry VI*
(dated by most scholars to 1590–1) and that in turn *Woodstock* influenced his *Richard II* (1595). The play's concern with the dilemma of
subjects under a weak or irresponsible king links it with a fashion
for plays with such concerns in the early 1590s such as *Edward II*,
the King John plays and Shakespeare's Henry VI plays as well as
Richard II.[22] There seems no compelling reason to doubt that it
belongs to this period. Dating by suppositions of literary or theatrical influence is, however, a hazardous business. Rossiter's case that
Thomas of Woodstock is directly dependent upon *2 Henry VI* must be
read in the light of both his wish to discredit the view that the main

influence on the *Woodstock* author was Marlovian and also his attempt to install Shakespeare as the main inventor of the well-constructed history play.[23] It is true that these two plays have certain features in common: it may be coincidental that both Shakespeare's 'Good Duke Humphrey' and 'Plain Thomas of Woodstock' were Dukes of Gloucester, but it is more significant that both plays are concerned with the murder of an 'Honest Man' who embodies traditional English values, who is trusted by the common people, who opposes forces of misgovernment and whose death threatens a popular uprising. However, such similarity does not prove that one play was dependent upon the other.

Rossiter's most convincing argument for the dependence of *Thomas of Woodstock* on *2 Henry VI* is that many of the salient features of the *Woodstock* dramatist's presentation of his central figure are entirely absent from his source material but are to be found in Shakespeare's presentation of Duke Humphrey. It may, however, be too large a claim to assert that the privileging of 'moral pattern' in *Thomas of Woodstock* over 'temporal sequence' must stem from Shakespeare's example. If there is influence, it certainly does not amount to a question of slavish imitation. 'Plain Thomas' is a fully considered icon of husbandry and aristocratic responsibility integral to the overall conception of the play, and occupies a much more central role than Shakespeare's Duke Humphrey. Similarly, comparison of the handling of parallel incidents in the two plays demonstrates the independence of *Thomas of Woodstock*. In Shakespeare's play, Humphrey dreams of his staff of office being broken by another before, in a later scene, being forced to resign his staff to the King; whereas, in *Woodstock*, Thomas's breaking of his staff in front of the King is a carefully orchestrated climax to a scene of high tension. Most tellingly of all, the sudden arrest of Woodstock in the theatrically resourceful masque scene, an invention of the playwright, contrasts with the much more straightforward arraignment of Humphrey in Shakespeare's play.

The difficulty of establishing influence in these matters is well illustrated by the parallel methods employed in the respective murders of Duke Humphrey and Woodstock. Rossiter argues that the stage direction which opens 3.2 of Shakespeare's *The First Part of the Contention* (*2 Henry VI*) suggests the use of the feather bed in 5.1 of *Thomas of Woodstock* as a technique to ensure the secrecy of the murder. But the text of *The Contention* may itself be influenced by a third play, Marlowe's *Edward II*, which also uses a similar tech-

nique.[24] Equally inconclusive is the attempt to show influence via
parallel passages; for example those offered by Rossiter from *The
Contention* are by no means compelling.[25] We cannot, therefore, conclude with any certainty that *The First Part of the Contention* provides
a *terminus a quo* for *Thomas of Woodstock*.

The limits for the composition of the play might be narrowed if
its relationship with Marlowe's *Edward II* could be determined.
Rossiter convincingly demolishes Keller's assumption that *Thomas
of Woodstock* depends upon Marlowe's play, demonstrating that most
of Keller's parallels are dubious and that others are common to the
historical source or to *The First Part of the Contention*. However,
Rossiter's argument for the reverse case—that Marlowe was dependent upon *Woodstock*—remains speculative since it is based on the
supposition that whereas Marlowe, an established dramatist with a
mature voice, would have been able to resist the influence of an
anonymous dramatist's style, the *Woodstock* dramatist would certainly not have been able to do so had *Edward II* been the earlier
play.[26]

Despite these difficulties in dating *Thomas of Woodstock*, it seems
most likely that its composition is earlier than that of *Richard II*. It
is certainly the case that modern audiences find the basis of the
quarrel between Mowbray and Bolingbroke, outlined in 1.1 of
Shakespeare's play, less than obvious; on occasions directors have
transposed the first two scenes of the play in order to clarify the
action. It is likely that Shakespeare depended upon his audience's
knowledge of Richard's plot against Woodstock, perhaps from
acquaintance with the Chronicles or *The Mirror for Magistrates* but
more probably from a familiarity with *Thomas of Woodstock* on the
stage. Certainly, experience of the earlier play allows the audience
to appreciate more fully the events which lie behind the opaque
opening of *Richard II* and Shakespeare may not have wished to
repeat material which had already been fully presented on stage.
Bolingbroke's initial charge is presented in general terms—Mowbray
is a traitor and a miscreant—and his first specific accusation concerns the fraudulent use of the King's moneys. The charge that
Mowbray was implicated in the murder of Woodstock is left until
last:

> Further I say, and further will maintain
> Upon his bad life, to make all this good,
> That he did plot the Duke of Gloucester's death,

Suggest his soon-believing adversaries,
And consequently, like a traitor-coward
Sluiced out his innocent soul through streams of blood;
Which blood, like sacrificing Abel's, cries
Even from the tongueless caverns of the earth
To me for justice and rough chastisement.

(1.1.98–106)

It is not until the following scene, in which Gaunt is confronted by the Duchess of Gloucester, that King Richard's shocking complicity in the murder is revealed.

Further evidence of *Thomas of Woodstock*'s influence on Shakespeare may be seen in the presentation of Gaunt, who appears to be modelled on Woodstock. Both characters are prone to coupling orthodox views of submission to kingly authority with sharp and direct criticism of their monarch's behaviour. The most striking evidence for this view is found when Gaunt expresses his dismay at the decline in English military prowess, the ills engendered by lawyers' 'inky blots and rotten parchment bonds' and the farming out of the realm to the King's favourites, charges which are central to Woodstock's criticism of Richard's misgovernment. Shakespeare appears even to have picked up telling phrases from *Thomas of Woodstock*, notably Richard's damaging admission:

And we his son, to ease our wanton youth,
Become a landlord to this warlike realm,
Rent out our kingdom like a pelting farm.
(*Woodstock*, 4.1.146–8)

This analysis and the language in which it is expressed resurfaces in Gaunt's lamentation of decline:

This land of such dear souls, this dear, dear land,
Dear for her reputation through the world,
Is now leased out—I die pronouncing it—
Like to a tenement or pelting farm.
(*Richard II*, 2.1.57–60)

together with his accusation to Richard's face: 'Landlord of England art thou now, not king' (*Richard II*, 2.1.113). The charge that Richard is 'landlord' of England occurs five times in *Thomas of Woodstock*, though, significantly, not in Holinshed, Shakespeare's source. Such 'borrowings' strongly suggest that Shakespeare was acquainted with *Thomas of Woodstock* and that it influenced his writing of *Richard*

II.[27] Thus, in so far as literary influence may help dating, it would seem probable that our play was written, and perhaps staged, some time before 1595.

THE SOURCES AND THEIR TREATMENT

Narrative structure

Readers familiar with Shakespeare's *Richard II* are likely to be confused on first reading *Thomas of Woodstock*. Whilst the broad historical outlines are recognisable—a weak and rapacious king, a group of manipulative flatterers, elder-statesmen uncles, Gaunt and York, dismayed by the King's behaviour and consequent widespread civil discontent—the detail of the action appears to be wholly muddled. The minions, Bushy, Greene, Bagot and Scroop, are overthrown, not by Bolingbroke but by an alliance of the King's uncles and other disaffected magnates after a battle (unhistorical) in which Greene is slain by the Earl of Arundel. Bolingbroke's historical return from exile and revolt against the crown in *Richard II* is here paralleled by an insurrection provoked by the murder of Woodstock at Calais and led by Lancaster (Gaunt) and York. Equally confusing is the dramatic prominence given to Robert Tresilian, Richard II's Lord Chief Justice, executed some nine years before Woodstock's murder in 1397. In addition, Richard's first queen, Anne of Bohemia (died 1394), lives until the eve of Woodstock's death, and the eight-year-old Isabella, Richard's second queen, is excluded. Thus the play's action presents the events of Richard II's reign in an apparently confused and jumbled selection. Although Renaissance dramatists frequently shape and re-order history to meet theatrical demands (for example Shakespeare transforms Richard's child-bride into a loving wife), the *Woodstock* dramatist's handling of history initially appears wayward, even careless.

The play's primary source, as in Shakespeare's *Richard II*, was Raphael Holinshed's *Chronicles of England, Scotland and Ireland*. Additionally we may recognise the influence (depending on the date assigned to the text) of Stow's *Annals of England* of 1592 in a number of episodes, and, as Rossiter has suggested,[28] it seems likely that the dramatist may also have consulted Grafton's *Chronicles*. The principal events of the play's action can be found in Holinshed: Richard's association with a group of flatterers and their misuse of the laws to farm the kingdom; the rebellion of the magnates (the Appellants) which led to the Merciless Parliament of 1388 and the removal of Richard's supporters from influence; the death of Anne of Bohemia followed by the King's grief and the destruction of the palace of Sheen; and the long-running enmity between the King and Woodstock which culminated in the Duke's murder in Calais. In addition we can follow the dramatist's incorporation of minor details from the Chronicles: Holinshed's mistaken report of the King's birth date, which is used to considerable dramatic effect;[29] the description of his negotiations with the French;[30] and the heavenly omens which precede Woodstock's abduction.[31] Woodstock's comment on the novel fashion for women to ride side-saddle[32] and Tresilian's attempt to disguise himself in order to avoid capture[33] appear to derive from Stow.

The treatment and handling of the source material are, however, by no means simple or straightforward. At first sight the dramatist appears to have confused the events of the late 1380s with those of the late 1390s. The minions who surrounded Richard in the 1390s are presented as in close alliance with Tresilian, the Lord Chief Justice executed in 1388. The power and influence of Greene, Bushy and Bagot, who became important only after Woodstock's murder, are ended by defeat in an unhistorical battle which recalls Radcot Bridge (1387) in which Robert de Vere, an *earlier* favourite of the King's, was put to flight by the Appellants. By the conflation of his source material, however, the dramatist has skilfully focused the drama on a number of significant issues which in a strictly chronological and linear narrative structure would be unfocused and disconnected. Concentrating upon *one* set of favourites, telescoping the action and presenting Woodstock, unhistorically, as a champion of moral and traditional values allows the play to explore with incisiveness and dramatic clarity the responsibilities of 'kingship', the proper administration of the law, the appropriate role of the King's council and the destructive attractions of pride and will.

Comparison with Marlowe's *Edward II* highlights the *Woodstock* dramatist's skill in narrative construction. *Edward II* presents the audience with a repetitive patterning in which first Gaveston and subsequently the Spencers manipulate a weak king to the detriment of the commonweal's governance. An audience watching *Edward II* cannot help but feel the play to be broken-backed when Gaveston, a character of considerable dramatic energy, is replaced by the less dynamic Spencers who provoke the barons to a second revolt against the monarchy. Thus, whereas Marlowe's play tends to emphasise the

king's personal inadequacies rather than stressing wider issues of
statecraft, *Thomas of Woodstock* sharply defines the criteria of good
government via its selection and organisation of source material,
contrasting the straightforward opposition of Woodstock and his
supporters with the extravagance and chicanery of the king and his
minions. That the fall of the flatterers is presented as a consequence
of Woodstock's murder, when historically it was Woodstock himself
who crushed de Vere, de la Pole etc. in 1388, accentuates the play's
moral structuring and underpins the view that disaster follows upon
regal misgovernment and the elevation of will over reason and
propriety.

Morality influence and The Mirror for Magistrates

Rossiter has argued for the influence of Tudor Morality drama on
the text, suggesting that Nimble, the lawyer's 'devil', derives from
the Vice of the Morality and that in Tresilian we may detect the ghost
of Cloaked Collusion or Crafty Conveyance in *Magnificence*, as in
4.1 where he persuades the King to sign away his kingdom and then
cheats the favourites of much of their expected gains.[34] The dramatist's handling of source material, however, may owe as much, if not
more, to *The Mirror for Magistrates*, a series of popular moralistic
verse 'biographies' first published in 1559 and subsequently reissued
with additions in the 1570s. Whilst *The Mirror for Magistrates* is not
a direct source for the play, it may be a significant influence on its
patterning, the shaping of relationships between major characters
and, further, the provision of a moral framework within which the
dramatist organised his source material.

In *The Mirror for Magistrates* the play's principal characters,
Richard II, Woodstock and Tresilian, are among those chosen to
relate their histories and warn their readers:

> For here as in a loking glas, you shall see (if any vice be in you) howe the
> like hath bene punished in other heretofore, whereby admonished, I trust
> it will be a good occasion to move you to the soner amendment. This is
> the chiefest ende, whye it is set furth, which God graunt it may attayne.[35]

The work offers an entirely orthodox and establishment statement
of Tudor political values which is made clear in the Preface:

> For the ambicious (that is to say prollers [prowlers] for power or gayne)
> seeke not for offices to helpe other, for whiche cause offices are ordayned,
> but with the undoing of other, to pranke up them selves. And therefore

bar them once of this bayte, and force them to do their duties, & they will geve more to be rid fro their charges, than they did at first to bye them: For they seke only their commodity and ease ... Thus the goodnes or badnes of any realme lyeth in the goodnes or badnes of the rulers.[36]

Such sentiments establish the tone and intent of *The Mirror for Magistrates*, and its invented testaments of Richard II, Tresilian and Woodstock articulate the personal failings and public misdemeanours which brought them down. In particular, Richard laments his poor governance, his exploitation of the people and luxury:

> For mayntenaunce wherof, my realme I polde
> Through Subsidies, sore fines, loanes, many a prest,
> Blanke charters, othes, & shiftes not knowen of olde,
> For whych my Subiectes did me sore detest.
> I also made away the towne of Brest,
> My fault wherin because mine uncle tolde
> (For Prynces vyces may not be controlde)
> I found the meanes his bowels to unbrest.
> The Piers and Lordes that did his cause uphold,
> With death, exile, or grevous fines opprest.
>
> (41–50)[37]

In turn Tresilian confesses his part in the manipulation of the law, his greed and abuse of privilege in the service of his King and also in the cause of lining his own pocket:

> The lawes we interpreted and statutes of the lande,
> Not trulye by the texte, but nuly by a glose:
> And wurds that wer most plaine whan thei by us were skande
> We turned by construction lyke a welchmans hose,
> Whereby many one both lyfe and lande dyd lose:
> Yet this we made a mean to mount aloft on mules.
> To serve kings in al pointes men must sumwhile breke rules ...
> So wurking lawe lyke waxe, the subiecte was not sure
> Of lyfe, lande, nor goods, but at the princes wyll:
> Which caused his kingdome the shorter tyme to dure,
> For clayming power absolute both to save and spyll,
> The prince therby presumed his people for to pyll:
> And set his lustes for lawe, and will had reasons place,
> No more but hang and drawe, there was no better grace.
>
> (71–91)[38]

Tresilian, concluding his testament by cursing the temptations of power and wealth and the corruption of flattery, urges his readers

to reject bribery and keep their hands pure since 'Ryches and pro-
mocion be vaine thynges and unsure'.

By contrast depiction of Woodstock, 'a man muche mynding the
common weale, & yet at length miserably made away', reflects on
the fickleness of fate and his over-trusting nature:

> Beyng by them, that should have been iust,
> Trayterously entrapt, ere I could mystrust.
> Ah wretched worlde what is to trust thee,
> Let them that wyll learne nowe hearken to mee.
>   (39–42)

> For whan Fortunes flud ran with full streame,
> I beyng a Duke descended of Kinges,
> Constable of Englande, chiefe officer in the realme,
> Abused with esperaunce in these vaine thinges,
> I wente without feete, and flewe without winges:
> Presumyng so far upon my high state
> That dread set aparte, my prince I would mate.
>   (71–7)[39]

Although Woodstock is presented as a man more sinned against
than sinning, a victim of both Fortune and the deceit of a corrupt
and malicious ruler, the poem also recognises his vainglorious
arrogance and limited vision, moral defects largely unexplored
in the play.

Dramatic treatment

Thomas of Woodstock, however, is a play not a narrow moral homily,
and the skill which the dramatist deploys in the compression and
elision of Chronicle material is paralleled by his dramatic in-
ventiveness. The play, after all, was written to attract and entertain
playgoers. The dramatist's resourcefulness is directed to two main
purposes: first, to enhance the dramatic vitality of the source material and, second, to ensure that the focus of the audience's criticism
is partially deflected from the King towards his minions and supporters. The invention of Nimble, Tresilian's servant, also develops
a series of comedic episodes which increases the range of dramatic
tone and widens the play's focus beyond the court and its political
machinations to the rural world of Cowtail, Simon Ignorance and
the Schoolmaster in which the depredations of regal corruption can
be presented at a local and immediate level. Further, Nimble's com-

ically exaggerated entrance wearing the latest fashion in footwear (3.1.113.1) provides a pointer to the way in which social barriers have been transgressed when a servant adopts the fashions of his betters. Similarly, the treatment of Woodstock's arrest at Plashy (4.2.) is presented in a markedly imaginative fashion. Where the sources suggest a relatively simple deception, the dramatist invents a splendidly dramatic masque to entrap Woodstock. This offers not only an opportunity for a theatrical *tour de force* but also a means of emblematising his abduction. The presentation of Richard's queen, Anne o' Beame, also demonstrates a skilful dramatic sensibility. Taking from the sources a hint of her concern for the stability of the state, the dramatist shows her in 2.3 engaged in charitable work and fearful for the future of the kingdom.

Each of these elaborations of source material and instances of dramatic invention demonstrates an ability to elevate historical narrative to a dramatically complex form which not only offers an audience a series of absorbing theatrical experiences but also imposes upon spectators the responsibility of judgement. The audience is not allowed to arrive at a simple condemnation of Richard, for the dramatist provides the King (unhistorically) with lines, addressed to his minions, which express his wish to cancel the order for Woodstock's execution:

> Send post to Calais and bid Lapoole forbear
> On pain of life to act our sad decree.
> For heaven's love, go prevent the tragedy.
> We have too much provoked the powers divine
> And here repent thy wrongs, good Uncle Woodstock,
> The thought whereof confounds my memory.
> If men might die when they would 'point the time,
> The time is now King Richard would be gone,
> For as a fearful thunderclap doth strike
> The soundest body of the tallest oak
> Yet harmless leaves the outward bark untouched,
> So is King Richard struck. Come, come, let's go.
> My wounds are inward; inward burn my woe.
>   *Exeunt omnes.* (4.3.172–84)

Richard's vulnerability is further highlighted here since it is evident to the audience that his followers have no intention of giving effect to his orders. Through the careful development of his sources the dramatist emphasises the manipulation of the repentant King by the

flatterers.[40] Such changes suggest a concern to emphasise the corruption and villainy of Richard's supporters rather than the personal
failings of the misled King, a strategy which reflects the reticence of
The Mirror in its care to present the King as a weak rather than a
malicious ruler.

The selection and handling of the play's source material, together
with the dramatist's theatrical invention, reveal a considerable level
of dramatic skill. The focused conflation and shaping of historical
events, the creation of scenes which explore the wider implications
of regal policy and the composition of episodes which present the
domestic and personal experience of the principal characters take
us far beyond the simple oppositions of morality drama. The exten-
sion of the action into the provinces suggests a writer responding to
the interests of a diverse audience and contributing a distinctive
voice to the vogue for historical drama in the early 1590s. The invention of an Ignorance, Cowtail or Whistler establishes a dual focus of
dramatic exploration, court and country, which provides a template
for subsequent chronicle drama and, it may be argued, made the
lives of 'ordinary' people an appropriate, if comedic, subject for the
theatre. In this sense the text presents a significant democratisation
of the drama, a movement from exclusivity of courts and magnates
(cf. Marlowe's *Edward II* in particular) to the immediate concerns
of the citizen who, oppressed and bamboozled by establishment
edict, finally appears on stage. In this, the play may be seen to reflect
the interests and concerns of its audience, no longer a remote
observer of state affairs but, through the drama, a judging spectator
of political events.

In this sense we may see *Thomas of Woodstock* as a significant
advance, a play which contributed to the opening up of government and decision-making to scrutiny by its audience. Kyd's
The Spanish Tragedy (1590?) initially presents us with kings and
viceroys, only to reveal that their actions are motivated by personal
will and vendetta; but *The Spanish Tragedy* dramatises a remote
and exotic play-world. In *Thomas of Woodstock* the audience is presented with its own national history, removed perhaps but none
the less raising issues of current relevance.[41] We need to be alert to
the skill with which the dramatist has organised his source material
in pointing up and exploring fundamental issues of statecraft whilst,
at the same time, recognising the sensitivities of the contemporary
establishment.

THE REIGN OF RICHARD II AND THE 1590S

It is clear that the exploration of Richard II's abuse of power and his subsequent deposition was a delicate issue in the 1590s, and it is likely that *Thomas of Woodstock* may have been controversial. Quarrels and events, then two hundred years in the past, continued to cast an alarming shadow over the last years of Elizabeth I's reign. If an 'anointed ' king could be forced from the throne and successfully usurped by Henry IV, the father of that Elizabethan 'worthie' and icon of chivalry, Henry V, then usurpation might appear to be legitimised. In the dying years of the century the question of Elizabeth I's successor was an issue which exercised many, although few were prepared to raise it in public debate.

One who was prepared to do so was Peter Wentworth, whose *A Pithie Exhortation to Her Majestie for Establishing Her Successor*, published posthumously in Edinburgh in 1598, represented the culmination of a campaign which resulted in his imprisonment in the Tower from 1593 until his death three years later. In his pamphlet Wentworth suggests that should the Queen die without a securely nominated successor the realm would descend into factionalism and civil war and her reign would be recalled as being infamous and pitiable. Wentworth's private agenda appears to have been the defence of the Protestant settlement, threatened, as he no doubt saw it, by the ambitions of domestic and Continental forces. None the less, discussion of the succession threatened the royal prerogative and was regarded as deeply treasonable, especially since Wentworth hoped that Essex, held by some to be a preferred candidate for the succession, might present his pamphlet to the Queen.

Whilst the immediate danger of invasion from Catholic Spain had been blunted by the defeat of the Armada in 1588, Spain remained a formidable threat; fleets could be and were rebuilt to reclaim England for the Catholic faith, a course to which Queen Mary (the late wife of King Philip II of Spain) had been committed in the 1550s. Yet the diplomatic and economically cautious policy which Elizabeth and her ministers adopted towards Spain lacked the aggression and dash for which some court factions hankered. In addition, many of those who had most influence over policy were courtiers and councillors of comparatively recent advancement who were drawn from families regarded by some as lacking relevant experience and appropriate pedigree. The world had changed: Elizabethan government was in the hands of bureaucrats rather than magnates whose authority and power had been based on a traditional ideal of military capability and a nationalistic belligerence which the exchequer could no longer afford to support. The difficulties which Elizabethan government faced in financing foreign adventures are well articulated in the opening movement of Shakespeare's *Henry V*, where the tensions between Church and State are explored in the clergy's desire to buy off the threat of the sequestration of their assets by offering a substantial contribution to the King's French enterprise. Such bargaining was a feature of the relationship between Elizabeth and her Parliaments, and in the late sixteenth century the monarch was in a weaker position than her forebears.

In broad terms the reign of Richard II, as dramatised in *Thomas of Woodstock*, presents an interesting parallel to the late Elizabethan political landscape: an established foreign enemy (Spain rather than France) which the 'government' was reluctant to confront directly, indeed was suspected of appeasing; a court riven by factional interests in which a small clique, regarded by some as *parvenus*, wielded unwarranted influence on the monarch; and, perhaps most important of all, the apparent betrayal of those nationalistic/religious ideals which would place England in the vanguard of a crusade against Catholicism.

The criticism expressed by the Farmer and the Butcher in 3.3 might suggest a contemporary relevance to some members of the play's first audience:

> *Farmer.* Ah, sirrah, and what said the good knight your landlord, neighbour?
> *Butcher.* Marry, he said—but I'll not stand to anything, I tell ye that aforehand; he said that King Richard's new councillors—God amend them—had crept into honester men's places than themselves were; and that the King's uncles and the old lords were all banished the court; and he said flatly we should never have a merry world as long as it was so. (3.3.65–73)

Although Elizabeth generally drew her court favourites from members of the aristocracy, their positions and prestige were likely to be swiftly terminated if they incurred her personal displeasure. Power and influence in matters of policy and government lay elsewhere, with a professional class of bureaucrats whose family origins were often humble, and whose influence was often resented by established aristocratic magnates. For example, William Cecil, the Queen's chief minister, was born into a lowly family whose *entrée* to the lower echelons of court was secured by his grandfather. Knighted eventually in 1551 at the late age of thirty-one, he rose on merit to administrative influence and was subsequently ennobled as baron of Burghley in 1571. Not infrequently, loyalty to the crown was buttressed by the gains of property and wealth which both established families and *parvenus* had accrued from the Henrican settlement in which church and monastery properties had been disbursed. Control of State business had passed into the hands of men who lacked noble pedigree—men such as Cecil, Walsingham, Elizabeth I's spy-master, and Hatton who had 'danced his way into the heart of Elizabeth' and was spoken of as 'a mere vegetable of the Court, that sprung up at night'.[42]

Thomas of Woodstock, together with other 1590s texts, demonstrates establishment sensitivity to the treatment of Richard II's reign and deposition. The anonymous play *The Life and Death of Jack Straw, a Notable Rebel* (1590–3), Shakespeare's *Richard II* (1595) and Sir John Hayward's *The First Parte of the Life and Raigne of King Henry IIII* (1599) all provoked interference from the authorities. *Jack Straw*, which appears to be directed towards a popular audience, dramatises the events of the Peasants' Revolt. Whilst there is no overt evidence of the censor's interference, the episodic and fragmentary nature of the text suggests that a censored prompt-book is the source of the printed text.[43] The focal points of the play as we have it are the Queen Mother's compassionate distress at the peasants' disloyalty to the throne, a series of homiletic observations on the duties of subjects by the nobility and clergy and, finally, the King's mercy, dispensed to all but Wat Tyler and Parson Ball. The peasants' grievances are presented but their validity is subsequently undermined. Straw's murder of the King's Tax Collector gives rise to Ball's endorsement of the crime and an analysis of the ills of the social structure:

> Neighbors, neighbors, the weakest now a dayes goes to the wall,
> But marke my words, and follow the councell of *John Ball.*
> England is growne to such a passe of late,
> That rich men triumph to see the poore beg at their gate.
> But I am able by good scripture before you to prove,
> That God doth not this dealing allow nor love.
> But when *Adam* delved and *Eve* span,
> Who was then a Gentleman . . .

Now tis come to a wofull passe,
The Widdow that hath but a pan of brasse,
And scarse a house to hide her head,
Sometimes no penny to buy her bread,
Must pay her Landlord many a groat,
Or twil be puld out of her throat.

$$(74-99)^{44}$$

Whilst such social criticism may draw a measure of audience sympathy, the rebels' position is disabled by their subsequent extravagant proposals to set up Ball as Archbishop of Canterbury and Straw as king, together with their half-comic antics as when the clown cheats one of the principal rebels out of a stolen goose (476ff.). At such points the text reveals an ambiguity of dramatic tone and focus between broad comedy and social comment. How far this is the result of the dramatist's concern to appeal to his audience is open to question; but that there was a measure of external intervention by the censor or of self-censorship on the part of the playwright(s) or the company seems likely.

Shakespeare's *Richard II* provides the most notable example of establishment apprehension provoked by the players' treatment of Richard's reign. The play appears to have been popular since three quarto editions were published, one in 1597 and two in the following year. None of these editions, however, prints the deposition scene (4.1), which was restored to the text only in the quarto of 1608 whose title-page advertises its 'new additions of the Parliament Sceane, and the deposing of King Richard. As it hath been lately acted by the Kinges Majesties servantes, at the Globe'.[45] To what extent the censorship of the deposition scene in the early printed texts reflects its censorship in performance is debatable. Both Peter Ure and Andrew Gurr[46] suggest that, on balance, it is more likely than not that the scene was performed, though Janet Clare, placing greater emphasis on the printer's claims for new additions 'lately acted', argues for the scene's suppression as there is evidence to indicate that the Master of the Revels was 'anxious to have the portrayal of seditious events abridged, or reported rather than enacted'.[47]

The political parallels drawn between Richard II's reign and that of Elizabeth I were most strongly emphasised at the time of Essex's attempted *coup d'état* in 1601. On 7 February, the day before the uprising, the Lord Chamberlain's Men were hired by a number of Essex's supporters to perform a play 'of the deposing and killing of

King Richard the Second'.[48] The actors initially appear to have been reluctant to stage a text 'so old and so long out of use' but were persuaded by the offer of a payment of forty shillings to cover potential losses. If, as is almost certain, the play was Shakespeare's *Richard II*, a number of contemporary parallels may be drawn: the ruined and exiled Bolingbroke mirrored the disgraced Essex banished from the court; the King's minions—Bushy, Greene and Bagot—recalled the Queen's councillors who held a tight grip on policy; whilst the military failures of Richard's reign reflected the Elizabethan regime's unwillingness to finance an aggressive foreign policy. The motives of the sponsors of the performance are unclear. It is possible that they hoped the play would provide an authoritative precedent for their *coup* rather than a spark to foment a general rebellion, although Schoenbaum suggests that the conspirators were attempting 'to buoy up their own spirits on the eve of a desperate adventure'.[49] Whatever the conspirators' motives, the authorities revealed a sharp sensitivity in calling the actors to account for their actions after the revolt was crushed. Although the Lord Chamberlain's Men escaped punishment—they performed at court again before the end of the month—the potency of the parallel between Richard II and the Queen was recognised by Elizabeth I herself. Examining the royal archives with the antiquarian, William Lambarde, the Queen 'fell upon the reign of King Richard II. saying, "I am Richard II. know ye not that?"', adding that 'this tragedy was played 40^{tie} times in open streets and houses'.[50] Whilst we can only guess at the tone of the Queen's comments, there is here a sense of offence that matters touching the Queen should have been rehearsed in public in the open streets.

A change in political climate may give rise to new and unexpected readings of a previously inoffensive text; *Richard II*, a historical tragedy sensitively exploring delicate issues in 1595, becomes potentially revolutionary and propagandist in 1601. Similarly Sir John Hayward's *The First Parte of the Life and Raigne of King Henry IIII*, which focuses on the malfeasance and deposition of Richard II, drew authority's wrath upon its author. Hayward appears to have been a naive victim of circumstance in that he dedicated his work to the Earl of Essex in a flamboyant and eulogistic Latin:

> To the best and most noble, says Euripides, at which thought you first and almost only came to mind, most illustrious Earl, whose name, should it shine on our Henry's forehead, he would more happily and more safely

go forth among the people. For you are great indeed, both in present judgement and in expectation of future time, in whom once blind fortune can seem now to have regained her sight, since she moves to heap with honours a man distinguished in all virtues ... Long may Almighty God keep Your Highness safe for us and for the state, so that we, avenged and protected in faith as well as in arms by your powerful right hand, may enjoy lasting security and glory. (trans. Manning)[51]

The phrase 'and in expectation of future time' (*& futuri temporis expectione*) was particularly provocative since it might be interpreted as a reference to the heir to the throne. Similarly the prayer that Essex would avenge and protect the faith, i.e. the Protestant faith, might suggest that the Protestant settlement was insecure with the lack of a nominated heir. Hayward's dedication thus appeared to impinge on the royal prerogative in matters of religious belief and practice. Licensed under the Bishop of London's authority by Samuel Harsnett as deputy censor, the volume became a best-seller. Half the initial print-run of a thousand copies was quickly sold and a second revised edition of fifteen hundred copies was planned. The proposed revisions were designed to rebut claims that the work afforded topical interpretation since the dedication to Essex had stimulated a good deal of speculative interest, as John Chamberlain records in a letter to Dudley Carleton:

> Here hath been much descanting about it, why such a story should come out at this time, and many exceptions taken, especially to the epistle which was a short thing in Latin dedicated to the Earl of Essex, and objected to him in good earnest, whereupon there was a commandment that it should be cut out of the book, yet I have got you a transcript of it that you may pick out the offence if you can. For my part, I can find no such bugswords, but that everything is as it is taken.[52]

In the first instance it was Hayward's dedication which aroused comment and there is some evidence that Essex was wary of accepting the author's compliments; the Earl had been acutely embarrassed by the dedication of *A Conference about the Next Succession to the Crown of England* (1595) which presented him as a kingmaker, the author claiming that 'no man [is] like to have a greater part or sway in deciding of this great affair (when time shall come for that determination) than your Honour'.[53] It seems that it was Essex himself who brought the authorities' attention to Hayward's dedication and thus led to the book's suppression. In the light of subsequent events, however, Hayward's work seemed, to the establishment, to reveal a propagandistic design. In late May 1599 remaining copies of the first edition were seized and in June all copies of the second edition were taken and burned.

It is clear that any discussion of Richard II's reign, and especially his deposition, had become intensely controversial in the late 1590s since it raised issues of monarchical legitimacy which directly related to the succession. By June 1599 the authorities were sufficiently alarmed to issue a decree prohibiting the publication of *any* historical work unauthorised by the Privy Council. Whilst Hayward escaped formal investigation at this time, Essex's arrest and examination after his unauthorised return from Ireland once more directed the government's attention to his *Henry IV*. Some passages in his history which parallel issues raised in *Thomas of Woodstock* are particularly provocative. Bolingbroke's view of a subject's loyalty is radically subversive in the sharpness of the tension between duty to society and allegiance to the monarch, a dilemma faced in the play by Woodstock and his brothers in the face of Richard's irresponsibility:

> A private man I am loath to be accompted, being designed to be a king by you; and a prince I cannot be esteemed, whilst another is in possession of the kingdome. Also your name is in suspence, whether to be tearmed rebels or subjects, until you have made manifest that your allegeance was bound rather to the state of the realme then the person of the prince.[54]

Similarly, the episode in Hayward in which Worcester, the Steward to the King's household, breaks his staff, dismisses his followers and defects to Bolingbroke challenges the essential title of monarchy: 'And thereupon, openly in the hall, in the presence of the kings servants, he break his white rodde, the ensigne of his office, and forthwith departed to the duke [Bolingbroke], willing every man to shift for himselfe in time.'[55] The persecution Hayward received for his treatment of Richard's reign indicates the sensitivity of the authorities to public discussion and examination of monarchical authority.

CENSORSHIP OF THE MANUSCRIPT

Whatever controversies may have been provoked by the play in the 1590s, any consideration of direct censorship of the manuscript must depend upon our understanding of its date and provenance. Previous editors of *Thomas of Woodstock* have assumed that the manuscript

belonged to the likely date of the play's composition,[56] but the conclusion of recent studies of stylistic features of the manuscript is that
it probably represents a Jacobean transcription of a play composed
and performed in the early 1590s.[57] Such a view radically affects
interpretation of the nature of any supposed censorial interventions
which have been 'detected' by previous editors and scholars. Clearly
if the manuscript is Jacobean, cuts and deletions which may be
attributable to censorship rather than literary or theatrical considerations must relate to Jacobean political circumstances rather than
those of the 1590s. For example, Clare's conjecture that Lapoole's
expression of horror at Woodstock's unlawful murder in 5.1 is
marked for cutting in order to forestall an audience drawing a coded
analogy between Lapoole's dilemma and that of Elizabeth I (in relation to her signing the death warrant of Mary Stuart in 1589)
requires modification if the manuscript belongs to a later date. An
alternative Jacobean parallel could, of course, be posited in order to
demonstrate topicality—James I's dilemma over Sir Walter Ralegh,
imprisoned in the Tower from 1603 and finally executed in 1618—
but such literal analogies must always remain speculative and largely
unnecessary since the play is not a *roman à clef*.

The manuscript contains a variety of interventions which might
be thought to support the likelihood of censorship: crossings out
and substitutions, passages marked for deletion, pencilled (and/or
inked) crosses, and the three-times iterated marginal comment 'out'.
However, caution must be exercised in reaching conclusions since
the evidence is by no means straightforward: for example interventions in the manuscript are not consistent; they appear to have no
overall coherence or rationale; moreover, they probably belong to
more than one revision of the text for performance.

In two places cuts are marked in the manuscript for passages
which are lacking speech prefixes (at 2.3.27–69 and 4.1.139–60). In
these cases we may be confident that the alteration occurred at such
an early stage of transcription that the scribe saved himself the
redundant labour of identifying the speakers and we must assume
either that the Master of the Revels was consulted before the com-
pletion of the process of adding the speech prefixes or that these
alterations are playhouse adjustments, whether for dramatic reasons
or out of self-censorship.

The first of these excisions precisely illustrates the difficulty of
drawing any clear inference as regards the nature of the censorship.
The 43-line cut in 2.3 develops the key theme of the scene: the chari-

table work of the Queen in relieving the poverty caused by Richard's government of England. It might thus be thought politically sensitive for its sharp censure of a monarch and, even more seriously perhaps, raising speculation as to the likelihood of rebellion by his subjects. Parfitt and Shepherd are surely right to question Frijlinck's view that this passage is marked for omission because it lacks dramatic interest; they note that it represents a significant addition by the dramatist to his source material and that 'A[nne]'s archetypal display of royal behaviour implicitly criticises Richard's royal conduct'.[58] Clare takes a similar view, adding that 'allusions to the commons' grievances against the King brought about by exorbitant taxation and the political influence of flatterers may well have been perceived as carrying dangerously contemporary associations'.[59] Clearly the playhouse would not have made a cut of this size in a short scene (with the attendant adjustments required to the text, including the delaying of Cheney's entry) without a compelling reason; but if we are to attribute the cut to the direct intervention of the censor, rather than self-censorship, we must assume a practice of consulting him before the process of copying out the manuscript had been fully completed.[60]

The second example of an excision made at an early stage in the preparation of the manuscript may suggest the operation of just such an arrangement with the censor. The 22-line cut is part of a scene in which Richard is shown farming out his kingdom to his favourites, and presents him as surprisingly relaxed about his shameful behaviour:

> And of the meanest subject of our land
> We shall be censured strangely when they tell
> How our great father toiled his royal person,
> Spending his blood to purchase towns in France;
> And we his son, to ease our wanton youth,
> Become a landlord to this warlike realm,
> Rent out our kingdom like a pelting farm
> That erst was held as fair as Babylon,
> The maiden conqueress to all the world.
>
> (4.1.142–50)

The repeated instruction 'out' written in the margin against this passage might possibly be playhouse in origin, indicating the players' extreme anxiety that on no account should the lines be included in a performance, but a more plausible explanation is that the repeated word 'out' represents the instruction of the censor. A similar instruction occurs in the margin against a passage which elaborates upon the exploits of the Black Prince against the French as part of an unfavourable comparison between Richard and his father,

> Whom the trembling French the Black Prince called,
> Not of a swart and melancholy brow,
> For sweet and lovely was his countenance,
> But that he made so many funeral days
> In mournful France: the warlike battles won
> At Crécy field, Poitiers, Artois and Maine
> Made all France groan under his conquering arm.
>
> (1.1.30–6)

Parfitt's suggestion that this cut may stem from sensitivity in the early 1590s to the expression of anti-French feeling at a time of more pro-French attitudes in government needs adjustment, as has already been argued, if the manuscript belongs to the Jacobean period. It is perfectly possible that the passage was thought objectionable in a Jacobean context because of its critical comparison between a monarch and his warlike predecessor which could have been interpreted as criticism of James I's attempted reconciliation with Spain (compared with the victories over Spain in Elizabeth's reign).

Some concerted adjustments in the manuscript to Lapoole's role in the murder scene (5.1) might seem to indicate playhouse alterations to suit the requirements of a particular performance, but even here external censorship may be suspected. As Parfitt and Shepherd have argued, the effects of these changes are 'both to tidy up and reduce the emotional power of Lapoole's inner struggle. (A blackening of L[apoole] lessens the implicit blame of the king).' Once again interpretation is not straightforward, for, if the intention was to reduce the impression of Richard's culpability, it is surprising that the reference to Lapoole's motivation to 'win King Richard's love with heaps of gold' (5.1.5) has not also been deleted. Two cuts in Lapoole's soliloquy before the murder seem especially indicative of censorship rather than a playhouse excision for artistic reasons. The first of these offers the audience a direct reminder that it is Richard who is the instigator of Woodstock's assassination:

> Horror of conscience with the king's command
> Fights a fell combat in my fearful breast.
>
> (5.1.34–5)

The second deleted passage concerns Lapoole's horrified recoil at the magnitude of such an unlawful murder:

A seven times crying sin. Accursèd man,
The further that I wade in this foul act
My troubled senses are the more distract,
Confounded and tormented past my reason.

(5.1.40–3)

It is not easy to imagine these powerful passages being willingly sacrificed by the actors since they add greatly to the depth and complexity of Lapoole's character; on the other hand, such overt expressions of the damnable consequences of the unlawful assassination of a subject by a king might well have excited the censor's concern.

Further evidence for the intervention of the Jacobean censor is to be found in the manuscript in the form of crosses, some pencilled, some inked, some both, some in the left-hand margin and some after speech prefixes. Howard-Hill has argued that the presence of such markings, which he finds also in three other prompt-books of plays of the period, together with our knowledge of the Jacobean censor Sir George Buc's habits of marking up copy, amount to strong proof that such interventions indicate the work of the Master of the Revels.[61] The most significant of these crosses occurs in the margin alongside the deletion of the phrase 'Superior Lord of Scotland' (2.2.110) and corresponds to the ink-over-pencil cross which Howard-Hill has established as characteristic of Sir George Buc. It is not difficult to see how such a glaring reference might have been spotted by Buc as offensive to James I after his accession to the English throne in 1603. However, the evidence of these crosses cannot be taken as conclusive since a number of them appear to have no apparent significance in terms of censorship, and it is possible that some of them were added at a much later date.[62]

Additional support for the notion of Jacobean censorship of the manuscript is to be found in other changes. The alteration of some of the oaths in the play suggests a response to the Act of 1606 restraining players from invoking God's name on stage.[63] Perhaps most telling of all, is the suppression of Woodstock's familiar and familial address to Richard as 'cuss' (i.e. 'coz' = cousin) at 2.2.34 and 39. In artistic terms the excising of Woodstock's wholly characteristic colloquialism and the substitution of the inappropriately respectful and formal 'my liege' makes no sense. Although, as Rossiter and Lancashire point out, 'cuss' is used on other occasions without being censored,[64] such inconsistency does not invalidate the likelihood of censorship since the censor tended to deal in broad directives rather than methodical or meticulous detail.[65]

Whilst it is impossible to ascertain the precise extent to which interventions in the manuscript are attributable to external censorship, it is sufficiently evident that this play could be read as displaying subversive tendencies both when performed originally, presumably in the 1590s, and at its subsequent Jacobean revival. Had the final leaf of the manuscript survived it might well have clarified matters by bearing the censor's licence.

THE PLAY

Structure

Woodstock reveals a remarkable sophistication in dramatic organisation and skill for a play which probably belongs to the early 1590s. The play is tightly but not mechanically structured. The text immediately inducts the audience into the warring factions of the play with the lords' panic reactions to the attempted *coup* by Richard's flatterers who have attempted to poison them at a banquet and the ensuing scene which shows the anger of Greene and others at the failure of their plot. These tensions having been established, the brief accord of the wedding celebration of the day following (2.1), is quickly disrupted when the enmity between the lords and the flatterers breaks into open dispute. This leads to a second and successful attempt by Richard's favourites to oust the magnates from their position of influence by means of Bushy's sharp interpretation of the chronicles to 'prove' Richard's age of majority, thus assuring the King full control of affairs of state (2.2). The uncles are dismissed from the council and Woodstock, under pressure, yields up his Protectorship, which allows Richard's favourites to acquire offices of influence. Act 2 scene 3 modulates the frantic mood and pace of the play's opening movement to the domestic concerns of Queen Anne and her ladies who are engaged in charitable work as they discuss the growing threat to the social fabric. They learn from a messenger how the King and his new council have devised policies of unprecedented court display and have embarked upon the financial pillage of the commons. The Queen's attempts in 3.1 to ameliorate Richard's excesses are quickly swept aside, and Tresilian's notorious blank charters, a novel form of taxation, are sent out throughout the realm. The two scenes which follow (3.2 and 3.3) explore the effect of these measures, firstly at Woodstock's residence, Plashy, and then upon the common people of Dunstable.

Having established and explored the consequences of Richard's misgovernment under the influence of his minions, the second half of the play focuses more directly on the fall of Woodstock and descent of England into civil war. We see Richard's council in unrestrained misgovernment in 4.1 as Tresilian misappropriates the proceeds of the blank charters, the kingdom is farmed out among the minions and plots are laid to arrest and dispose of the opposition. Woodstock's arrest at Plashy is prefigured by the Duchess's ominous dream, whilst the Queen's sickness and subsequent death presage the final act of the play which presents the murder of Woodstock and the defeat of the minions. The intervention of the ghosts of Edward III and the Black Prince, Richard's grandfather and father, present a savage context for the murder which is handled in the longest scene in the play in a manner which highlights the magnitude of Richard's crimes. The ghosts embody notions of honour and chivalry which are in stark contrast to the ignominy of Richard's betrayal and murder of Woodstock, his kinsman and subject. The concluding battlefield sequence is presented episodically in a series of quick-moving scenes which shift from the grotesquery of Nimble's clownish betrayal of Tresilian to the pathos of Greene's death and Richard's grief.

Stage imagery

In this way the play's structure emphasises the central issues of misrule, ungoverned appetite and intemperate will, opposed by traditional values of established order, compassion and communal responsibility. Such oppositions are articulated and underpinned both linguistically and visually in images of clothing and in terms of stage costume. Woodstock is characterised by his peers as an almost exasperating example of straightforwardness:

> How does thy master, our good brother Woodstock,
> Plain Thomas, for by th'rood so all men call him
> For his plain dealing and his simple clothing?
> 'Let others jet in silk and gold', says he,
> 'A coat of English frieze best pleaseth me'.
>
> (1.1.98–102)

It is with great difficulty that his brothers persuade him, out of a sense of decorum, to 'sumpter a gaudy wardrobe' (1.1.211) at the wedding celebration. The favourites' comments on his uncharacteristic '*very brave*' appearance in 2.1 corroborate his sharp condemnation of extravagant and absurd display:

> A hundred oaks upon these shoulders hang
> To make me brave upon your wedding day,
> And more than that, to make my horse more tire,
> Ten acres of good land are stitched up here.
>
> (1.3.95–8)

Woodstock's jibe is apposite since it exactly encapsulates the ostentation and immorality of their conspicuous expenditure on costume which is used by the dramatist as an index of irresponsibility and misgovernment. Greene's value judgements are entirely based on superficial appearance ('it shall henceforth be counted high treason for any fellow with a grey beard to come within forty foot of the court gates'), supported by Bagot's determination to banish those who wear a 'great bellied doublet', in favour of foreign and exotic fashions. The absurdity of these fashions is confirmed by Nimble:

> *Enter* NIMBLE [*in peaked shoes with knee-chains*].
>
> *Nimble.* As nimble as a morris-dancer now my bells are on.
>   How do ye like the rattling of my chains, my lord?
>
> (3.1.113.1–15)

The plot to arrest Woodstock provides a further opportunity for the dramatist to extend the clothing imagery, not only in the spectacular appearance of the masquers but also in the masquing suit which Woodstock is forced to wear when arrested. The text does not specify the nature of this costume but we may assume that it is designed to maximise in its costliness the antithesis of all that Woodstock represents. Conversely, Tresilian in his conservative retention of his beard and his legal robes disguises his individualistic rapacity beneath the conventional costume of integrity. Significantly, when later in fear of capture, Tresilian abandons the robes of authority for an inconspicuous disguise. The dramatist may well have intended to follow Stow's description of the disguised Tresilian, 'a poore weak man, in frize coat, all old and torne, and had artificially made himselfe a long beard', thus ironically recalling Woodstock's beard and frieze costume.

Play-world

Woodstock presents its audience with a complex and coherent play-world which encompasses a variety of locations—court, council chamber, noble household, legal bureaucracy, rural backwater, foreign prison and field of battle. Each reflects the play's political power struggles and exhibits the way in which Richard's actions radically affect everyone from the baronial magnates to the lower orders of society—schoolmasters, minor officials, butchers and farmers. The play suggests that England *itself* is a significant character in the drama in a manner very different from Shakespeare's *Richard II* where the play-world is socially restricted to the activities of the court and nobility and where even the gardeners (3.4), who emblematise the wider implications of the action, speak in verse.[66] This sense of the nation's significance is reinforced by Woodstock's continual concern for the 'commons', the ordinary people of England, and his fear that they will make revolutionary head against Richard's rule.[67]

The dramatist ensures that each segment of the play-world directly illustrates the effect of regal irresponsibility whether it be located in the court of Anne o' Beame or in Dunstable marketplace. Thus in 2.3 we encounter Queen Anne with her maids, engaged in charitable work for the poor, lamenting the current state of the realm:

> Alack the day! Though I am England's queen
> I meet sad hours and wake when others sleep.
> He meets content, but care with me must keep.
> Distressèd poverty o'erspreads the kingdom:
> In Essex, Surrey, Kent and Middlesex
> Are seventeen thousand poor and indigent
> Which I have numbered; and to help their wants
> My jewels and my plate are turned to coin
> And shared amongst them. O riotous Richard,
> A heavy blame is thine for this distress
> That dost allow thy polling flatterers
> To gild themselves with others' miseries.
>   (2.3.15–26)

In 3.3 we witness at first hand the oppressive effects on ordinary country-folk of extortionate taxes such as blank charters levied to support regal extravagance:

> *Nimble.* Here, ye bacon-fed pudding eaters, are ye afraid of a sheep-skin?

Cowtail. Mass, 'tis somewhat darkly written.
Farmer. Ay, ay, 'twas done i'th' night, sure.
Cowtail. Mass, neighbours, here's nothing that I see.
Butcher. And can it be any harm, think ye, to set your hands to nothing?
These blank charters are but little pieces of parchment. Let's set our
marks to them and be rid of a knave's company.
Farmer. As good at first as last; we can be but undone.
Cowtail. Ay, and our own hands undoes us, that's the worst on't. Lend's
your pen, sir.
Butcher. We must all venture, neighbours, there's no remedy.
Nimble. [*Aside*] They grumble as they do it. I must put them down for
whisperers and grumblers.

                                                        (3.3.115–29)

Tresilian's chicanery comically draws the peasantry into frighten-
ing legal tangles in order to finance the King's fascination with
'Polonian' shoes and sumptuous feasting. Not only can they be
charged for 'whispering' and 'murmuring' but even for the act of
'whistling' (3.3.232.1ff.). Whilst the Dunstable market scene is
essentially comic, presenting the audience with a dull Constable,
an overweening schoolmaster and a catalogue of unsophisticated
provincials, the humour is sharply mediated by the audience's
experience of the minions' conniving and Tresilian's rapacity. This
is graphically dramatised at the opening of Act 4 when Tresilian
enters *'with writings and a* Servant *with bags of money'*:

       So, seven thousand pounds
    From Bedford, Buckingham and Oxford shires,
    These blanks already have returned the king.
    So then there's four for me and three for him:
    Our pains in this must needs be satisfied.
                                                        (4.1.5–9)

Dramatic style

A major feature of the dramatist's skill is the ability to deploy
and control dramatic tone. Such tonal variety sustains our involvement as the tone modulates from the tensions of the assassination
plot of the play's opening scene through a variety of shifts of feeling.
The dramatic mood oscillates from the gravity of statecraft and
political debate to the comedy provided by Nimble's malapropisms
and the Bailey's stupidity. In the final act we move from the tension

of the murder scene to the turmoil of the final military confrontation between the King's party and the magnates, punctured by the ironic comedy of Tresilian's cowardice and Nimble's parodistic betrayal of his master. The blending of the serious with the comic is sharply illustrated in 3.2 in which Woodstock and his brothers, York and Lancaster, have retired from London to Plashy. Here Woodstock's country estate is presented as a haven of tranquillity and traditional values in contrast to the febrile power-jockeying and conspicuous consumption of Richard's court. Yet the pressure of events is felt even within these idyllic surroundings as Cheney enters with news of the imposition of blank charters. The party quickly breaks up as York and Lancaster leave for their estates to restrain the commons' protest and potential rebellion. Woodstock is left darkly ruminating on the ruination of the Kingdom and his fears of insurrection. At this moment of foreboding the King's messenger enters to recall Woodstock to court where the King can control him:

> We'll have him near us. Within his arrow's length
> We stand secure. We can restrain his strength.
> (3.1.105–6)

The despotic court physically penetrates the play-world's only oasis of harmony. Whilst an audience might expect the drama to darken at this point, the dramatist shifts the tone with the arrival of the comic 'spruce' Courtier. Fastidious and unwilling to dismount beyond the courtyard, he enters on horseback attired in the modish exaggerated fashions designed by the King and his minions; a forebear perhaps of that 'neat and trimly dress'd' lord who demands Hotspur's prisoners at Holmedon.[68] This surprising modulation to comedy allows the dramatist to explore a telling parallel between the Courtier and the King's minions. Like them, he fails to recognise true authority and honour, mistaking Woodstock, plainly dressed as ever, for a groom, and offering him a tester to walk his horse. The consequent stage image, Plain Thomas performing a groom's role, visually emphasises one of the text's central concerns, the ousting of tried and established counsellors in favour of a group of worthless *parvenus*. The point is extended when, in response to Woodstock's mocking enquiry, the Courtier reveals the time and trouble spent in devising novel fashions, praising the design of his 'Polonian' footwear:

> For these two parts being in operation and quality different, as for example: the toe a disdainer or spurner; the knee a dutiful and most humble orator; this chain doth, as it were, so toeify the knee and so kneeify the toe that between both it makes a most methodical coherence or coherent method. (3.2.220–6)

The concentration of Richard's new council, packed by favourites, on trivial business is thus contrasted with the lords' earlier discussion of potential civil disorder, even rebellion, provoked by the blank charters, an issue immediately illustrated in the following 'Dunstable' scene (3.3).

The dramatist's rhetorical style displays a similar inventive flexibility for, as Clemen argues, the dialogue is 'far superior to the bareness of language characteristic of earlier chronicle plays'.[69] Woodstock's dialogue, in particular, frequently emulates conversational patterns of speech in an unforced and natural manner—in his address to the 'spruce' Courtier's horse he is even allowed to drop into prose; the dramatist avoids or limits set-pieces and rhetorical devices so that high dramatic rhetoric quickly modulates into plain and workaday speech structures. Woodstock's dismissal from the Protectorship on Richard's assumption of power, for example, does not provoke a high-flown rhetorical response but a measured and regretful reply:

> Was this the trick, sweet prince? Alack the day,
> You need not thus have doubled with your friends.
> The right I hold, even with my heart I render
> And wish your grace had claimed it long ago.
> Thou'dst rid mine age of mickle care and woe,
> And yet I think I have not wronged your birthright;
> For if the times were searched I guess your grace
> Is not so full of years till April next;
> But be it as it will. Lo, here, King Richard,
> I thus yield up my sad Protectorship. *Gives the mace up.*
> (2.2.94–103)

Even when Woodstock is deprived of his membership of the Council and is pressured into breaking his staff of office in public, an action which will preclude him from all political influence, the presentation is managed with effective dramatic restraint. High words are initially spoken but Woodstock's final lines return to a mixture of familial solidarity and seeming proverbial wisdom:

Farewell, King Richard. I'll to Plashy. Brothers,
If ye ride through Essex call and see me.
If once the pillars and supporters quail
How can the strongest castle choose but fail?

(2.2.165–8)

Woodstock's matter-of-fact dialogue is a significant element in the creation of his character and supports his plain dress and concern for the 'commons' in arousing audience sympathy, not only for the character but for what he represents. In addition, it suggests a linkage with the very practical worries expressed by the farmers and tradesmen of 3.3. In contrast, Nimble's Dogberry-like comic malapropisms and the Baily of Dunstable's indiscriminate dependence on his catch-word 'pestiferous' suggest a relationship between pretentious language and extravagant fashion as signifying a destructive and uncaring individualism whilst plain and unadorned speech represents communal values and concerns.

The play, then, reveals a singular dramatic skill in providing its audience with a variety of dramatic tone and linguistic register which focuses its central concerns. Equally skilful is the deployment of established devices. The dramatic build-up to Woodstock's assassination (5.1) is a case in point. We may presume that a contemporary audience would have been familiar with the conclusion from *The Mirror for Magistrates* or the Chronicles, yet, so carefully has our sympathy for Woodstock been aroused, that the text allows, even encourages, the hope that he may survive the plot against him. Lapoole's moral qualms, the murderers' fear that his rhetoric might blunt their purpose and, most significantly, the ghostly warnings of the Black Prince and Edward III, each offer hope for Woodstock's survival. The process of the assassination is subtly drawn out, paralleling episodes from *Richard III* of Clarence's murder (1.4) and the ghosts of Richard's victims (5.5). The sleeping Woodstock appears to respond to the apparitions in his dream:

1 Ghost. O yet for pity, wake, prevent thy doom!
 Thy blood upon my son will surely come;
 For which, dear brother Woodstock, haste and fly,
 Prevent his ruin and thy tragedy.   *Exit* GHOST.

Thunder. Enter Edward the Third's GHOST.

Woodstock. Oh!
2 *Ghost.* Sleepst thou so soundly and pale death so nigh?
   Thomas of Woodstock, wake, my son, and fly!
                                                (5.1.72–8)

On waking, he characteristically dismisses the ominous experience
as 'fancy'. Since they embody the legitimacy and authority of
responsible kingship, the ghosts of Edward III and the Black Prince
lend gravity and import to the action. Their appearance, heralded
by thunder and lightning, demonstrates the disastrous consequences
facing the throne, whilst Edward III's lamentation of Richard's
misgovernment—depriving his uncles of their offices and power,
renting out the crown's revenues and racking his subjects—draws
the audience back to the play's dominant issues. Whilst their primary
function is that of the conventional ghost warning of imminent cat-
astrophe, the dramatist has refined the device. The Black Prince's
despairing recognition both invokes pathos and increases dramatic
tension:

                Oh, I am nought but air!
        Had I the vigour of my former strength . . .
        I'd shake these stiff supporters of thy bed
        And drag thee from this dull security.
                                                (5.1.65–71)

Here is no Senecan excessiveness as reported in the Induction to
the anonymous tragedy, *A Warning for Fair Women* (1599):

        Then [too] a filthy whining ghost
        Lapt in some foul sheet, or a leather pilch
        Comes screaming like a pig half-stick'd
        And cries Vindicta!—Revenge, Revenge![70]

The focus of the ghosts' concern in *Woodstock* is not the primitive
revenge of familial grief or honour but rather the impending ruination of the royal line and the consequent crisis in the English social
structure. Personal motivation has largely been subsumed into a
wider political arena. The dramatist's handling of the ghosts is drawn
in part from The *Mirror for Magistrates* in which a range of historical figures relate their history for the reader's moral education.
Similarly, both ghosts refer to their military triumphs, Crécy and
the capture of the French king for the Black Prince and the conquest of France for Edward III. However, where in *The Mirror for
Magistrates* the reader is encouraged to learn from its protagonists'

transgressions, here the audience is invited to compare the prowess of royal ancestors with King Richard's manifest failures. That the Black Prince and Edward III should be summoned from their graves in a vain attempt to save Woodstock secularises the Morality device of the Good Angel who attempts to save the hero from his fate in Marlowe's *Dr Faustus*.

At a basic level we may explore *Thomas of Woodstock* as a moral history, drawing on the structures and conventions of the Tudor Interlude[71] and earlier dramas such as Skelton's *Magnificence*[72] and the medieval *Everyman*.[73] In such an analysis Richard II would stand for Magnificence whilst Woodstock might be interpreted as Measure and the minions as Cloaked Collusion, Courtly Abusion, Fancy or Crafty Conveyance etc. Such an interpretation can be supported by the play's potential emblematic staging: the Queen (Charity) and her maids collecting clothes for the poor (2.3), Richard's elevation of his supporters at the opening of 3.1, and Tresilian (Crafty Conveyance) '*with writings and a servant with bags of money*' (4.1). But whilst we may recognise such underlying structures, the text complicates our response in a number of ways. Woodstock is not a simple figure of virtue since he is continually at war with himself, attempting to preserve loyalty to the crown in others and yet failing to control his own temper at moments of crisis:

> *Queen Anne.* The king but jests, my lord, and you grow angry.
> *Woodstock.* T'other hose! Did some here wear that fashion
>   They would not tax and pill the commons so.
> *York.* [*to Lancaster*] 'Sfoot, he forewarned us and will break out
>   himself.
>
> (1.3.110–13)

Neither are Richard or Anne o' Beame simple exempla of vices or virtues. The dramatist provides the characters with individual traits which allow the actors to present more complex portraits. Anne's character has sufficient flexibility to convey a sense of insecurity and even embarrassment on her introduction to the English court (1.3), while Richard's distress at Anne's death and his repentance for his treatment of Woodstock (4.1), together with his grief for Greene's death (5.4), draw the audience's sympathy towards his personal suffering if not his political acumen. Thus the play makes an essential distinction between the *role* of those who exercise power and the *individual* who bears the responsibility, whether it be Woodstock or Richard. The play lays the weight of opprobrium, of course, on

Richard but it allows sufficient space for an audience to find in the character a measure of empathy for his grief at his wife's death and his distress on the death of his closest friend, Greene.[74]

Although the dramatist may have drawn on the dramatic work of his time, he has enhanced the work of his forebears. He is entirely innovative in his handling of the masque scene in which Woodstock is arrested (4.1) for, as Janet C. Stravopoulos has argued, the play initiates the dramatic practice of using the masque deceitfully as a cover for treason and murder.[75] In a plot devised by Tresilian, the King and his favourites disguise themselves as masquers and gain entry to Plashy, purporting to be a group of country gentlemen who wish to provide the Duke with entertainment. Despite his Duchess's earlier foreboding dream, the naive Woodstock welcomes them, prepares a banquet and calls for lights and music. Thus a series of dramatic ironies is created as Woodstock's fellowship and traditional hospitality are turned against him. Here the masque, an occasion designed to compliment the host and celebrate order and social harmony, is perverted by the King and his supporters to destroy the very model of responsible, trustworthy and compassionate governance.[76] The masquers, disguised as hunters, are introduced by Cynthia as knights who have travelled from afar to honour Woodstock as 'a faithful prince and peer' who maintains a 'court of love and pity' before they embark on a hunt for 'a cruel tuskèd boar' which has terrorised the kingdom. Tresilian's plotting and the Duchess's foreboding dream have already alerted the audience to the likely outcome of the masque, and a contemporary audience's association of the dukedom of Gloucester with the emblem of the boar[77] would confirm Woodstock as the victim of the hunt.

Courtesy, ceremony and decorum, the *raisons d'être* of the masque, are subverted as Woodstock, instead of being invited to participate in the celebration, is bundled into a masquing suit and carried off to Calais where he will meet his death. As has been suggested, the masquing suit into which Woodstock is forced would be wholly in keeping with the play's sensitivity to costume if it were elaborate enough to offer a sharp contrast to plain Thomas's habitual modesty. At a surface level the masque provides a dramatically spectacular episode allowing the audience to witness an aristocratic event closed to all outside the court. As such it offers the play's spectators a tantalising glimpse of stately entertainment, just as the play as a whole allows its audience to look beneath the façade of 'establishment' ceremony and public relations iconography to examine the naked ambition and jockeying for power and influence which characterises the *realpolitik* and falsehood of statecraft. The corruption which lies below the ceremonious surface of public life, a central feature of the text, and the King's perversion of privilege and custom are thus directly articulated in stage action.

THE ENDING

Woodstock has long been recognised as being remarkably critical of kingship among Elizabethan history plays; Rossiter noted that 'it is unorthodox, and its author an independent thinker';[78] Armstrong describes it as 'rather a challenge to orthodoxy than a confirmation of it';[79] Mannheim acknowledges that 'the possibility of deposition hardly seems unwelcome';[80] Heinemann sees it as 'in some ways the boldest and most subversive of all Elizabethan historical plays'.[81] Whilst the orthodox notion of adherence to the divine authority of the crown is repeatedly advocated by Woodstock himself, the tone of such avowals is increasingly desperate and the circumstances in which they are uttered make such policy appear progressively untenable. Technically, Woodstock remains loyal to the orthodox theory that a tyrant must be endured and dies a martyr to this belief, but his doctrinal passivity in the face of Richard's excesses serves to emphasise the limitations of such conventional views and conduct. Furthermore, no other play of the period is so peppered with references to the mutiny of the people[82] and, remarkably, all parties, including Richard's favourites and even the King himself, seem to concur that such rebellious thoughts are perfectly reasonable:

> *Greene.* 'Sfoot, what need you care what the world talks? You still retain the name of king, and if any disturb ye, we four comes presently from the four parts of the kingdom with four puissant armies to assist you.
> *King Richard.* You four must be all then, for I think nobody else will follow you, unless it be to hanging.
>
> (4.1.138–42)

So insistent are references to the mutiny of the commons that the Duchess of Gloucester's attempt to comfort the Queen is seen to be mere wishful thinking:

> Fear not that, madam, England's not mutinous:
> 'Tis peopled all with subjects, not with outlaws.
>
> (2.3.38–9)

It seems unlikely, however, that the lost ending of the play could actually have involved the deposition of Richard since his successor, Bolingbroke, is not active in the drama (or even mentioned) so no preparation for a change of monarch has been established. The most likely scenario is that Nimble's comic interlude with which the manuscript breaks off would have been followed by York's entry with the defeated King. York is a much more conciliatory character than his brothers, regarded by Richard as 'gentle, mild and generous' (2.1.127), and he has already interceded between Richard and Woodstock. It is fitting, therefore, that he should perform the delicate business of leading in the 'captive' Richard and effect a general reconciliation with the King. York's absence from the victorious entry at the beginning of 5.6 has puzzled previous editors but would be perfectly explained if this final role for him were assumed. It seems necessary that the play should end on a note of reconciliation, modifying the success of the rebels and the defeat of Richard, and thus restoring order and decorum. Allegiance could be restored to Richard if he were to reinstate York and Lancaster to the Council and affirm his intention to be a more responsible monarch in the future. Such a reconciliation is supported by Holinshed's account of the negotiations between the King and the magnates after Woodstock's death:

> At length, by the intercession and meanes of those noble men that went to and fro betwixt them, they were accorded, & the king promised from thencefoorth to doo nothing but by the assent of the dukes: but he kept small promise in this behalfe, as after well appeared. (1397, p. 490)

Audiences would be aware that Richard was eventually deposed because of his failure to reform; so that it is likely that there might have been a touch of irony in any promises he might give.[83]

STAGE HISTORY

The opening scene of Shakespeare's *Richard II* seems to have been written with an expectation that the Elizabethan audience would have been familiar with a play dealing with Woodstock's murder, probably *Thomas of Woodstock*.[84] If, as seems likely, Shakespeare was influenced by elements in the play[85] it is reasonable to assume that our play had a successful theatrical life, though no record of an actual performance has come down to us. It is possible that a performance of *Thomas of Woodstock* is indicated by a letter from

Sir Edward Hoby to Sir Robert Cecil, promising some form of entertainment where 'as late as it shal please you a gate for your supper shal be open; & K. Richard present himself to your view'. Many editors of Shakespeare's *Richard II* have assumed that the allusion is to a private performance of Shakespeare's play but the allusion could equally well apply to *Woodstock*, or, as some scholars have suggested, a portrait or tract on the subject of either Richard II or Richard III.[86] Simon Forman's account of details of a performance of 'Richard the 2 At the Glob 1611 the 30 of Aprill' makes it clear that the play is very different in its emphasis and treatment from either *Thomas of Woodstock* or Shakespeare's *Richard II*[87] but is further testimony to the continuing interest in Richard's reign as a subject for dramatic representation during the period. Any of these three plays about Richard II, or another on the same theme which is now lost to us, may be meant by the reference to an amateur performance of a play organised by William Keeling, Captain of the East India Company's ship *Dragon* off Sierra Leone who on 30 September 1607 entered in his diary: 'Captain Hawkins dined with me, when my companions acted King Richard the Second'.[88]

Further evidence to support a vigorous early stage history of *Woodstock* is to be found in the manuscript itself, which may well have been transcribed for the purposes of a Jacobean revival.[89] The intervention in the manuscript, whether by the theatre company or the Jacobean censor, Sir George Buc, is compelling evidence of preparation for performance; the variety of additional marginal notes in the manuscript, including those relating to properties needed for production such as 'Booke', 'Peticions', 'A bed for / woodstock'[90] also points to its having served, possibly over a period of time, as a book-keeper's copy.[91] The addition of stage directions relating to sound and music would seem to suggest a revival in which there was some attempt to embellish these effects, particularly in the masque scene, for an elaborately staged revival. The addition of act divisions, in an italic hand in the manuscript, may relate to the division of the play for the purposes of musical interludes at such a revival, possibly staged at an indoor private theatre. There is also a likelihood that the names 'George', 'Toby' and 'G ad' (*sic*) which the book-keeper has noted in the margins of the manuscript relate to actors hired to take on particular small parts for a specific performance. However, attempts to suggest that these names can be associated with a later revival in the second or third decade of the seventeenth century are very speculative, depending, as they do, upon similarities of names

which are not uncommon.[92] The condition of the manuscript itself
with erosions at the edges of the pages suggests its being in frequent
use, and repeatedly thumbed by the book-keeper in a number of
revivals.

A telling allusion in Jonson's *The Devil Is an Ass* provides supple-
mentary evidence of the play's impact on the play-going public:

> *Fitzdottrel.* But Thomas of Woodstock,
> I'm sure, was Duke, and he was made away
> At Calais; as Duke Humphrey was at Bury;
> And Richard the third, you know what end he came to.
> *Meercraft.* By my'faith you are cunning i'the chronicle, sir.
> *Fitzdottrel.* No, I confess I ha't from the play-books,
> And think they're more authentic.
>
> (2.4. 8–15)

In view of Fitzdottrel's direct reference to the murder of 'Thomas
of Woodstock' and his insistence that his knowledge comes via
'play-books' rather than the chronicles, it is likely that our play is
indicated, possibly available in a printed version in 1616 when
Jonson wrote the play.[93]

We do not know which acting company owned and played
Thomas of Woodstock, though various speculations have been made
by scholars.[94] Although the play deploys a large number of characters, it could with judicious doubling be played by a company of
sixteen actors, with the possible addition of one or two supernu-
meries to make up numbers for the guard of archers, attendants,
soldiers etc.[95] No modern revivals have been traced[96] but it would
be perfectly feasible to revive the play (with a supplied ending), in
tandem, perhaps, with Shakespeare's *Richard II*.[97]

THIS EDITION

Since her edition for the Malone Society in 1929 all editors and
scholars who have worked on the play have been indebted and to
some degree reliant upon Wihelmina Frijlinck's transcription of the
text and her work on the handwriting and inks used in the manuscript. Frijlinck detected eight hands which were distinguishable
in the manuscript apart from that of the main scribe. In addition to
the pale brown ink which the scribe used for the text and directions
as first written, she identified also ten further inks, five brown and
five grey, three of which may also have been scribal. As Frijlinck

acknowledged, not all of these discriminations are secure. Recent inspection of the manuscript confirms that some of her specific identifications must remain only speculative. Especially in the case of inks, variations inevitably occur in the process of dipping which can give a false impression of a change to a different ink. In the light of this it would be unwise to rely on identification of the variety of inks as a basis for a coherent theory of the manuscript's development.

All changes in the manuscript have been recorded in the textual collation but in many cases where words or passages have been crossed out or marked for deletion the original text has been retained on the grounds that the deletion may have been the result either of direct intervention by the censor or of self-censorship by the theatre company in anticipation of difficulties with the authorities. Where minor adjustments have been made in the manuscript for what appear to be stylistic or metrical reasons, these have, in some cases, been accepted, but the editors have reserved the right to ignore such changes where they seem to impair the emphasis or flow of a particular speech. In one case (3.2.63–6) the order of the lines of the manuscript appear to have been miscopied and are reversed in this edition.

Additional marginal stage directions in the manuscript, have, where they seem suggestive of staging possibilities, been incorporated into the text of this edition.[98] Although it is impossible to be sure of their date or status, such additions are valuable in suggesting how the text might have been realised on the Renaissance stage. Where speech prefixes or words in the text are missing because of erosion in the manuscript, conjectural readings are presented without the use of square brackets, but this edition follows Frijlinck in using in the textual collation angle brackets to indicate that the right ('mon<') or left ('>ll') edge, or sometimes the middle of the page ('<...>'), is eroded or torn, making letters either obscure or impossible to read. Where letters are given inside an angle bracket this indicates that they are conjectural ('<har>te' or 'Rigo<r').

The text as recorded by Frijlinck in her diplomatic edition for the Malone Society contains some readings and conjectures which it is now impossible to verify by examination of the manuscript in its present state. Such readings have been recorded in the collation and have been taken into account in arriving at the present text since it is possible that the manuscript was in a better condition in 1929. Accordingly, a distinction is sometimes made in the textual collation between the manuscript as it now appears and Frijlinck's version of it (e.g. 'credit] *conj. Frijlinck*; c< *Frijlinck; MS now obliterated*'). Because of the probability that the manuscript has declined in legibility over the years some variant readings by editors prior to Frijlinck are also collated, though it is obvious at times that these previous editors were prone to misreading.[99]

Rossiter, in his edition, made an interesting case for the scribe's punctuation in the manuscript as the equivalent to a form of musical notation, designed to indicate particular nuances and rhythms of the speaking voice. He attempted to carry this into his own modernised text by liberal use of dashes, colons and italics, whilst at the same time acknowledging the inadequacy of modern syntax-based punctuation to operate with the freedom and suggestiveness of the Elizabethan theatre script.[100] Since, however, the manuscript appears to be a Jacobean transcription it is hard to be sure that its punctuation is faithful to authorial intentions. Moreover, as both Frijlinck and Partridge observe, commas and full stops are often difficult to distinguish in the manuscript, and what now appear as periods may have been in the original draft 'imperfectly tailed commas'.[101] The problem of pointing is further compounded by the scribe's habit of rarely using punctuation at the end of a line and often omitting to provide punctuation where it is clearly needed; stretches of text as long as ten to twelve lines are found at times with no pointing at all.[102]

We have made a close study of the pointing for the entire text, the result of which indicates that the scribal pointing is as likely to be arbitrary as it is to be significant, and for this reason have treated it with great caution.[103] However, there do appear to be specific places where the manuscript pointing can make a significant contribution to the emphasis, tone or nuance of a speech. In such cases, in so far as modern conventions of punctuation allow, the present text attempts to reflect these indications. For example, in Woodstock's speech in 1.3, the manuscript's staccato mid-line pointing seems to convey Woodstock's sense of the chaos of affairs and the urgency of the crisis which engulfs him:

> the commons they rebell: & the king all careless
> heeres wrong on wrong. to stirr more mutiny
> a fore my god I knowe not what to doe
>
> (1.3.244–6)

an effect which is repeated later:

The commons will rebell wthout all questione
& fore my god. I have no eloquence
to stay this vproore. I must tell them playne
we all are strocke. but must not stricke agayne

(3.2.110–14)

Prose passages, too, including some of Tresilian's and Nimble's speeches, appear to be carefully pointed. The most striking case of this occurs in the dialogue of the first murderer:

lett him sprall & hang. hees sure enough for speakeing,
pull of the bed now. smooth downe his hayre & beard.
close his eyes. & sett his necke right: why so: all fine & cleanely,
who can say that this man was murderd now,

(5.1.242–6)

Here the heavy pointing in the manuscript seems to reflect the tension and urgency of the stage action.

Rossiter was undoubtedly right to lament the inadequacies of modern conventions of punctuation to capture the freedom and suggestiveness of Elizabethan dramatic pointing, but modern-day directors and actors must be trusted to make their own contribution in realising a Renaissance play-text. The editor can only hope to have produced a text which facilitates reading but does not iron out complexity and ambiguity.

NOTES

1 See also Partridge, *Orthography*, pp. 34–42.
2 For a discussion of the surviving Renaissance theatre manuscripts see Long, *Few*, and also Long, *Bed*.
3 For a detailed discussion of the status of the marginalia of the manuscript see Long, *Bed*.
4 Marginal interventions in the text are recorded and discussed in Appendix D.
5 See T. Howard-Hill, pp. 168–77, and the discussion under 'Censorship' below.
6 See Long, *Few*, p. 416.
7 Rossiter, p. 178.
8 Long, *Bed*, p. 96.
9 See discussion under 'Date and Literary Influences' below.
10 See Partridge, *Orthography*, pp. 34–42.
11 See Lake, pp. 133–43.
12 See discussion under 'Censorship' below.
13 Ed. W. I. Carpenter (1900).
14 Ed. J. O. Halliwell-Phillips (1870).

15 Ed. W. Keller (1899).
16 Ed. W. P. Frijlinck (1929).
17 Ed. W. A. Armstrong (1965) and eds E. B. Everitt and R. L. Armstrong (1965).
18 Ed. A. P. Rossiter (1946).
19 Eds George Parfitt and Simon Shepherd (1977).
20 Rossiter, pp. 26–7.
21 Although Tresilian, as Vice or Machiavel, is presented as the chief archi-tect of England's wrongs, his dramatic presentation, accompanied con-stantly with his comic side-kick Nimble, is relatively light weight.
22 Mannheim, pp. 71–80, treats these plays as a group reflecting public anxiety about the crown at this time.
23 See Rossiter, pp. 66–71.
24 See Marlowe, *Edward*, pp. 35–6.
25 See Rossiter's discussion, p. 68 and his commentary notes to the text.
26 Rossiter, pp. 53–65.
27 Melchiori, pp. 170–1, argues that Shakespeare 'undoubtedly intended to counteract' the presentation of Richard found in *Woodstock* and in order to do so focused on the later developments of Richard's reign.
28 Rossiter, p. 18.
29 Bushy gives Holinshed's version at 2.1.105–6, but Woodstock appears to know the correct date at 2.2.100–1.
30 4.1.122–4.
31 4.2.66–8.
32 1.3.59–61.
33 5.5.0.1.
34 Rossiter, pp. 24–5.
35 *Mirror*, p. 50.
36 *Mirror*, pp. 63–4.
37 *Mirror*, pp. 113–14.
38 *Mirror*, pp. 77–8.
39 *Mirror*, pp. 93–4.
40 See, for example, 4.1.18–63 and 4.3.126–35.
41 See below.
42 Quoted by Neale, p. 306. Cf. 4.1.160 n.
43 Clare, pp. 58–60.
44 *Jack Straw*, eds Kenneth Muir and F. P. Wilson.
45 The details of Richard II's deposition were also excised from the 1586/7 edition of Holinshed's *Chronicles* although they had been thoroughly narrated in the earlier 1577 edition.
46 *King Richard II*, ed. Peter Ure (London, 1956), p. xiv, and *King Richard II*, ed. Andrew Gurr (Cambridge, 1984) p. 9.
47 Clare, pp. 68–72. Dutton, p. 125, conjectures that the 'abdication' scene may be an element of Shakespeare's revision of the text.
48 Chambers, *ES*, p. 205.
49 Schoenbaum, p. 87.
50 Quoted in *King Richard II*, ed. Peter Ure, p. lix.
51 Hayward, p. 61. Translation from Latin by John J. Manning, p. 61. Manning's introduction provides a detailed account of the circum-stances surrounding the publication and suppression of Hayward's book; see especially pp. 17–34.

52 Chamberlain, I, p. 70.
53 Quoted by Manning in Hayward, p. 20.
54 Hayward, p. 121.
55 Hayward, p. 124; cf. *Woodstock*, 2.2.161.
56 See the editions of Rossiter, and Parfitt and Shepherd; and see also Clare, pp. 64–7, and Dutton, p. 148.
57 See the discussion under 'The Manuscript' above.
58 P. 28.
59 P. 66.
60 Clare, p. 66, seems to suggest that the Master of the Revels might well have perused manuscripts at an early stage of their preparation but offers no concrete evidence in support.
61 See Howard-Hill, pp. 168–77.
62 All of the crosses are recorded in Frijlinck's Malone Society edition, either in her text or noted in her collation, with the exception of crosses which we have noted in the manuscript at 2.3.101 and 4.2.157.
63 See for example 1.1.133.
64 See Rossiter, p. 189, and *Second Maiden*, p. 285.
65 See Clare, p. 66.
66 Whilst *Richard II* lacks a wide canvas, the *Henry 4* plays parallel *Thomas of Woodstock* in their social range. It may be that Shakespeare was influenced by the earlier play's example.
67 There are numerous references in the play (at least fifteen) to the commons' discontent as a potential cause of rebellion.
68 *1H4*, 1.3.28–68.
69 Clemen, pp. 207–10.
70 Quoted by Hunter, *Seneca*, p. 23.
71 Discussed by Rossiter, pp. 9–10. See also *Tudor Interludes*.
72 John Skelton, *Magnificence*.
73 *Everyman*.
74 Melchiori presents an alternative view that *Woodstock* shows an 'utterly negative presentation of the figure of the king', pp. 170–1.
75 See Stravopoulos, pp. 1–14. She suggests a possible source in Holinshed (1587) where it is related that in 1400 Richard II's supporters mounted an abortive plot to murder Henry IV during a masque (p. 9).
76 The masque performed for Woodstock does not follow the elaborate patterning of the Jacobean masque but is closer to the 'disguising' in which Henry VIII courts Anne Boleyn in *Henry VIII (All Is True)*, 1.4.64.1–112.
77 The boar was the emblem of Richard, Duke of Gloucester, later Richard III.
78 P. 32.
79 *Elizabethan History Plays* (Oxford, 1965), p. xi.
80 Manheim, p. 73.
81 Heinemann, p. 184.
82 See 1.1.157–9, 1.3.122–5, 232–56, 2.2.4–6, 41–50, 2.3.18–21, 36–7, 3.3.67–87, 131–2, 4.1.81–2, 121–2, 4.2.147–8, 161–3, 204–6, 5.1.99, 5.3.32–6.
83 See Manheim, p. 73.
84 This impression is reinforced by the fact that some modern directors of

Richard II feel the need to reverse the first two scenes of Shakespeare's play for the sake of audience comprehension.

85 See discussion under 'Date and Literary Influences' above.

86 See David M. Bergeron, 'The Hoby Letter and *Richard II*: A Parable of Criticism', *SQ* 26 (1975), pp. 477–80 and also A. N. Kincaid, 'Sir Edward Hoby and "K. Richard": Shakespeare Play or Morton Tract?', *N&Q* (April 1981), pp. 124–7.

87 See Chambers, *WS*, II, pp. 339–40.

88 See Dover Wilson, New Cambridge edition of *Richard II*, p. lxxviii.

89 See discussion under 'The Manuscript' above.

90 See Long, *Bed*.

91 'There are over twenty prompt directions added in different hands pointing to several revisers and repeated revivals of the play' (Frijlinck, p. xxi).

92 See commentary notes at 1.1.124, 3.2.109 and 4.2.95. Long, *Few*, suggests that these names relate to a revival around 1633 on the grounds that the hand is the same as that of the book-keeper who made marginal entries in the manuscript of Mountfort's *The Launching of the Mary*, licensed by Sir Henry Herbert on 22 June 1633.

93 The death is referred to as a past event in Shakespeare's *Richard II*, but the phrase 'Thomas of Woodstock' is not employed; no mention of Woodstock's death is given in Simon Forman's summary of the plot of the play at the performance mentioned above.

94 See Chambers, *ES*, IV, pp. 42–3.

95 See Appendix E for a conjectural casting and doubling plot for the play.

96 No mention of the play is to be found in Lisa Cronin, *Professional Productions in the British Isles since 1880 of Plays by Tudor and Early Stuart Dramatists (excluding Shakespeare)*, Renaissance Drama Newsletter Supplement Seven (University of Warwick, 1987), nor in William Hindle, 'Shakespeare's Contemporaries in the Theatre 1890–1968', unpublished University of Birmingham MA, 1969.

97 A 'rehearsed reading' of the text was given by the Royal Shakespeare Company in The Swan Theatre, Stratford-upon-Avon on 19 August 2000 with a cast including Samuel West as Richard II, Ian Hogg as Lancaster and David Troughton as Tresilian.

98 All such directions appear in the textual collation.

99 Frijlinck acknowledges that it 'is possible that when Halliwell's edition was prepared some words may have been more legible than they are now' (p. xxx).

100 See pp. 174–8.

101 Partridge, *Orthography*, p. 42; see also Frijlinck, p. x.

102 See, for example, 1.1.27–33, 2.1.63–74, 3.1.61–71.

103 Disregarding cases where MS's pointing clearly relates to and confirms the obvious needs of the syntax, a study was made of all MS's more contentious pointing with the following result: roughly 44 per cent of such cases were inconclusive; in some 40 per cent of cases MS's punctuation seemed distinctly erratic or unhelpful; in roughly 16 per cent of cases, though, MS's punctuation did seem to indicate a specific purpose in terms of emphasis, rhythm or tone.

THOMAS OF WOODSTOCK
or RICHARD THE SECOND, PART ONE

DRAMATIS PERSONAE

[THOMAS OF WOODSTOCK, Duke of
   Gloucester, *Lord Protector*
DUKE OF LANCASTER, John of Gaunt
DUKE OF YORK, Edmund of Langley
EARL OF ARUNDEL, *Lord Admiral of*
   England
EARL OF SURREY

} *uncles to the king*

5

DRAMATIS PERSONAE] No cast list is provided in the MS. The cast-list is a re-arrangement and expansion of Parfitt and Shepherd's edition.

1. *WOODSTOCK*] Also Earl of Buckingham (1355–97). One of Richard II's main opponents who, with other Appellants, defeated De Vere, one of Richard II's favourites, at Radcote Bridge in 1388 and had considerable influence on the Merciless Parliament which established the Appellant's control of the affairs of the realm until 1389 when Richard II wrested control of the kingdom from him. Most editors of Shakespeare's Histories follow York's genealogy of the sons of Edward III (*2H6*, 2.2.10–17) which gives Woodstock as the 'sixth' son, followed by the elusive William of Windsor who died in infancy. Woodstock was, however, the *seventh* son of Edward III, for William was the elder of the two; see *DNB* and McKisak. Shakespeare's genealogy cannot always be trusted. For the source of this error see Karl P. Wentersdorf, 'Shakespeare's Richard II: Gaunt's Part in Woodstock's Blood', *ELN* 18, no. 2 (1980), p. 99.

3. *LANCASTER*] John of Gaunt (Ghent, his birthplace), 1340–99, the fourth son of Edward III; his eldest son, Henry Bolingbroke (later Henry IV), deposed Richard II in 1399.

4. *YORK*] Fifth son to Edward III and first Duke of York (1341–1402); he plays a significant role in Shakespeare's *R2*.

5. *ARUNDEL*] Richard Fitzalan (1346–97), also Earl of Surrey and Admiral of the West. One of the Lords Appellant, he was a close ally of Gloucester. He won a naval victory over the French, Spanish and Flemings at Cadzand (off Margate) in 1387 in which he captured a hundred vessels laden with wine for the French forces at Sluys. He was executed on Tower Hill in 1397.

7. *SURREY*] There is some confusion here; the Earl of Surrey was Arundel's alternative title. Thomas Holland, Earl of Kent (1374–1400), a supporter of Richard II, was created *Duke* of Surrey in 1597 and executed for conspiring against Henry IV. It appears that the dramatist has created a ghost character by a misunderstanding.

SIR THOMAS CHENEY, *supporter of Woodstock and his brothers*
LORD MAYOR EXTON, *Lord Mayor of London*
KING RICHARD II, *King of England, son of the Black Prince* 10
and grandson of Edward III

SIR HENRY GREENE ⎫
SIR EDWARD BAGOT ⎪
⎬ *favourites of the king*
SIR WILLIAM BUSHY ⎪
SIR THOMAS SCROOP ⎭ 15

SIR ROBERT TRESILIAN, *a lawyer, subsequently Lord Chief*
Justice of England
NIMBLE, *his man*
A Servant *to Tresilian*
CROSBY ⎫
⎬ *Tresilian's law officers* 20
FLEMING ⎭

---

8. CHENEY] Although Rossiter describes Cheney as Woodstock's 'atten-dant', his role is more extensive since he plays a significant part in the battle in Act 5 and is also the bearer of messages and news at significant points in the play. Whilst no Thomas Cheney is associated with Woodstock historically, a Sir John Cheyne of Beckford, Gloucestershire, who was allied with Wood-stock, was proceeded against by Richard after the latter's death (see Saul, p. 381 n.).

10. KING RICHARD II] 1367–99; he became king in 1377 and was known as Richard of Bordeaux after his place of birth.

12. GREENE] Member of Parliament for Northamptonshire, royal coun-cillor and member of the Regency Council during the king's Irish campaign; he was executed at Bristol by Bolingbroke in 1399.

13. BAGOT] Sheriff of Leicester and Member of Parliament, royal coun-cillor and member of the Regency Council. Escaped to Ireland after Bol-ingbroke's rebellion, was later imprisoned but released to die in retirement.

14. BUSHY] Sheriff of Lincoln, Speaker of the House of Commons and member of the Regency Council. Executed at Bristol in 1399 by Bolingbroke.

15. SCROOP] Historically, Sir William Scrope (1351?–99), Earl of Wilt-shire, Treasurer of England and member of the Regency Council; he was executed at Bristol in 1399 by Bolingbroke.

16. TRESILIAN] The first victim of the Appellants (the faction of mag-nates who took power from the King); he was executed in 1388. He tried and condemned John Ball and his followers at the time of the Peasants' Revolt. One of Richard II's advisers, he was hanged at Tyburn for treason, having been dragged from the sanctuary of Westminster Abbey by Woodstock.

18. NIMBLE] Whilst reflecting his nimbleness in sharp practice, Nimble's name also carries bawdy implications appropriate to his frequent sexual punning. See Rubinstein, 'Nimble = Lusty. ME "nimel": quick at seizing' (p. 170). Cf. Marston, *The Dutch Courtesan*, 2.1. 'a puncke . . . smooth thigh, and the nimble Divell in her buttocke'.

Master IGNORANCE, *the Baily of Dunstable*
A Farmer
A Butcher
COWTAIL, *a grazier*   25
A Schoolmaster
A Serving-man
A Whistler
A Servant *at Plashy House*
A Courtier   30
CYNTHIA, *prologue to the masque*
THE SHRIEVE *of Kent*
THE SHRIEVE *of Northumberland*
LAPOOLE, *Governor of Calais*
1 GHOST (*of the Black Prince*)   35
2 GHOST (*of King Edward III*)
1 Murderer
2 Murderer
Soldiers *of the Calais garrison*

ANNE O' BEAME (Anne of Bohemia), *Queen of England*   40

---

22. Baily] Bailiff; a law officer under the authority of a sheriff.

31. *CYNTHIA*] Probably played by the boy actor taking the part of Anne O' Beame; see commentary note at 4.2.101.4 and Appendix E.

32. *SHRIEVE*] Sheriff; an officer appointed by the crown to be the monarch's representative in a county and having wide powers in legal and administrative affairs.

34. *LAPOOLE*] Michael de la Pole, first Earl of Suffolk (1320?–89). The young King Richard's most trusted adviser, he was driven into exile by the Appellants in 1387 and died in Paris. His brother, not the play's Lapoole, held the governorship of Calais early in Richard's reign. Thomas Mowbray held the governorship at the time of Woodstock's death.

35. Black Prince] Edward, Prince of Wales (1330–76), eldest son of Edward III and father of Richard II, most famous for his role in the battle of Crècy, where he commanded the vanguard.

36. Edward III] Richard II's grandfather (1312–77). He was held to be a model of chivalry and waged war in Scotland, France and Spain whilst maintaining peace at home.

40. *ANNE O' BEAME*] Richard II's first queen (1366–94). She married him in 1382 and earned a reputation for humanity and charity, interceding on the part of some of the rebels during the Peasants' Revolt and, in 1392, on behalf of the City of London in its quarrel with the King. It appears that she and her large Bohemian retinue were instrumental in introducing lavish changes in fashion and costume, and that the resulting expense had much

DUCHESS OF GLOUCESTER, *wife of Thomas of Woodstock*
DUCHESS OF IRELAND, *wife of the deceased Robert de Vere, the*
    King's former favourite
A Maid-in-waiting *to the Queen*

Courtiers, Masquers, Officers, Gentlemen, Servants, Maids,   45
    Soldiers, Archers]

---

to do with the disagreements between Richard and his Parliaments. The historical Queen Anne died before the plotting of Woodstock's murder.
   41. *DUCHESS OF GLOUCESTER*] Eleanor Bohun, daughter of Bohun, Earl of Hereford.
   42. *DUCHESS OF IRELAND*] Philippa de Coucy, married de Vere in 1378.

Act I

Enter hastily at several doors: DUKE *of* LANCASTER,
DUKE *of* YORK, *the* EARLS *of* ARUNDEL *and* SURREY,
with napkins on their arms and knives in their hands;
and SIR THOMAS CHENEY, *with others bearing torches,*
and some with cloaks and rapiers.

All. Lights, lights! Bring torches, knaves!
Lancaster.   Shut to the gates!
　Let no man out until the house be searched.
York. Call for our coaches! Let's away, good brother.
　Now by th'blest saints, I fear we are poisoned all.
Arundel. Poisoned, my lord?   5
Lancaster. Ay, ay, good Arundel, 'tis high time begone.
　May Heaven be blest for this prevention.
York. God for thy mercy! Would our cousin king
　So cozen us, to poison us in our meat?
Lancaster. Has no man here some helping antidote   10
　For fear already we have ta'en some dram?
　What thinkest thou, Cheney? Thou first broughtst the
　　tidings;
　Are we not poisoned, thinkest thou?
Cheney.   Fear not, my lords.
　That mischievous potion was as yet unserved:

1.1 Act I] (i) *Sceane MS.* 1. *All*] *Omnes MS.* 2–3. Shut ... searched]
Rossiter; one line in MS. 7. *May*] ma *altered from* m *in slightly darker ink in*
MS. *Heaven*] heaven *MS (replacing deleted* god*);* heaven *interlined above*
deletion in same hand but in a slightly darker ink.

　1.1.01–5.] The alarm with which the play begins is admirably caught by the
confusion of the characters' entrances, some just departed from the table (cf.
Heywood, 8.21.1–2) and others having snatched up rapiers for their defence.
　6. *time begone*] i.e. time to be gone.
　9. *cozen*] cheat, deceive.
　in our meat] during our meal.
　14–17. *That mischievous ... health*] It is likely that the contemporary audi-

It was a liquid bane dissolved in wine,   15
Which after supper should have been caroused
To young King Richard's health.
Lancaster. Good i'faith! Are his uncles' deaths become
Health to King Richard? How came it out?
Sir Thomas Cheney, pray resolve us.   20
Cheney. A Carmelite friar, my lord, revealed the plot
And should have acted it, but, touched in conscience,
He came to your good brother, the Lord Protector,
And so disclosed it, who straight sent me to you.
York. The Lord protect him for it, ay, and our cousin king. 25
High Heaven be judge, we wish all good to him—
Lancaster. A heavy charge, good Woodstock, hast thou had
To be Protector to so wild a prince,
So far degenerate from his noble father,
Whom the trembling French the Black Prince called,   30
Not of a swart and melancholy brow,
For sweet and lovely was his countenance,
But that he made so many funeral days

---

20. resolve us] *MS (*this doubt *following* resolve us *deleted), us* interlined
before deletion in different ink. 30–6. Whom . . . arm] *marked for deletion by
the word* out *in the margin at l. 33 and the lines crossed out in MS, seemingly in
the same ink as the alterations at l. 12.*

---

ence would have been outraged by such a plot since poisoning seems to have
been regarded with singular abhorrence. In October 1615 Sir John Throck-
morton, commenting on the murder of Sir Thomas Overbury, reported that
foreigners 'begin to brand and mark us with that hideous and foul title of
poisoning one another, and ask if we become Italians, Spaniards or of what
other vile, murderous nation', Somerset, p. 462. Since it is alleged that the
poison was to be administered by a Carmelite friar, it is possible that the
episode also provoked an anti-Roman Catholic response.

   21. *Carmelite friar*] a member of the Carmelite order of mendicant friars
who derived their origin from a colony founded on Mount Carmel.

   23. *Lord Protector*] Historically inaccurate since no formal office of Lord
Protector was created during Richard II's minority.

   31. *of*] because of.

   swart] black, dark complexioned.

   brow] aspect, appearance.

   33.] The status of the marginal instruction 'out' accompanying the deletion of ll. 30–6 is not certain; it may be a playhouse cut or, possibly, the mark
of the censor; see 'Censorship' section in Introduction. It should be noted
that if these lines are deleted ll. 37–8 also need to be cut since they make no
sense on their own.

In mournful France: the warlike battles won
At Crécy field, Poitiers, Artois and Maine   35
Made all France groan under his conquering arm.
But Heaven forestalled his diadem on earth
To place him with a royal crown in Heaven.
Rise may his dust to glory! Ere he'd've done
A deed so base unto his enemy,   40
Much less unto the brothers of his father,
He'd first have lost his royal blood in drops,
Dissolved the strings of his humanity
And lost that livelihood that was preserved
To make his—unlike—son a wanton king.   45
York. Forbear, good John of Gaunt; believe me, brother,
We may do wrong unto our cousin king:
I fear his flattering minions more than him.
Lancaster. By the blest Virgin, noble Edmund York,
I'm past all patience. Poison his subjects,   50
His royal uncles! Why, the proud Castilian,
Where John of Gaunt writes king and sovereign,
Would not throw off their vile and servile yoke
By treachery so base. Patience, gracious Heaven!
Arundel. A good invoke. Right princely Lancaster,   55
Calm thy high spleen. Sir Thomas Cheney here
Can tell the circumstance; pray give him leave.

---

45. unlike] (vnlike) *MS.*   51. Castilian] Castillyan *MS;* Castilians *Arm-strong.*   53. vile] vyle *Halliwell;* vyld *MS.*   55. A] a *MS;* O *Halliwell, Keller.*

34–5. *battles . . . Maine*] Crécy, a small town near the mouth of the Somme, where the French were defeated by Edward III in 1346; Poitiers, the capital of the province of Poitou where the Black Prince defeated the army of Jean II of France in 1356; Artois, a province of northern France whose capital was Arras; Maine, a French province, capital Le Mans, which lay between Normandy and Anjou. The dramatist takes a measure of dramatic licence in exaggerating the conquering role of Richard II's father in order to emphasise the son's failings. The MS's spelling of French place names, e.g. 'Cressey', 'poyteeres' and 'Artoyse', may indicate contemporary Elizabethan pronunciation.

43. *strings . . . humanity*] i.e. heartstrings of his life; cf. *Lear* (*History*), 24.213.

44. *livelihood*] animation, life.

45. *unlike*] MS's brackets serve to emphasise the stark contrast with Richard's father.

51–4. *proud Castilian . . . base*] Gaunt claimed the throne of Castile through his marriage to Constanza, the daughter of Pedro, King of Castile and Leon, although he failed to acquire sovereignty of the kingdom.

55. *invoke*] invocation, prayer; not recorded in this form in *OED.*

Lancaster. Well, let him speak.

Cheney. 'Tis certainly made known, my reverend lords,
  To your loved brother and the good Protector,   60
  That not King Richard but his flatterers,
  Sir Henry Greene, joined with Sir Edward Bagot,
  And that sly machiavel, Tresilian,
  Whom now the king elects for Lord Chief Justice,
  Had all great hands in this conspiracy.   65

Lancaster. By blessèd Mary, I'll confound them all!

York. Your spleen confounds yourself.

Lancaster. By kingly Edward's soul, my royal father,
  I'll be revenged at full on all their lives.

York. Nay, if your rage break to such high extremes   70
  You will prevent yourself and lose revenge.

Lancaster. Why, Edmund, canst thou give a reason yet
  Though we so near in blood, his hapless uncles,
  His grandsire Edward's sons—his father's brothers—
  Should thus be made away? Why might it be   75
  That Arundel and Surrey here should die?

Surrey. Some friend of theirs wanted my earldom sore.

Arundel. Perhaps my office of the Admiralty!
  If a better and more fortunate hand could govern it
  I would 'twere none of mine.   80
  Yet thus much can I say, and make my praise
  No more than merit: a wealthier prize
  Did never yet take harbour in our roads
  Than I to England brought. You all can tell
  Full threescore sail of tall and lusty ships   85
  And six great carracks fraught with oil and wines
  I brought King Richard in abundance home;
  So much that plenty hath so staled our palates

---

77. sore] *Frijlinck; either* svre *or* sore *MS;* sure *Carpenter.*   79–80. If . . .
mine] *MS;* If . . . hand / Could . . . mine *Keller.*   88. so staled] so stailed
MS; to staild *Halliwell, Keller.*

---

67. *spleen*] fiery temper.
71. *prevent*] frustrate, bring to nought (*OED* II.10).
77. *sore*] sorely.
82–90. *a wealthier prize . . . money*] Parfitt notes that the dramatist con-
fuses or compresses two of Arundel's raids as recorded in Holinshed and Stow.
86. *carracks*] armed merchant-men, galleons.
fraught] freighted, loaded.
88. *staled*] made stale, cheapened.

As that a tun of high-prized wines of France
Is hardly worth a mark of English money.   90
If service such as this done to my country
Merit my heart to bleed, let it bleed freely.
Lancaster. We'll bleed together, warlike Arundel.
Cousin of Surrey, princely Edmund York,
Let's think on some revenge: if we must die   95
Ten thousand souls shall keep us company.
York. Patience, good Lancaster. Tell me, kind Cheney,
How does thy master, our good brother Woodstock,
Plain Thomas, for by th'rood so all men call him
For his plain dealing and his simple clothing?   100
'Let others jet in silk and gold', says he,
'A coat of English frieze best pleaseth me'.
How thinks his unsophisticated plainness
Of these bitter compounds? Fears he no drug
Put in his broth? Shall his healths be secure?   105
Cheney. Faith, my lord, his mind suits with his habit,
Homely and plain, both free from pride and envy,
And therein will admit distrust to none.

Enter THOMAS *of* WOODSTOCK *in frieze, the mace*
[carried before him]; the LORD MAYOR EXTON
and others with lights afore them.

89. high-prized] hye prizd *MS;* high-priced *Rossiter.* 101. jet] Iett *MS;*
sett *Halliwell, Keller.* 102.] *A word written over and perhaps deleted is now*
indecipherable in the left-hand margin of MS. 105. be] *MS;* best *Halliwell,*
Keller. 108.2. SD add.] *This ed.; MS is eroded at this point.* 108.2. LORD
MAYOR EXTON] *Rossiter;* Lord Mayre & Exton *MS.*

90. *mark*] coin valued at two-thirds of a pound sterling.
101. *jet*] swagger, walk pompously.
102. *English frieze*] a kind of coarse woollen cloth with a nap, usually on
one side only. Woodstock's preference for English cloth is an aspect of his
patriotism and makes a forcible contrast with the flatterers' indulgence in
excessive foreign fashion; cf. the proverbial expression 'The English are the
Frenchman's apes' (Tilley E153).
103. *unsophisticated*] uncorrupted, genuine.
104. *compounds*] mixed substances as opposed to 'simples' (drugs of one
ingredient only).
108.1. *mace*] The symbol of authority, carried before Woodstock, which
signifies his office as Protector.
108.2. *EXTON*] Although the MS announces the Lord Mayor and Exton
as separate characters, Richard Exton, according to Holinshed, was Lord

And see, his grace himself is come to greet you.
By your leave there. Room for my Lord Protector's grace!   110
York, Lancaster. Health to your grace.
Woodstock. I salute your healths, good brothers; pray pardon
    me,
I'll speak with you anon. Hie thee, good Exton,
Good Lord Mayor, I do beseech ye prosecute
With your best care a means for all our safeties.   115
Mischief hath often double practices;
Treachery wants not his second strategem;
Who knows but steel may hit though poison fail?
Alack the day, the night is made a veil
To shadow mischief. Set, I beseech,   120
Strong guard and careful to attend the city.
Our Lady help, we know not who are friends,
Our foes are grown so mighty; pray be careful.
Lord Mayor. Your friends are great in London, good my lord.
I'll front all dangers, trust it on my word.   125
      Exit LORD MAYOR [EXTON *with others*].

124.] G ad *written in darker ink and different hand in left-hand margin
over something illegible, the original letter showing between* G *and* ad *is illegible.* great] 'Greate' *written over the word* strong *in MS in sligtly darker
ink.*

Mayor of London at this time. As Rossiter points out, the exit at l. 125.1 is
a single one; moreover, Woodstock's remarks appear to be addressed to one
person.
  116. *double*] with a play on deceitful.
  practices] invariably carrying machiavellian overtones of intrigue in
Renaissance literature.
  117. *wants . . . stratagem*] i.e. does not lack alternative plots.
  120. *shadow*] conceal.
  124.] Frijlinck suggests that the MS's marginal note may be intended
to indicate Grad, i.e. Gradell (Henry Gradwell) an actor associated
with Prince Charles's company; G. E. Bentley suggests 'Goad' for
Christoper Goad whose name appears in the list of actors of a touring
company of 1635; see Bentley, II, pp. 444–5. If this is a reference to an
actor, and assuming that he played the part of the Lord Mayor, it is
interesting that the note appears opposite his sole speech rather than his
entrance.
  great] the substitution in the MS of 'great' for 'strong' may appear to be
of marginal significance, but it may indicate a desire to associate Woodstock
with aristocratic rather than common support.
  125. *front*] confront, oppose.

Woodstock. Thanks from my heart. I swear, afore my God,
I know not which way to bestow myself
The time's so busy and so dangerous too.
Why, how now, brothers? How fares good John o'Gaunt?
Thou'rt vexed I know; thou griev'st, kind Edmund York.   130
Arundel and Surrey, noble kinsmen,
I know ye all are discontented much;
But be not so. Afore my God, I swear
King Richard loves you all; and, credit me,
The princely gentleman is innocent   135
Of this black deed, and base conspiracy.
Speak, speak, how is't with princely Lancaster?
Lancaster. Sick, Gloucester, sick. We all are weary,
And fain we would lie down to rest ourselves,
But that so many serpents lurk i'th' grass   140
We dare not sleep.
Woodstock.   Enough, enough,
Good brother, I have found out the disease:
When the head aches, the body is not healthful.
King Richard's wounded with a wanton humour,
Lulled and secured by flattering sycophants;   145
But 'tis not deadly yet, it may be cured:
Some vein let blood where the corruption lies
And all shall heal again.
York. Then lose no time, lest it grow ulcerous.

127–8. I . . . too] *marked, apparently, for deletion in darker ink in MS.*
133. my God] *deleted in MS.* 136. deed, and base] *This ed.;* deed. and,
base *MS.* 141–2. Enough . . . disease] *one line in MS.*

127–8. *I know . . . too*] Possibly marked for deletion because of the repetition of l. 127 at 1.3.240.

133. *my God*] Possibly the oath was deleted in response to the 'Acte to
restraine Abuses of Players' of 1606 which forbad the familiar use of 'the
holy Name of God or of Christ Jesus, or of the Holy Ghoste or the Trinitie'
in stage plays. If this is the case the removal of the such oaths in this text is
half-hearted.

136. *deed . . . conspiracy*] The nouns 'deed' and 'conspiracy' are not syn-
onymous; Rossiter paraphrases Woodstock's meaning as 'the king is innocent
of this black deed (in particular) and equally of conspiracy (in general)'.

142–9. *Good . . . ulcerous*] Woodstock draws on contemporary medical
belief to diagnose the corruption of the king as representative of the state;
cf. *R2*, 1.1.152–7.

147. *Some . . . blood*] i.e. 'May some vein let blood'.

The false Tresilian, Greene, and Bagot　　　　　150
Run nought but poison, brother. Spill them all.
Lancaster. They guide the nonage king; 'tis they protect him.
Ye wear the title of Protectorship
But like an under-officer, as though
Yours were derived from theirs. 'Faith, you're too plain!　155
Woodstock. In my apparel, you'll say.
Lancaster.　　　　　　　　　　　Good faith, in all.
The commons murmur 'gainst the dissolute king.
Treason is whispered at each common table
As customary as their thanks to Heaven.
Men need not gaze up to the sky to see　　　　160
Whether the sun shine clear or no; 'tis found
By the small light should beautify the ground.
Conceit you me, a blind man thus much sees:
He wants his eyes to whom we bend our knees.
Arundel. You all are princes of the royal blood,　　165
Yet like great oaks ye let the ivy grow
To eat your hearts out with his false embraces.
Ye understand, my lord?
Woodstock. Ay, ay, good coz, as if ye plainly said,
'Destroy those flatterers and tell King Richard　170
He does abase himself to countenance them.'
Soft, soft.

---

156. you'll] youle *MS;* yould *Halliwell.*　157. dissolute] *Rossiter;* dessolat
MS.　163. Conceit] consaite *MS;* counsaile *conj. Carpenter.*　169. coz]
Cuss *MS;* cussen *Halliwell, Carpenter.*　171-2. He . . . soft] *one line in MS.*

---

151. *run*] discharge.
spill] destroy.
152. *They . . . they*] Lancaster's stress on the pronoun 'they' expresses his
deep anxiety at Woodstock's overly diplomatic role.
nonage] under-age, hence immature.
157. *commons*] the common people as distinguished from the nobility.
159. *thanks to Heaven*] i.e. as grace before meals.
162. *small light . . . ground*] This is obscure, but the meaning seems to be
that the 'small light' is the diffused light of the sun upon the ground just as
Richard, as a divinely appointed monarch, should metaphorically reflect the
greater light of God's justice, nurturing rather than corrupting the kingdom.
163. *conceit*] conceive, understand.
164. *He*] i.e. King Richard.
wants] lacks.
169. *coz*] colloquial form of cousin; see 2.2.34.
171. *countenance*] favour.

Fruit that grows high is not securely plucked;
We must use ladders and by steps ascend
Till by degrees we reach the altitude.   175
You conceit me too? Pray be smooth awhile.
Tomorrow is the solemn nuptial day
Betwixt the King and virtuous Anne o' Beame,
The Emperor's daughter, a right gracious lady
That's come to England for King Richard's love.   180
Then, as you love his grace—and hate his flatterers—
Discountenance not the day with the least frown,
Be ignorant of what ye know. Afore my God,
I have good hope this happy marriage, brothers,
Of this so noble and religious princess,   185
Will mildly calm his headstrong youth to see
And shun those stains that blurs his majesty.
If not, by good King Edward's bones, our royal father,
I will remove those hinderers of his health,
Though't cost my head.   190

York, Lancaster. On these conditions, brother, we agree.
Arundel. And I.
Surrey.   And I.
Lancaster. To hide our hate is soundest policy.
York. And, brother Gloucester, since it is your pleasure
To have us smooth our sullen brows with smiles,   195
We'd have you suit your outside to your heart,
And like a courtier cast this country habit,
For which the coarse and vulgar call your grace
By th'title of Plain Thomas: yet we doubt not
Tomorrow we shall have good hope to see   200
Your high Protectorship in bravery.
Woodstock. No, no, good York, this is as fair a sight;
My heart in this plain frieze sits true and right.
In this I'll serve my king as true and bold

---

189. those] *MS;* these *Halliwell.*   of] *MS;* to *Halliwell, Carpenter.*

176. *smooth*] calm, mild.
178. *Anne o' Beame*] see note under *Dramatis Personae.*
179. *Emperor's daughter*] Her father was Charles IV, the Holy Roman Emperor (1347–78).
197. *country*] unsophisticated.
201. *in bravery*] splendidly dressed.

As if my outside were all trapped in gold.   205
Lancaster. By Mary, but you shall not, brother Woodstock!
What, the marriage-day to Richard and his queen,
And will ye so disgrace the state and realm?
We'll have you brave, i'faith.
Woodstock.   Well, well,
For your sakes, brothers, and this solemn day,   210
For once I'll sumpter a gaudy wardrobe, but 'tis more
Than I have done, I vow, this twenty years.
Afore my God, the king could not have entreated me
To leave this habit, but your wills be done.
Let's hie to court, you all your wishes have: 215
One weary day Plain Thomas will be brave.

                                        Exeunt omnes.

[1.2]

              Enter GREENE *in rage,* BAGOT *and* TRESILIAN.

Tresilian. Nay, good Sir Henry, King Richard calls for you.
Bagot. Prithee, sweet Greene,
Visit his highness and forsake these passions.
Greene. 'Sblood, I am vexed; Tresilian, mad me not.
Thyself and I and all are now undone.   5
The lords at London are secured from harm,
The plot's revealed. Black curses seize the traitor!
Bagot. Eternal torments whip that Carmelite!

209–10. Well . . . day] *Rossiter; one line in MS.* 212. this] *MS;* these
Rossiter, Armstrong.

[1.2]] 2 *sceane MS.* 0.1. SD] *This ed.; Enter* . . . Tressillian *in Rage MS.*

_____

205. *trapped*] tricked out.
207. *to*] of.
211. *sumpter*] A sumpter is a packhorse or mule; here Woodstock
expresses his scorn by using the word as a verb to mean 'wear' in the sense
of saddling himself like a packhorse; *OED* cites this unique usage of
'sumpter' as a verb.

1.2.0.1. Enter . . . rage] Despite the ordering of the manuscript's stage
direction, it is Greene who is initially enraged; Tresilian and Bagot become
so only when they learn the cause of Greene's anger.
TRESILIAN] Tresilian must be bearded; see 3.1.26.

Tresilian. A deeper hell than *Limbo Patrum* hold him,
    A fainting villain! Confusion crush his soul!   10
Bagot. Could the false slave recoil and swore their deaths?
Greene. Mischief devour him! Had it but ta'en effect
    On Lancaster, and Edmund Duke of York,
    (Those headstrong uncles to the gentle king)
    The third brother, Plain Thomas the Protector,   15
    Had quickly been removed; but since 'tis thus,
    Our safeties must be cared for, and 'tis best
    To keep us near the person of the king.
    Had they been dead, we'd ruled the realm and him.
Bagot. So shall we still so long as Richard lives.   20
    I know he cannot brook his stubborn uncles.
    Come, think not on't. Cheer thee, Tresilian,
    Here's better news for thee: we have so wrought
    With kingly Richard that by his consent
    You are already mounted on your footcloth,   25
    Your scarlet or your purple, which ye please,
    And shortly are to underprop the name—
    Mark me, Tresilian—of Lord Chief Justice of England.
Tresilian. Hum, hum, hum, *legit* or *non legit*? Methinks already
    I sit upon the bench with dreadful frowns, frighting the   30

---

10. fainting] faynting *MS;* fayrting *Halliwell, Keller.*   19. we'd] *Parfitt;*
we'had *MS;* we had *Rossiter.*   29–36. Hum . . . ornament] *as prose in MS;*
Rossiter and Armstrong print in verse lines but without capitals at the beginning
of the lines.

---

9. Limbo Patrum] the limbo of the Church Fathers—an area of Hell
where the just who died before Christ's coming waited for the Last Judgement. Limbo is a Roman Catholic rather than a Protestant concept.
   10. *fainting*] faint-hearted.
   11. *and . . . deaths*] having sworn to murder them.
   21. *brook*] endure, tolerate.
   25. *footcloth*] richly ornamented cloth laid over the back of a horse indicating the mount of a dignitary; cf. 'Cade. . . . Thou dost ride in a foot-cloth,
dost thou not? / *Saye.* What of that? / *Cade.* Marry, thou oughtest not to let
thy horse wear a cloke, when honester men than thou go in their hose and
doublets' (*Contention,* 4.7.43–8).
   26. *scarlet . . . purple*] colours associated with high office. Parfitt also suggests an allusion to the robes of cardinals of the Catholic Church and hence
the exploitation of anti-Catholic feeling.
   29. legit *or* non legit] 'can he read or can't he?' The question is whether
the accused can read the 'neck-verse' (usually the beginning of Psalm 51) in
order to plead 'benefit of clergy', whereby those able to read came under the
jurisdiction of the ecclesiastical courts and usually escaped the noose.

lousy rascals, and when the jury once cries 'Guilty' could
pronounce 'Lord, have mercy on thee', with a brow as
rough and stern as surly Rhadamanth; or when a fellow
talks, cry 'Take him, jailer; clap bolts of iron on his heels
and hands'. Chief Justice, my lords? Hum, hum, hum. I   35
will wear the office in his true ornament.
Greene. But, good your honour, as 'twill shortly be,
You must observe and fashion to the time
The habit of your laws. The King is young,
Ay, and a little wanton—so perhaps are we.   40
Your laws must not be beadles then, Tresilian,
To punish your benefactors, look to that.
Tresilian. How, sir, to punish you, the minions to the King,
The jewels of his heart, his dearest loves?
'Zounds, I will screw and wind the stubborn law   45
To any fashion that shall like you best.
It shall be law what I shall say is law,
And what's most suitable to all your pleasures.
Bagot. Thanks to your lordship which is yet to come!
Greene. Farewell, Tresilian, still be near the court;   50
Anon King Richard shall confirm thy state.
We must attend his grace to Westminster
To the high nuptials of fair Anne o' Beame,
That must be now his wife and England's queen.
          Exeunt GREENE *and* BAGOT. *Manet* TRESIL[IAN].
Tresilian. So, let them pass. Tresilian, now bethink thee.   55
Hum, Lord Chief Justice! Methinks already
I am swelled more plump than erst I was.
Authority's a dish that feeds men fat,
An excellent delicate. Yet best be wise:

---

31. *lousy*] i.e. infected by lice.

32. *Lord . . . thee*] The final phrase of the death sentence.

33. *Rhadamanth*] one of the judges in the underworld, the son of Zeus
and Europa. See Kyd, *The Spanish Tragedy*, 1.1.33 (Revels ed.).

39. *habit*] custom, with a pun on clothing.

41. *beadles*] parish law officers with power to punish petty offences.
Greene is putting Tresilian firmly in his place.

43. *minions*] favourites.

45. *'Zounds*] God's wounds.

57. *erst*] formerly.

59. *delicate*] delicacy.

No state's secure without some enemies.   60
The dukes will frown; why, I can look as grim
As John of Gaunt and all that frown with him.
But yet until mine office be put on
By kingly Richard, I'll conceal myself,
Framing such subtle laws that Janus-like   65
May with a double face salute them both.
I'll search my brain and turn the leaves of law:
Wit makes us great, greatness keeps fools in awe.
My man there, ho! Where's Nimble?

[*Enter*] NIMBLE.

Nimble. As nimble as an eel, sir. Did ye call, sir?   70
Tresilian. 'Sir?' Look out some better phrase: salute again.
Nimble. I know no other, sir, unless you'll be frenchified and
    let me lay the monsieur to your charge, or sweet signior.
Tresilian. Neither. 'Tis higher yet. Nimble, thou buckram
    scribe, think once again.   75
Nimble. [*Aside*] Neither 'sir', nor 'monsieur', nor 'signior'?
    What should I call him, trow? He's monstrously trans-
    lated suddenly. At first, when we were schoolfellows, then
    I called him 'sirrah', but since he became my master, I
    pared away the 'ah' and served him with the 'sir'. What   80
    title he has got now, I know not, but I'll try further.—
    Has your worship any employment for me?

69.1. SD] *Rossiter*; Nimble] *(written in eroded left hand margin in MS at
l. 69)*; Nimble! *(as part of Tresilian's speech) Keller; calls Nimble (as SD)
Halliwell.* 76. [*Aside*]] *This ed.* 77. him, trow?] *Parfitt*; hime tro, *MS*;
him? Troth *Rossiter.* 80. 'ah'] *This ed*; Ah *Rossiter*; Ah's *conj. Rossiter*; .a.
MS.

---

65. *Janus-like*] Janus, Roman god of doorways and passages, depicted in
art with two heads facing opposite ways; thus ambiguous.
    70. *As . . . eel*] proverbial (see Tilley E59, E60).
    74. *buckram*] strong coarse linen cloth which furnished the clothes of
minor law officers; thus a term of abuse.
    77. *trow*] in truth.
    79. *sirrah*] a form of address to inferiors. The shifting and confusing
alterations of social status presented by the King's favourites, guyed here
by Nimble, emphasise the instability created by Richard II's regime and seem
designed to encourage audience sympathy for Woodstock's party.
    80. *'ah'*] Rossiter speculates that there may be a pun on 'arse'.

Tresilian. Thou gross uncaput, no, thou speakest not yet.

Nimble. [*Aside*] My mouth was open, I'm sure.—If your
    honour would please to hear me—   85

Tresilian. Ha, 'honour', sayst thou? Ay, now thou hittest it,
    Nimble.

Nimble. [*Aside*] I knew I should wind about ye, till I had your
    honour.

Tresilian. Nimble, bend thy knee: 90
    The Lord Chief Justice of England speaks to thee.

Nimble. The lord be praised, we shall have a flourishing com-
    monwealth, sir.

Tresilian. Peace, let me speak to thee.

Nimble. Yes, anything, so your honour pray not for me. I care   95
    not, for now you're Lord Chief Justice, if ever ye cry 'Lord
    have mercy' upon me, I shall hang for't, sure.

Tresilian. No, those fearful words shall not be pronounced
    'gainst thee, Nimble.

Nimble. Thank ye, my lord. Nay, and you'll stand between me   100
    and the gallows, I'll be an arrant thief, sure. If I cannot
    pick up my crumbs by the law quickly, I'll cast away my
    buckram bags and be a highway lawyer now certainly.

Tresilian. Canst thou remember, Nimble, how by degrees I
    rose, since first thou knewst me. I was first a schoolboy—   105

Nimble. Ay, saving your honour's speech, your worshipful tail
    was whipped for stealing my dinner out of my satchel.
    You were ever so crafty in your childhood, that I knew
    your worship would prove a good lawyer.

Tresilian. Interrupt me not. Those days thou knewst, I say,   110
    From whence I did become a plodding clerk,

---

84. [*Aside*]] *This ed.* 88. [*Aside*]] *This ed.* 97. sure] Shure *MS* ('h
inserted).

---

83. *uncaput*] fool, literally headless.

88. *wind about ye*] manage your humour.

92–3. *we . . . sir*] Nimble's comment points up 'common' to emphasise
Tresilian's arbitrary elevation.

103. *buckram bags*] bags made of coarse cloth in which lawyers carried
their papers. See Barry, 1.4.369, in which buckram bags and lawyers are
closely associated with sharp practice.

    highway lawyer] i.e. a highway thief; a further criticism of the rapacity of
lawyers.

From which I bounced as thou dost now in buckram
To be a pleading lawyer, and there I stayed,
Till by the king I was Chief Justice made.
Nimble, I read this discipline to thee   115
To stir thy mind up still to industry.
Nimble. Thank your good lordship.
Tresilian. Go to thy mistress—'lady' you now must call her—
Bid her remove her household up to London;
Tell her our fortunes and with how much peril   120
We have attained this place of eminence.
Go and remove her.
Nimble. With a Habis Corpus or a Surssararis, I assure ye.
And so I leave your lordship, always hoping of your
wonted favour: 125
That when I have passed the London Bridge of Affliction
I may arrive with you at the Westminster Hall of
Promotion.
And then I care not.
Tresilian. Thou shalt; thou hast an executing look
And I will put the axe into thy hand.   130
I rule the law: thou by the law shalt stand.
Nimble. I thank your lordship, and a fig for the rope then.
                                        Exeunt.

---

113. To . . . lawyer] *inserted by a different hand in a space left by the scribe in MS.*   123. Habis] habis *MS;* Habeas *Rossiter.*   Surssararis] surssararys *MS;* Certiorari *Rossiter.*   132. rope] Roope *MS (or possibly* Rape*);* Roope *Frijlinck;* Raxe *Halliwell;* Raixe *Keller;* raxe *Carpenter (conj.* rack*).*

113. *To . . . lawyer*] The fact that a space was left in the MS for this phrase to be added later suggests that the scribe could not read the original at this point.
115. *discipline*] lesson.
123. *Habis . . . Surssararis*] Habeas Corpus, a writ requiring the body of a person to be brought before a judge or into court; Certiorari, a writ from a superior court to an inferior one requesting records. Rossiter's emendations are unnecessary because Nimble's pronunciation of these legal Latin phrases is part of the character's comic malapropism.
125. *wonted*] accustomed.
126. *London . . . Affliction*] London Bridge had a gruesome reputation since the heads of traitors were publicly displayed there.
132. *a fig for*] expression of contempt; 'fig' was used as a type of anything small, valueless.
rope] Attempts to emend MS 'Roope' are needless since Nimble's fears of execution relate to hanging, the form of execution appropriate for the lower orders; the axe or sword was reserved for the execution of the nobility.

[1.3]

> *Sound a sennet.* Enter, in great state, KING RICHARD,
> QUEEN ANNE *crowned,* LANCASTER; YORK, ARUNDEL;
> SURREY, GREENE, BAGOT; *and* WOODSTOCK *very*
> *brave; the* DUCHESS of GLOUCESTER *and the*
> DUCHESS *of* IRELAND.

King Richard. Bagot and Greene, next to the fair Queen Anne
    Take your high places by King Richard's side,
    And give fair welcome to our queen and bride.
    Uncles of Woodstock, York, and Lancaster,
    Make full our wishes and salute our queen.   5
    Give all your welcomes to fair Anne o' Beame.
Lancaster. I hope, sweet prince, her grace mistakes us not
    To make our hearts the worser part of us;
    Our tongues have in our English eloquence—
    Harsh though it is—pronounced her welcomes many   10
    By oaths and loyal protestations,
    To which we add a thousand infinites;
    But in a word, fair Queen, forever welcome.
Woodstock. Let me prevent the rest, for mercy's sake!
    If all their welcomes be as long as thine   15
    This health will not go round this week, by th'Mass!
    Sweet Queen, and cousin—now I'll call you so—
    In plain and honest phrase, welcome to England.
    Think they speak all in me, and you have seen
    All England cry with joy: 'God bless the Queen!'   20
    And so, afore my God, I know they wish it.

1.3.2. your] yor *MS;* you *Halliwell.*

   1.3.0.1. Sound a sennet] A frequent stage direction in Elizabethan texts;
a fanfare played within on a trumpet or cornet when important characters
enter (see Dessen and Thomson).
   in great state] in ceremonial costume and with great formality. The
MS punctuation suggests that the characters enter in several groups and
may offer some indication of the staging of this formal stage entry
with Greene and Bagot elevated to the company of Surrey and the striking
appearance of Woodstock emphasised by his separate place in the
procession.
   0.4. brave] finely arrayed.
   1–2. *Bagot . . . side*] Richard's pointed departure from decorum by ele-
vating Bagot and Greene to a high place at his side suggests the dramatist's
care in creating a visual statement of the play's power dynamic.

Only I fear my duty not misconstr'd—
Nay, nay, King Richard, 'fore God I'll speak the truth!
Sweet Queen, you've found a young and wanton choice,
A wild-head, yet a kingly gentleman;   25
A youth unsettled, yet he's princely bred,
Descended from the royal'st bloods in Europe,
The kingly stock of England and of France.
Yet he's a hare-brain, a very wag i'faith,
But you must bear, madam—'las, he's but a blossom,   30
But his maturity I hope you'll find
True English bred, a king loving and kind.
King Richard. I thank ye for your double praise, good uncle.
Woodstock. Ay, ay, good coz, I'm Plain Thomas, by th'rood,
    I'll speak the truth.   35
Queen Anne. My sovereign lord, and you true English peers,
Your all-accomplished honours have so tied
My senses by a magical restraint
In the sweet spells of this your fair demeanours
That I am bound and charmed from what I was.   40
My native country I no more remember
But as a tale told in my infancy,
The greatest part forgot; and that which is
Appears to England's fair Elysium
Like brambles to the cedars, coarse to fine,   45

---

22. Only . . . misconstr'd] *MS;* Only I fear lest duty be misconstr'd *conj.*
Rossiter. 39. this] *MS;* these *Rossiter.* 45. coarse] *Rossiter;* curse *MS.*

---

22. *Only . . . misconstr'd*] i.e. 'I fear lest my duty, in speaking the truth
about Richard's misdemeanours, should be misconstrued'. There appears to
be some gesture of interruption from the King at this point but Woodstock
persists in his statement.

29. *hare-brain*] wild or crazy person; hares were thought to be mad especially at spring mating time, 'As mad as a March Hare' (Tilley H148).

30. *bear*] tolerate, with a pun on 'bearing' children.

33. *double*] Richard puns on 'double' in the sense of deceptive or
deceitful.

40. *bound and charmed*] i.e. spell-bound and bewitched; cf. *Temp.*,
1.2.489.

44. *Elysium*] Heaven; also a punning reference and compliment to
Elizabeth I.

45. *cedars*] Cedars, much celebrated in the Scriptures, were regarded
in the sixteenth and seventeenth centuries as noble trees with royal
associations.

Or like the wild grape to the fruitful vine.
And having left the earth where I was bred,
And English made, let me be Englishèd.
They best shall please me, shall me English call:
My heart, great king, to you; my love to all.   50
King Richard. Gramercy, Nan; thou highly honour'st me.
York. And blest is England in this sweet accord.
Woodstock. Afore my God, sweet Queen, our English ladies
And all the women that this isle contains
Shall sing in praise of this your memory   55
And keep records of virtuous Anne o' Beame,
Whose discipline hath taught them womanhood.
What erst seemed well by custom now looks rude;
Our women till your coming, fairest cousin,
Did use like men to straddle when they ride,   60
But you have taught them now to sit a-side.
Yet, by your leave, young practice often reels:
I have seen some of your scholars kick up both their heels.
Duchess of Gloucester. What have you seen, my lord?
Woodstock.   Nay, nay, nothing, wife.
I see little without spectacles thou knowst.   65
King Richard. Trust him not, aunt, for now he's grown so
      brave
He will be courting—ay, and kissing too.
Nay, uncle, now I'll do as much for you,
And lay your faults all open to the world.
Woodstock. Ay, ay, do, do.   70
King Richard. I'm glad you're grown so careless: now by my
      crown

70. Ay . . . do] I. I doe doe *MS;* Ay. I do. Do. *conj. Rossiter.*

---

51. *Gramercy*] literally, 'God grant you mercy', i.e. 'Thank you'.
   Nan] a familiar form of Anne. Richard's affectionate form of address prepares for the extremity of his grief on Anne's death in 4.3.
   58. *rude*] unrefined, uncultured.
   59–61. *Our women . . . sit a-side*] 'Also noble women . . . rode on side-
saddles, after the example of the Queene who first brought that fashion into
this land, for before women were used to ride astride like men' (Stow, p. 295).
   62. *young . . . reels*] i.e. new customs often go astray.
   63. *kick up . . . heels*] bawdy, relating to a woman's posture in intercourse
(Williams).
   64. *nothing*] also carrying the meaning 'vagina' (Williams).
   71. *careless*] carefree, gamesome.

I swear, good uncles York and Lancaster,
When you this morning came to visit me
I did not know him in this strange attire.
How comes this golden metamorphosis   75
From home-spun huswifery? Speak, good uncle,
I never saw you hatched and gilded thus.
Woodstock. I am no Stoic, my dear sovereign cousin,
To make my plainness seem canonical,
But to allow myself such ornaments   80
As might be fitting for your nuptial day
And coronation of your virtuous queen;
But were the eye of day once closed again
Upon this back they never more should come.
King Richard. You have much graced the day; but, noble
    uncle,   85
I did observe what I have wondered at.
As we today rode on to Westminster,
Methought your horse, that wont to tread the ground
And pace as if he kicked it scornfully,
Mount and curvet like strong Bucephalus,   90
Today he trod as slow and melancholy
As if his legs had failed to bear his load.
Woodstock. And can ye blame the beast? Afore my God,
He was not wont to bear such loads, indeed.
A hundred oaks upon these shoulders hang   95
To make me brave upon your wedding day,
And more than that, to make my horse more tire,

---

88. that] *MS;* that's *Rossiter.*   94. to] *Keller;* be *MS.*

---

77. *hatched*] decorated, usually with reference to inlaid gold or silver work.
78–82. *I . . . queen*] i.e. 'I am not such a Stoic (one who practices patient endurance) as to demand that everyone adopts plain dress, but I am being stoical by decking myself out for the wedding'.
90. *Mount*] rise up.
curvet] leap, prance.
Bucephalus] Alexander the Great's warhorse.
95–8. *A . . . here*] i.e. Woodstock estimates the cost of his clothing at that of a hundred felled oaks. It was a common complaint in Elizabethan times that land and natural resources were squandered in supporting such conspicuous consumption. See Marlowe *Edward*, 1.4.401–18, and Tourneur, 2.1.215–226.
97. *tire*] tired; punning on the secondary sense of 'attired'.

Ten acres of good land are stitched up here.
You know, good coz, this was not wont to be.
King Richard. In your t'other hose, uncle?   100
Greene. No, nor his frieze coat neither.
Woodstock. Ay, ay, mock on. My t'other hose, say ye?
There's honest plain dealing in my t'other hose.
Should this fashion last I must raise new rents,
Undo my poor tenants, turn away my servants   105
And guard myself with lace; nay, sell more land
And lordships too, by th'rood. Hear me, King Richard:
If thus I jet in pride, I still shall lose,
But I'll build castles in my t'other hose.
Queen Anne. The King but jests, my lord, and you grow
      angry.   110
Woodstock. T'other hose! Did some here wear that fashion
They would not tax and pill the commons so.
York. [*to Lancaster*] 'Sfoot, he forewarned us and will break
      out himself.
Lancaster. [*to York*] No matter, we'll back him though it
      grows to blows.
Woodstock. Scoff ye my plainness, I'll talk no riddles. Plain
      Thomas   115
Will speak plainly. There's Bagot there and Greene—
Greene, Bagot. And what of them, my lord?
Woodstock. Upstarts, come down; you have no places there.
      Here's better men to grace King Richard's chair

---

113. SD] *Rossiter subst.* 'Sfoot] sfoote *MS;* ffoole *Halliwell, Carpenter;*
Foote *Keller.* 114. SD] *Rossiter subst.* grows] growes *MS;* grow *Rossiter.*
118. there] *Halliwell, Keller;* th'are *MS.*

---

106. *guard*] protect, punning on the sense of 'guard' as an ornamental
border or trimming of a garment.
109. *I'll build castles*] Woodstock's intemperate riposte is a direct challenge
to the King's authority since nobles needed the monarch's permission to
erect fortifications. In 1386 Sir Edward Dalynrigge applied for and received
a royal licence to crenellate his manor house at Bodiam in Sussex as a
defence against French raids on the area. In the event he chose to build a
new castle, which still stands. The royal licence is extant; see Paul Johnson,
British Castles (London, 1978), p. 132.
112. *pill*] plunder, rob. See *R2,* 2.1.247.
113. *'Sfoot*] By God's foot.
break out] lose his temper.
114. *back*] support.

If't pleased him grace them so.

King Richard.   Uncle, forbear.   120

Woodstock. These cuts the columns that should prop thy
    house.
    They tax the poor and I am scandaled for it
    That by my fault those late oppressions rise
    To set the commons in a mutiny
    That London even itself was sacked by them.   125
    And who did all these rank commotions point at?
    Even at these two: Bagot here and Greene,
    With false Tresilian whom your grace, we hear,
    Hath made Chief Justice. Well, well, be it so:
    Mischief on mischief sure will shortly flow.   130
    Pardon my speech, my lord. Since now we're all so brave
    To grace Queen Anne, this day we'll spend in sport;
    But in my t'other hose, I'll tickle them for't.

Greene. Come, come, ye dote, my lord.

Lancaster. Dote, sir! Know ye to whom ye speak?   135

King Richard. No more, good uncles—Come, sweet Greene,
    ha' done;
    I'll wring them all for this by England's crown.
    —Why is our Lord Protector so outrageous?

Woodstock. Because thy subjects have such outrage shown
    them
    By these thy flatterers. Let the sun dry up   140
    What th'unwholesome fog hath choked the ground with.

---

121. cuts] cutts *MS;* cut *Rossiter.*

---

121. *cuts . . . house*] Rossiter's emendation is doubly unnecessary since the
third person plural often ends in *s* in Elizabethan grammar (see Abbott, pp.
235–7) and 'cuts' can be read either as a verb or as a noun, i.e. wounds or
slashes, with a further reference to the slashes in rich garments which develops Woodstock's attack on fashion. Thus the passage may be read as either,
'These favourites destroy the columns which support the throne' or 'These
overdressed favourites should be supporters rather than wreckers of the
throne'.

    122. *scandaled*] disgraced, defamed.

    123–5. *late oppressions . . . them*] reference to the Peasants' Revolt of 1381.

    133. *tickle*] beat, chastise.

    137. *wring*] vex, distress (*OED* 5).

    138. *outrageous*] violent, excessively fierce.

    140–1. *Let . . . with*] The King is compared to the sun; his kingly radiance
should disperse the unhealthy influence of his flatterers. Rossiter cites *R2*,
3.2.37ff.

Here's Arundel, thy ocean's admiral,
Hath brought thee home a rich and wealthy prize,
Ta'en three score sail of ships and six great carracks
All richly laden. Let those goods be sold   145
To satisfy those borrowed sums of coin
Their pride hath forcèd from the needy commons;
To salve which inconvenience, I beseech your grace
You would vouchsafe to let me have the sale
And distribution of those goods.   150
King Richard. Our word, good uncle, is already passed,
Which cannot with our honour be recalled.
Those wealthy prizes already are bestowed
On these our friends.
All Lords.   On them, my lord?
King Richard. Yes. Who storms at it?
Woodstock.   Shall cankers eat the fruit   155
That planting and good husbandry hath nourishèd?
Greene, Bagot. Cankers!
York, Arundel.   Ay, cankers! caterpillars!
Lancaster. Worse than consuming fires
That eats up all their furies falls upon.
King Richard. Once more be still!   160
Who is't that dares encounter with our will?
We did bestow them. Hear me, kind uncles:
We shall ere long be past Protectorship,
Then will we rule ourself and even till then
We let ye know those gifts are given to them.   165
We did it, Woodstock.
Woodstock. Ye have done ill then.
King Richard.   Ha, dare ye say so?

146–7. *borrowed . . . commons*] Richard II's raising of revenue by obliga-
tory loans, which required the consent of the lender but which could not be
refused, was not a novel device. Such loans were first raised by Edward III
and later in 1379 by the Council during Richard's minority.

149. *vouchsafe*] allow or permit as an act of favour.

155–6. *cankers . . . nourishèd*] The image of the ruined state as a neglected
garden is a commonplace in the period, see *R2*, 33.4, and *H5*, 5.2.36–55. Here
'cankers' bears a number of meanings; canker-worms which destroy buds
and leaves, canker-roses or wild dog-roses regarded as weeds, and 'cankers'
as spreading and persistent ulcers.

157. *caterpillars*] rapacious persons; cf. Bolingbroke: 'By Bushy, Bagot,
and their complices, / The caterpillars of the commonwealth, / Which I have
sworn to weed and pluck away' (*R2*, 2.3.164–6).

Woodstock. Dare I? Afore my god, I'll speak, King Richard,
Were I assured this day my head should off.
I tell ye, sir, my allegiance stands excused   170
In justice of the cause. Ye have done ill.
The sun of mercy never shine on me
But I speak truth. When warlike Arundel,
Beset at sea, fought for those wealthy prizes
He did with fame advance the English cross,   175
Still crying 'Courage, in King Richard's name'.
For thee he won them, and do thou enjoy them.
He'll fetch more honours home—but had he known
That kites should have enjoyed the eagle's prize
The fraught had swum unto thine enemies.   180
King Richard. So, sir, we'll soothe your vexèd spleen, good
        uncle,
And mend what is amiss. To those slight gifts
Not worth acceptance, thus much more we add:
Young Henry Greene shall be Lord Chancellor;
Bagot, Lord Keeper of our Privy Seal;   185
Tresilian, learned in our kingdom's laws,
Shall be Chief Justice. By them and their directions
King Richard will uphold his government.
Greene. Change no more words, my lord, ye do deject
Your kingly majesty to speak to such   190

180. fraught] *MS;* freyght *Halliwell;* frayght *Keller.*

---

173. *But*] unless.
175. *the English cross*] the Cross of St George.
180.] i.e. He would have thrown the booty overboard or allowed the captured ships to founder.
fraught] freight, cargo.
184–5. *Greene . . . Seal*] Lord Chancellor and the Lord Keeper of the Privy Seal were positions of great power, the former effectively the king's principal secretary, the latter a position of considerable influence in financial and legal procedures. The elevation of Greene and Bagot, although unhistorical, mirrors the advancement of Richard II's friends, Burley, de la Pole (Earl of Suffolk) and de Vere (Duke of Ireland) earlier in the reign. All were driven from power by the faction led by Woodstock (Gloucester). Burley was executed, de la Pole and de Vere exiled. Woodstock's part in the fall of Richard's supporters was the basis of his quarrel with the King. Thus, the dramatic reshaping of historical events retains the spirit of the antagonism. Cf. Marlowe *Edward*, 1.1.153–5.
189. *Change*] exchange.
deject] degrade.

Whose home-spun judgements, like their frosty beards,
Would blast the blooming hopes of all your kingdom.
Were I as you, my lord—
Queen Anne. Oh, gentle Greene, throw no more fuel on
   But rather seek to mitigate this heat.   195
   Be patient, kingly Richard; quench this ire.
   Would I had tears of force to stint this fire.
King Richard. Beshrew the churls that makes my queen so
   sad.
   But by my grandsire Edward's kingly bones,
   My princely father's tomb, King Richard swears   200
   We'll make them weep these wrongs in bloody tears.
   Come, fair Queen Anne o' Beame; Bagot and Greene
   Keep by King Richard's side. But as for you
   We'll shortly make your stiff obedience bow.
                 Exeunt KING, QUEEN [*and the Duchesses*].
Bagot. Remember this, my lords,   205
   We keep the Seal: our strength you all shall know.
                                             Exit BAGOT.
Greene. And we are Chancellor: we love you well, think so.
                                             Exit GREENE.
York. God for his mercy, shall we brook these braves,
   Disgraced and threatened thus by fawning knaves?
Lancaster. Shall we that were great Edward's princely sons   210
   Be thus outbraved by flattering sycophants?
Woodstock. Afore my God and holy saints, I swear,
   But that my tongue hath liberty to show
   The inly passions boiling in my breast,
   I think my overburdened heart would break.   215
   What then may we conjecture? What's the cause
   Of this remiss and inconsiderate dealing
   Urged by the King and his confederates
   But hate to virtue, and a mind corrupt

---

209. fawning] fawneing *MS;* frowneing *Halliwell.*   210. sons] sonns *MS;*
fame *Halliwell, Keller (Keller noting perhaps* sand).   214. inly] Inlye *MS;*
Julye *Halliwell;* Iulye *Keller.*

197. *of force*] sufficient.
203. *you*] i.e. Woodstock.
208. *braves*] insults.
214. *inly*] inward, heartfelt.

With all preposterous rude misgovernment?   220
Lancaster. These prizes ta'en by warlike Arundel
    Before his face are given those flatterers.
Surrey. It is his custom to be prodigal
    To any but to those do best deserve.
Arundel. Because he knew you would bestow them well,   225
    He gave it such as for their private gain
    Neglect both honour and their country's good.
                    Wind horns within.
Lancaster. How now, what noise is this?
York. Some posts it seems. Pray Heaven the news be good.
Woodstock. Amen. I pray for England's happiness.   230

             Enter CHENEY.

Speak, speak, what tidings, Cheney?
Cheney. Of war, my lord, and civil dissension.
    The men of Kent and Essex do rebel.
Woodstock. I thought no less and always feared as much.
Cheney. The shrieves in post have sent unto your grace   235
    That order may be ta'en to stay the commons,
    For fear rebellion rise in open arms.
Woodstock. Now, headstrong Richard, shalt thou reap the fruit
    Thy lewd licentious wilfulness hath sown.
    I know not which way to bestow myself.   240
York. There is no standing on delay, my lords.
    These hot eruptions must have some redress
    Or else in time they'll grow incurable.
Woodstock. The commons they rebel—and the King all
    careless.

221–2.] *'A reviser began by crossing out these lines, then smudged out his marks and added the speech-rule and speaker's name' (Frijlinck).* 227.1. SD] *In left-hand margin at ll. 225–6 in MS.* 229. posts] postes *MS;* post *Rossiter.*

---

220. *preposterous*] turned upside down.
226. *such*] to such.
233. *The men . . . rebel*] as in the case of the Peasants' Revolt of 1381 which was also centred in the counties of Kent and Essex.
235. *shrieves*] sheriffs; king's officers appointed to maintain order in cities and counties.
    in post] in haste.
236. *stay*] check.
244. *careless*] indifferent.

Here's wrong on wrong to stir more mutiny.   245
Afore my God, I know not what to do.
Lancaster. Take open arms. Join with the vexèd commons
And hale his minions from his wanton side.
Their heads cut off, the people's satisfied.
Woodstock. Not so, not so. Alack the day, good brother,   250
We may not so affright the tender prince.
We'll bear us nobly for the kingdom's safety
And the King's honour. Therefore list to me:
You, brother Gaunt and noble Arundel,
Shall undertake by threats, or fair entreaty,   255
To pacify the murmuring commons' rage;
And whiles you there employ your service hours
We presently will call a parliament
And have their deeds examined thoroughly,
Where, if by fair means we can win no favour,   260
Nor make King Richard leave their companies,
We'll thus resolve for our dear country's good
To right her wrongs or for it spend our bloods.
Lancaster. About it then. We for the commons, you for the
     court.
Woodstock. Ay, ay, good Lancaster, I pray be careful.   265
Come, brother York, we soon shall right all wrong
And send some headless from the court ere long.
                                             Exeunt omnes.

---

245. Here's] *MS;* Heepes *Keller.*

257–8. *And . . . parliament*] Woodstock's intention in calling a parliament
is to arraign the King's flatterers for their actions.
257. *service hours*] i.e. hours in that service.
267. Exeunt omnes] Woodstock leaves the stage with York, and presumably Lancaster with Cheney, via different stage exits.

Act 2

Trumpets sound [a] flourish.
Enter KING RICHARD, GREENE, BAGOT, BUSHY
[carrying a book], SCROOP, TRESILIAN *and others.*

King Richard. Thus shall King Richard suit his princely train
Despite his uncles' pride. Embrace us, gentlemen.
Sir Edward Bagot, Bushy, Greene and Scroop,
　　　　　　　　　　　　　[Embracing them in turn]
Your youths are fitting to our tender years
And such shall beautify our princely throne.　　　　　　5
Fear not my uncles, nor their proudest strength,
For I will buckler ye against them all.
Greene. Thanks, dearest lord. Let me have Richard's love
And like a rock unmoved my state shall stand
Scorning the proudest peer that rules the land.　　　　　10
Bushy. Your uncles seeks to overturn your state,
To awe ye like a child, that they alone
May at their pleasures thrust you from the throne.
Scroop. As if the sun were forcèd to decline
Before his dated time of darkness comes.　　　　　　　15
Bagot. Sweet king, set courage to authority
And let them know the power of majesty.

2.1.3. Edward] *Rossiter;* Thomas *MS.* 3.1. SD] *This ed.* 14. decline]
declyne *Keller (not as emendation);* delyne *MS.*

2.1.0.1. flourish] a trumpet fanfare played within to signal the entrance
of the King.
　1. *suit*] agree with, accord with.
　3. *Edward*] Some confusion over Bagot's first name is evident from the
manuscript; it is given correctly as 'Edward' at 1.1.62 and 4.1.182, but it is
given as 'Thomas' here and again at 4.3.99 where it has been corrected to
'Edward'.
　7. *buckler*] shield, defend; cf. ''Tis not the king can buckler Gaveston',
Marlowe, *Edward,* 1.4.288.
　11–13.] Keller notes the parallel with *Contention,* 2.3.28ff.
　11. *seeks*] See note to 1.3.121.

Greene. May not the lion roar because he's young?
          What are your uncles but as elephants
          That set their agèd bodies to the oak?   20
          You are the oak against whose stock they lean;
          Fall from them once and then destroy them ever.
          Be thou no stay, King Richard, to their strength,
          But as a tyrant unto tyranny,
          And so confound them all eternally.   25
Tresilian. Law must extend unto severity
          When subjects dare to brave their sovereign.
King Richard. Tresilian, thou art Lord Chief Justice now;
          Who should be learnèd in the laws but thee?
          Resolve us therefore what thou thinkst of them   30
          That under title of Protectorship
          Seek to subvert their king and sovereign.
Tresilian. As of the King's rebellious enemies;
          As underminers of his sacred state,
          Which in the greatest prince or mightiest peer,   35
          That is a subject to your majesty,
          Is nothing less than treason capital,
          And he a traitor that endeavours it.
King Richard. Attaint them then; arrest them and condemn
          them.
Greene. Hale them to th'block and cut off all their heads,   40
          And then, King Richard, claim the government.
King Richard. See it be done, Tresilian, speedily.
Tresilian. That course is all too rash, my gracious lord.
All. Too rash for what?

24. tyranny] *Rossiter;* teranaye *MS.* 35. Which] *Rossiter;* wth *MS.*
36.] Book *is written in left margin of MS.* 37. Is] *MS;* 'Tis *conj. Carpenter.*
42. Tresilian] *Rossiter;* Tissillian *MS.*

18–25.] 'Perhaps suggested by Stow's report of the dressing-down Richard
gave certain lords for supporting the Lollards' (Rossiter).
    21. *stock*] trunk.
    22. *Fall from*] forsake.
    23. *stay*] prop, support.
    35. *in*] i.e. even in.
    39–42. *Attaint . . . speedily*] Richard's enthusiasm to arrest and execute his
uncles is unequivocal here. The fact that the passage is not marked for deletion weakens Parfitt's argument that some of the manuscript's cuts are
designed to avoid showing Richard to be as culpable as his advisers; see
Introduction under 'Censorship'.

Tresilian. It must be done with greater policy 45
    For fear the people rise in mutiny.
    [BUSHY *consults a book.*]
King Richard. Ay, there's the fear: the commons love them
      well
    And all applaud the wily Lancaster,
    The counterfeit relenting Duke of York,
    Together with our fretful Uncle Woodstock, 50
    With greater reverence than King Richard's self.
    But time shall come when we shall yoke their necks
    And make them bend to our obedience.
    How now! What readst thou, Bushy?
Bushy. The monument of English Chronicles 55
    Containing acts and memorable deeds
    Of all your famous predecessor kings.
King Richard. What findst thou of them?
Bushy. Examples strange and wonderful, my lord;
    The end of treason even in mighty persons, 60
    For here 'tis said your royal grandfather,
    Although but young and under government,
    Took the Protector then, proud Mortimer,

46.1. SD] *This ed.; 'Bushy reads a book' (at l. 39) Rossiter.* 55. Chronicles]
MS; my lord *deleted in MS.*

46.1. SD] Rossiter suggests that Bushy reads the book from l. 39, but this
would distract attention from Richard's initial aim to punish his uncles
and would deny Bushy's joining in the general response to Tresilian's statement at l. 44. It is more likely that Bushy consults the Chronicles after Tresilian has pointed out the difficulties in acting against Richard's uncles. The
book-keeper's marginal note 'Book' at l. 36 is more likely to be a memo about
a prop required for the scene than a specific prompt at that point of the
action.
    49. *relenting*] compassionate.
    50. *fretful*] peevish.
    55. *monument*] record.
    English Chronicles] Rossiter observes that Bushy appears to read from a
composite of Holinshed, Stow and Grafton.
    60–5. *The end . . . treachery*] Roger Mortimer of Wigmore who became
Lord Protector on Edward II's imprisonment (the Young Mortimer, lover of
Queen Isabella in *Edward II*, see 5.6.20–66) was hanged at Tyburn by Edward
III. Rossiter suggests that the detail of the fifty-foot gallows was drawn from
Holinshed's description of the execution of Hugh Spencer, Earl of Glouces-
ter, one of Edward's favourites.

And on a gallows fifty foot in height
He hung him for his pride and treachery.   65
King Richard. Why should our proud Protector then presume
And we not punish him whose treason's viler far
Than ever was rebellious Mortimer's?
Prithee, read on; examples such as these
Will bring us to our kingly grandsire's spirit.   70
What's next?
Bushy. The battle full of dread and doubtful fear
Was fought betwixt your father and the French.
King Richard. Read on, we'll hear it.
Bushy. Then the Black Prince, encouraging his soldiers, being   75
in number but 7,750, gave the onset to the French King's
puissant army, which were numbered to 68,000, and in
one hour got the victory, slew 6,000 of the French soldiers, took prisoners of dukes, earls, knights and gentlemen to the number 1,700, and of the common sort   80
10,000; so the prisoners that were taken were twice so
many as the Englishmen were in number. Besides, the
thrice renowned prince took with his own hand King
John of France and his son prisoners. This was called
the Battle of Poitiers, and was fought on Monday the   85
nineteenth of September 1363, my lord.

68. Mortimer's] *Parfitt;* mortimer *MS.* 76. 7,750] 5,750 *Halliwell, Keller;*
'*The first figure was originally 7, but is blotted out and presumably deleted, and
may have been altered before deletion: the second figure was originally 0 and has
been altered to 7: the alterations are in different ink' (Frijlinck).* 77. puissant]
Rossiter; pvesant *MS (or* presant*);* presant *Halliwell, Keller.* 86. 1363]
MS; 1356 *Rossiter.* my lord] *added in darker ink by the same hand in MS
(Frijlinck).*

76. *7,750*] Frijlinck's reading seems preferable in the light of the information from the Chronicles; Holinshed states that 'all the princes company
passed not the number of 8000 men' and Stow reports that 'in all the whole
armie of the prince there was not above foure thousand men of armes, one
thousand armed souldiers, and two thousand Archers'.
    onset] signal to attack.
85–6. *Poitiers . . . 1363*] The battle was actually fought in 1356. Contemporary audiences may have been familiar with the dramatic presentation of
the battle in scenes 3–7 of Act 4 of *Edward III* (c. 1592–3 according to Melchiori, ed., *Edward III*, New Cambridge Shakespeare, 1998), in which King
John and his son are taken prisoner.

King Richard. A victory most strange and admirable.
　Never was conquest got with such great odds.
　O princely Edward, had thy son such hap,
　Such fortune and success to follow him,　　　　　　　90
　His daring uncles and rebellious peers
　Durst not control and govern as they do.
　But these bright shining trophies shall awake me,
　And as we are his body's counterfeit
　So will we be the image of his mind　　　　　　　　95
　And die but we'll attain his virtuous deeds.
　What next ensues? Good Bushy, read the rest.
Bushy. Here is set down, my princely sovereign,
　The certain time and day when you were born.
King Richard. Our birthday, sayst thou? Is that noted there?　100
Bushy. It is, my lord.
King Richard.　　　　Prithee, let me hear't,
　For thereby hangs a secret mystery
　Which yet our uncle strangely keeps from us.
　On, Bushy.
Bushy. Upon the third of April 1365 was Lord Richard, son　105
　to the Black Prince, born at Bordeaux.
King Richard. Stay. Let me think awhile. Read it again.
Bushy. Upon the third of April 1365 was Lord Richard, son
　to the Black Prince, born at Bordeaux.
King Richard. 1365? What year is this?　　　　　　　110
Greene. 'Tis now, my lord, 1387.
King Richard. By that account the third of April next
　Our age is numbered two-and-twenty years.
　O treacherous men that have deluded us!
　We might have claimed our right a twelve month since.　115
　Shut up thy book, good Bushy. Bagot, Greene,

---

105. third] 3 *MS.* 106. Bordeaux] Burdex *MS;* Burdox *Carpenter.*
108–9. Upon . . . Bordeaux] *as verse in MS.* 112. third] 3 *MS.* 113.
two-and-twenty] *Parfitt;* 22 *MS.* 116. book] blooke *MS.*

---

89. *hap*] fortune.
93. *trophies*] examples, tokens of valour.
94. *counterfeit*] image, likeness; with, perhaps, an ironic pun as
'fake'.
96. *but*] unless.
105. *1365*] Richard was actually born on 6 January 1367; the dramatist
exploits differing views as to this date, see 2.2.100–1.

King Richard in his throne will now be seen.
This day I'll claim my right, my kingdom's due.
Our uncles well shall know they but intrude,
For which we'll smite their base ingratitude.   120

       [Enter a Messenger *who gives a note to*
          BAGOT *and exits.*]

Bagot. Edmund of Langley, Duke of York, my lord,
    Sent from the Lord Protector and the peers
    Doth crave admittance to your royal presence.
King Richard. Our Uncle Edmund? So. Were it not he
    We would not speak with him. But go admit him.   125
    Woodstock and Gaunt are stern and troublesome
    But York is gentle, mild and generous
    And therefore we admit his conference.

               Enter YORK.

Bagot. He comes, my lord.
King Richard. Methinks 'tis strange, my good and reverend   130
    uncle,
    You and the rest should thus malign against us
    And every hour with rude and bitter taunts
    Abuse King Richard and his harmless friends.
    We had a father that once called ye brother;
    A grandsire, too, that titled you his son;   [YORK *kneels.*]   135
    But could they see how you have wronged King
      Richard
    Their ghosts would haunt ye, and in dead of night
    Fright all your quiet sleeps with horrid fears.
    I pray stand up, we honour reverend years
    In meaner subjects. Good uncle, rise, and tell us   140
    What further mischiefs are there now devised

---

117. in] *altered from* is *in darker ink (Frijlinck).*   120.1–2. SD] *This ed.;*
A knock within. BAGOT *to the door and returns. Rossiter.*   128.1. *Enter*
YORK] *in the right margin between ll. 126 and 127 in MS.*   135,142. SDs] *This*
ed.

118. *due*] just title.
137–8. *Their . . . fears*] Ironically, the ghosts of Edward and the Black
Prince do appear to Woodstock in 5.1 but take his part in warning him of
Richard's threat to his life.

To torture and afflict your sovereign with. [YORK *rises.*]
York. My royal lord, even by my birth I swear,
My father's tomb, and faith to Heaven I owe,
Your uncles' thoughts are all most honourable,   145
And to that end the good Protector sends me
To certify your sacred majesty
The peers of England now are all assembled
To hold a parliament at Westminster,
And humbly crave your highness would be there   150
To sit in council touching such affairs
As shall concern your country's government.
King Richard. Have they so soon procured a parliament?
Without our knowledge, too? 'Tis somewhat strange.
Yet say, good uncle, we will meet them straight.   155
York. The news to all will be most wished and welcome.
I take my leave and to your grace I swear,
As I am subject loyal, just and true,
We'll nothing do to hurt the realm nor you.
King Richard. We shall believe you, uncle. Go attend him.   160
                         Exit YORK [*attended*].
Yes, we will meet them, but with such intent
As shall dismiss their sudden parliament
Till we be pleased to summon and direct it.
Come, sirs, to Westminster attend our state:
This day shall make you ever fortunate.   165
The third of April—Bushy, note the time—
Our age accomplished, crown and kingdom's mine.
                         Flourish. Exeunt omnes.

162–3.] 'Petitions / : Mace' *in left-hand margin in MS. A word is deleted before* Mace; *probably* Tisd *or possibly* Wd.   165–7.] Enter the Queen / Duchess of Gloucester / Ireland *in left-hand margin of MS, written in a different ink and deleted in yet another ink.*   167.1. Flourish] *in left-hand margin at l. 164 in MS.*

---

147. *certify*] inform.
148–9. *The peers . . . Westminster*] Keller comments that nothing in any chronicle supplies this parliament.
165–7.] The marginal entry for the Queen and the Duchesses of Gloucester and Ireland is premature; its deletion presumably indicates the scribe's awareness of the mistake (their entry occurs at the beginning of 2.3).

[2.2]

Enter LANCASTER, ARUNDEL, SURREY, *the* QUEEN
[ANNE], WOODSTOCK [*with petitions and the mace
carried before him*], *and his* DUCHESS [*and*
CHENEY]. YORK *meets them in haste.*

Woodstock. Now, brother York, what says King Richard, ha?
York. His highness will be here immediately.
Woodstock. Go, cousin Surrey, greet the parliament;
   Tell them the King is coming; give these petitions
   To th'knights and burgesses o'th' lower house,   5
   Sent from each several shire of all the kingdom.
   These copies I will keep and show his highness.
   Pray make haste.
Surrey. I will, my lord.   *Exit* SURREY.
Queen Anne. Pity King Richard's youth, most reverend
   uncles,   10
   And in your high proceedings gently use him.
   Think of his tender years. What's now amiss
   His riper judgement shall make good and perfect
   To you and to the kingdom's benefit.
York. Alack, sweet Queen, you and our lord the King   15
   Have little cause to fear our just proceedings.
   We'll fall beneath his feet and bend our knees
   So he cast off those hateful flatterers

2.2.0.1–4. SD] *Add. this ed.*   5. knights] *Carpenter;* knight *MS.*

2.2.0.2. the mace] a staff of office resembling a metal-headed club
and the symbol of Woodstock's authority which signifies his office as
Protector. The importance of this prop to the scene is signalled by the
book-keeper's marginal reminder at 2.1.162–3 in the MS. It seems appropriate that the petitions and the mace should be carried on stage by an attendant since Woodstock carries the staff of office as a councillor which he
breaks at l. 161.
   5. *burgesses*] members of parliament for boroughs, towns and universities
as distinct from the knights of the shires, gentlemen representing a shire or
county in parliament.
   6. *Sent . . . kingdom*] It is unclear whether this line refers to the petitions or to the knights and burgesses, or to both. Lines 44–5 emphasise that it is not only the petitions which have come from every
province.
   18. *So*] provided that.

That daily ruinate his state and kingdom.
Woodstock. Go in, sweet ladies; comfort one another.   20
This happy parliament shall make all even
And plant sure peace betwixt the King and realm.
Queen Anne. May Heaven direct your wisdoms to provide
For England's honour and King Richard's good.
York. Believe no less, sweet queen. [*To Duchess*] Attend her
highness.   25

                  Ex[*eunt* QUEEN ANNE *and* DUCHESS
                      of GLOUCESTER].

Arundel. The King is come, my lords.
Woodstock. Stand from the door then. Make way, Cheney.

      Sound [*a*] *flourish. Enter* KING RICHARD, BAGOT,
        BUSHY [*with* papers], GREENE, *and*
        SCROOP *and others.*

Greene. Yonder's your uncles, my lord.
King Richard.   Ay, with our plain Protector,
Full of complaints, sweet Greene, I'll wage my crown.
Bagot. Give them fair words, and smooth awhile: 30
The toils are pitched, and you may catch them quickly.
King Richard. Why how now, uncle? What, disrobed again
Of all your golden rich habiliments?
Woodstock. Ay, ay, good coz, I'm now in my t'other hose,
I'm now myself, Plain Thomas, and by th'rood   35
In these plain hose I'll do the realm more good
Than these that pill the poor to jet in gold.
King Richard. Nay, be not angry, uncle.

27.1. *flourish*] *in left-hand margin at l. 24 in MS; a word, possibly* flourish *has been eroded in right-hand margin at l. 27.*   34. coz] cuss *MS, over which is written* my *with* leege *interlined above caret mark.*

27.2. with papers] the trick petition required at l. 65 and noted in the margin of the MS by the book-keeper at l. 60.
    30. *smooth*] flatter, humour.
    31. *The toils are pitched*] the trap is set; see below ll. 66ff.
    33. *habiliments*] attire.
    34. *coz*] The alteration to 'my leege' is made by a different hand, possibly that of the Jacobean censor Sir George Buc, Master of the Revels. See 'Censorship' section in Introduction.
    37. *pill*] pillage.
    jet] swagger.

Woodstock. Be you then pleased, good coz, to hear me speak
　　And view thy subjects' sad petitions.   40
　　See here, King Richard: whilst thou liv'st at ease,
　　Lulling thyself in nice security,
　　Thy wrongèd kingdom's in a mutiny.
　　From every province are the people come
　　With open mouths exclaiming on the wrongs   45
　　Thou and these upstarts have imposed on them.
　　Shame is deciphered on thy palace gate,
　　Confusion hangeth o'er thy wretched head;
　　Mischief is coming and in storms must fall:
　　Th'oppression of the poor to Heaven doth call.   50
King Richard. Well, well, good uncle, these your bitter taunts
　　Against my friends and me will one day cease.
　　But what's the reason you have sent for us?
Lancaster. To have your grace confirm this parliament
　　And set your hand to certain articles   55
　　Most needful for your state and kingdom's quiet.
King Richard. Where are those articles?
Arundel. The states and burgesses o'th' parliament
　　Attend with duty to deliver them.
York. Please you ascend your throne, we'll call them in.   60
King Richard. We'll ask a question first and then we'll see
　　　them;
　　For trust me, reverend uncles, we have sworn

---

39. coz] cuss *deleted in MS in same ink as at l. 34.*   41–3. See ... mutiny]
*Lines are ruled above l. 41 and below l. 43 in darker ink, possibly the same as used
for* cuss *omissions.*   41. whilst] *Halliwell, Keller;* whist *MS.*   60.] Paper
written in the right-hand margin in MS.

39. *coz*] The MS deletion is possibly an intervention by the censor which,
as at l. 34 above, interferes with the metrical line.

40. *sad*] serious, grave.

41–3. *See ... mutiny*] The marking off of these lines may indicate an
intention to omit them perhaps because they openly criticise the King's
behaviour and raise the prospect of rebellion; the deletion of these lines
would not jeopardise the flow and sense of the speech.

42. *nice*] Several possible meanings may attach to Woodstock's scornful
use of 'nice' here; i.e. foolish, lascivious, idle or unmanly.

47. *deciphered*] ciphered, written, either literally or metaphorically.

54. *confirm this parliament*] It is the king's prerogative alone to summon
and dissolve parliament.

58. *states and burgesses*] persons of rank and commoners.

We will not sit upon our royal throne
Until this question be resolved at full.
Reach me that paper, Bushy. Hear me, princes: 65
We had a strange petition here delivered us.
A poor man's son, his father being deceased,
Gave him in charge unto a rich man's hands
To keep him and the little land he had
Till he attained to one-and-twenty years.   70
The poor revènue amounts but to three crowns,
And yet th'insatiate churl denies his right
And bars him of his fair inheritance.
Tell me, I pray, will not our English laws
Enforce this rich man to resign his due?   75
Woodstock. There is no let to bar it, gracious sovereign.
Afore my God, sweet prince, it joys my soul
To see your grace in person thus to judge his cause.
York. Such deeds as this will make King Richard shine
Above his famous predecessor kings   80
If thus he labour to establish right.
King Richard. The poor man then had wrong, you all confess?
Woodstock. And shall have right, my liege, to quit his wrong.
King Richard. Then, Woodstock, give us right; for we are
        wronged.
Thou art the rich, and we the poor man's son.   85
The realms of England, France and Ireland
Are those three crowns thou yearly keepst from us.
Is't not a wrong when every mean man's son
May take his birthright at the time expired,
And we the principal, being now attained   90

70. one-and-twenty] *Rossiter;* (2i) *MS.*   82–4.] *Speech prefixes are missing
probably because part of the page has eroded at this point. Halliwell supplies the
King's name as speaker at ll. 82 and 84.*   83. Woodstock] *conj. Frijlinck;* [*All:*]
Halliwell; All Lords. Keller.

---

65. *Reach*] hand.
71. *three crowns*] referring to the coin (25p) with a pun on 'crown' as a kingdom; the three kingdoms are England, France and Ireland (see ll. 86–7 below).
76. *let*] hindrance.
78. *his*] i.e. the poor man's son.
83. Woodstock] It is appropriate that Woodstock is given the speech,
rather than all of the uncles, since he bears the burden of the argument with
Richard and the king addresses him directly in the next line.
90. *principal*] i.e. the chief protagonist in the dispute and also punning
on 'prince'.

Almost to two-and-twenty years of age,
Cannot be suffered to enjoy our own,
Nor peaceably possess our father's right?
Woodstock. Was this the trick, sweet prince? Alack the day,
You need not thus have doubled with your friends.   95
The right I hold, even with my heart I render
And wish your grace had claimed it long ago.
Thou'dst rid mine age of mickle care and woe,
And yet I think I have not wronged your birthright;
For if the times were searched I guess your grace   100
Is not so full of years till April next;
But be it as it will. Lo, here, King Richard,
I thus yield up my sad Protectorship. *Gives the mace up.*
A heavy burden hast thou ta'en from me.
Long mayst thou live in peace and keep thine own   105
That truth and justice may attend thy throne.
King Richard. Then in the name of Heaven we thus ascend
it,
And here we claim our fair inheritance
Of fruitful England, France and Ireland,
Superior Lord of Scotland, and the rights   110
Belonging to our great dominions.
Here, uncles, take the crown from Richard's hand
And once more place it on our kingly head.
This day we will be new enthronishèd.
Woodstock. With all our hearts, my lord. Trumpets be ready.   115
                                        A flourish.
All. Long live King Richard of that name the second,
The sovereign lord of England's ancient rights!
King Richard. We thank ye all. So now we feel ourself.

---

91. two-and-twenty] *Rossiter;* (22) *MS.* 98. Thou'dst] *Rossiter;* thadst
MS. 110. Superior . . . Scotland] *deleted in MS; a large cross is written in the
left-hand margin.* 114. enthronishèd] Inthronished *MS;* enthronised *Halliwell, Keller.*

---

95. *have doubled*] i.e. have been ambiguous, hence tricked, deceived.
98. *mickle*] great, much.
103. *sad*] burdensome.
110. *Superior Lord of Scotland*] The adjacent cross in the margin, coupled
with the deletion of this phrase in the MS, may indicate the intervention of
the Jacobean censor, Sir George Buc; the phrase was likely to be seen as
offensive to the Stuarts after King James's accession in 1603. See 'Censorship' section in Introduction.

Our body could not fill this chair till now,
'Twas scanted to us by Protectorship.   120
But now we let ye know King Richard rules
And will elect and choose, place and displace
Such officers as we ourself shall like of.
And first, my lords, because your age is such
As pity 'twere ye should be further pressed   125
With weighty business of the commonweal,
We here dismiss ye from the council table,
And will that you remain not in our court.
Deliver up your staves and hear ye, Arundel,
We do discharge ye of the Admiralty.   130
Scroop, take his office and his place in council.
Scroop. I thank your highness.
York. Here, take my staff, good cousin. York thus leaves
     thee:
Thou leanst on staves that will at length deceive thee.
Lancaster. There lie the burden of old Lancaster,   135
And may he perish that succeeds my place.
King Richard. So, sir, we will observe your humour.
Sir Henry Greene, succeed our uncle York—
And, Bushy, take the staff of Lancaster.
Bushy. I thank your grace: his curses frights not me; 140
I'll keep it to defend your majesty.
Woodstock. What transformation do mine eyes behold
As if the world were topsy-turvy turned!
Hear me, King Richard.
King Richard.   Plain Thomas, I'll not hear ye.
Greene. Ye do not well to move his majesty.   145
Woodstock. Hence, flatterer, or by my soul I'll kill thee!
Shall England that so long was governèd
By grave experience, of white-headed age,
Be subject now to rash unskilful boys?
Then force the sun run backward to the east,   150

---

120. *scanted*] reduced, restricted.
129. *staves*] wood or ivory wands used as badges of office by crown officials.
135. *There . . . burden*] i.e. Lancaster gives up his staff of office.
137. *observe your humour*] tolerate your mood.
145. *move*] exasperate.

Lay Atlas' burden on a pigmy's back,
Appoint the sea his times to ebb and flow
And that as easily may be done as this.
King Richard. Give up your council staff; we'll hear no more.
Woodstock. My staff, King Richard? See, coz, here it is;   155
Full ten years' space within a prince's hand,
A soldier and a faithful councillor,
This staff hath always been discreetly kept;
Nor shall the world report an upstart groom
Did glory in the honours Woodstock lost;   160
And therefore, Richard, thus I sever it. [*Breaks his staff.*]
There let him take it—shivered, cracked, and broke,
As will the state of England be ere long
By this rejecting true nobility.
Farewell, King Richard. I'll to Plashy. Brothers,   165
If ye ride through Essex call and see me.
If once the pillars and supporters quail
How can the strongest castle choose but fail?
All Lords. And so will he ere long. Come, come, let's leave
    them.
Bushy. Ay, ay, your places are supplied sufficiently.   170
                Exeunt the lords [and CHENEY].
Scroop. Old doting greybeards!
'Fore God, my lord, had they not been your uncles,

---

153. as this.] *MS; as this . . . Rossiter.*   171–3.] *Rossiter; as prose MS.*

151. *Atlas' burden*] in Greek myth Atlas, a Titan, was compelled to support
the sky.
153. *this*] i.e. appointing Greene and Bushy to such high positions.
Rossiter's reading seems to imply that Woodstock's speech is unfinished and
that Richard interrupts him.
158–61. *This staff . . . I sever it*] It was traditional for court officials to
break their staffs of office over the coffin of their deceased lord; thus Woodstock's gesture before the King suggests his rejection of the king's legitimate
authority. In his *The Life and Raigne of King Henrie IIII* Hayward reports
Worcester's defection to Bolingbroke: 'Thomas Percie, Earle of Worcester
and steward of the king's household . . . openly in the hall, in the presence
of the kings servants, he brake his white rodde, the ensign of his office, and
forthwith departed to the duke [Bolingbroke], willing every man to shift for
himselfe in time' (Hayward, p. 124). Cf. *R2*, 2.2.58–9. Rossiter compares
Contention, 2.3.32–6, where Duke Humphrey gives up his staff of office.
159. *groom*] servant, base fellow.
165. *Plashy*] Plashy House, north-east of Chelmsford in Essex.

I'd broke my council staff about their heads.

Greene. We'll have an act for this: it shall be henceforth
    counted high treason for any fellow with a grey beard to   175
    come within forty foot of the court gates.

Bagot. Ay, or a great-bellied doublet; we'll alter the kingdom
    presently.

Greene. Pox on't, we'll not have a beard amongst us; we'll
    shave the country and the city too, shall we not, Richard?   180

King Richard. Do what ye will, we'll shield and buckler ye.
    We'll have a guard of archers to attend us
    And they shall daily wait on us and you.
    Send proclamations straight in Richard's name
    T'abridge the laws our late Protector made.   185
    Let some be sent to seek Tresilian forth.

Bagot. Seek him? Hang him! He lurks not far off I warrant;
    and this news come abroad once, ye shall have him here
    presently.

King Richard. Would he were come. His counsel would direct
    you well.   190

---

173. I'd] *Rossiter;* Ile *MS;* Ild *Halliwell.* 175. treason] *Halliwell;* trea<s *MS*
eroded at this point. 178. presently] *Rossiter;* per[force] *Halliwell, Keller;*
psent *MS.* 180. shave] *conj. Frijlinck;* sh<a *MS (or* Ch<a*);* rule *Halliwell;*
ch[ange] *Keller.* 187. warrant] warrant [you] *Rossiter;* warrant< *MS.*
189. presently] *conj. Frijlinck;* p<s *MS.*

---

177. *great-bellied doublet*] The reference here is to the size of the
belly rather than the fashioning of the doublet; thus Bagot wishes to
banish Richard's uncles who, as older men, have more substantial figures.
The aspersion is in line with Greene's comment on greybeards. Cf. *LLL,*
3.1.17.

178. *presently*] immediately.

180. *shave*] punning on the word in the sense of 'fleece'.

Richard] Greene's familiarity of address to the King is shocking in that,
unlike Woodstock, he lacks any familial connection with the King; thus his
behaviour serves to emphasise the destruction of hierarchical values, pre-
dicted by Woodstock.

182. *guard of archers*] Richard raised a select body of up to two thousand
Cheshire archers as his personal bodyguard. According to Saul, 'Never before
had the king surrounded himself by so massive a personal bodyguard, let alone
one so exclusively recruited'; Saul quotes the Kenilworth chronicler who
reports that 'the corps leaders' were on intimate terms with the King, 'Dycun,
slep sicury quile we wake, and dreed nouzt quile we lyve sestow' (Saul, p. 394).

185. *T'abridge*] to curtail or reduce.

188. *and*] if.

Greene. Troth, I think I shall trouble myself but with a few
counsellors.
What cheer shall we have to dinner, King Richard?
King Richard. No matter what today; we'll mend it shortly.
The hall at Westminster shall be enlarged   195
And only serve us for a dining-room,
Wherein I'll daily feast ten thousand men.
Greene. An excellent device. The commons has murmured
against us a great while and there's no such means as
meat to stop their mouths.   200
Scroop. 'Sfoot, make their gape wider: let's first fetch their
money and bid them to dinner afterwards.
Greene. 'Sblood, and I were not a councillor, I could find in
me to dine at a tavern today, sweet king.
Shall's be merry?   205
Scroop. We must have money to buy new suits, my lord;
The fashions that we wear are gross and stale.
We'll go sit in council to devise some new.

---

192. few counsellors] few c[ounsellors] *Halliwell;* few [counsellors] *Keller;*
friends *conj. Rossiter;* few< *MS.*   199. against us] *Rossiter;* a[ngrily] *Halli-*
well; ang[rily] *Keller;* a gainst you *conj. Frijlinck;* a g< *MS.*   200. stop their
mouths] *Rossiter;* stopp [them] *Halliwell, Keller;* stopp< *MS.*   201. gape]
This ed.; gate *MS.*   202. money] mon[ey] *Halliwell, Keller;* mon< *MS.*
204. me] *Parfitt;* myself *Rossiter;* ty[me] *Halliwell, Keller;* <. *MS.* king]
MS; Richard *Halliwell, Keller.*   206. Scroop] *Halliwell, Keller; missing in MS.*
206–8. We must . . . new] *as prose Parfitt.*   207. fashions] *Rossiter;* fash-
ione *MS.*

191–2. *few counsellors*] The MS is eroded at this point; Halliwell's 'counsellors' seems appropriate since it picks up Richard's 'counsel' in the previous line.
195–7. *The hall . . . men*] The Great Hall at Westminster was rebuilt at
great expense between 1393 and 1400. It is 240 ft in length and 70 ft wide.
Whilst Richard constructed it specifically for the purpose of great feasts and
ceremonial occasions, by the late sixteenth century it was the venue for the
Courts of Justice. Thus, for the play's contemporary audience it might have
seemed a shocking proposal to use such a building for comparatively trivial
purposes and such conspicuous consumption.
201. *gape*] MS's 'gate' is obscure; assuming Rossiter's conjecture 'their
mouths' in l. 200 is correct, one would expect Scroop to be referring to the
commons' appetite; it seems probable that the scribe has misread his copy here.
fetch] bring in, realise, but also with the subsidiary sense of 'steal'.
206. Scroop] Parfitt argues that the speaker is probably Scroop since he
has already shown interest in money.

Greene. A special purpose to be thought upon. It shall be the
    first thing we'll do. 210
King Richard. Come, wantons, come: if Gloucester hear of
    this
    He'll say our Council guides us much amiss.
    Dismiss the parliament our uncles called
    And tell the peers it is our present pleasure
    That each man parts unto his several home. 215
    When we are pleased they shall have summons sent
    And with King Richard hold a parliament.
    Set forward.
Greene. You of the Council, march before the King.
    I will support his arm.
King Richard.   Gramercy, Greene. 220
    Trumpets sounds [a flourish]. Exeunt omnes.

[2.3]

> *Enter the* QUEEN [ANNE], *the* DUCHESS *of*
> GLOUCESTER, *the* DUCHESS *of* IRELAND *and other*
> Maids *with shirts and bands and other lining [in trunks].*

Queen Anne. Tell me, dear aunt, has Richard so forgot
    The types of honour and nobility
    So to disgrace his good and reverend uncles?

---

209. *Greene] This ed.; All Halliwell;* [A]*ll Keller;* >*ll MS.* 209–10.] *one line
in MS;* A . . . upon! / It . . . do. *Armstrong.* 217–18.] *Rossiter; one line in MS.*
220.1. [a flourish]] Flourish *in left-hand margin at l. 216 in MS.*

2.3.0.3. *lining]* lyneing *MS;* linen *Rossiter.* 3. reverend] 'Reverent' *written
over some other word, possibly* vertious *(Frijlinck).*

---

209. Greene] Keller's conjecture 'All' seems a plausible reading of what
remains in the MS, but it seems unlikely that this line is a group response
to Scroop's suggestion. In view of Greene's self-confidence and dominance
during this scene it is appropriate to give him the line.

2.3.0.2–3. other Maids] i.e. other court ladies attending upon the Queen.
0.3. bands] neck-bands or collars.
lining] Parfitt points out that Rossiter's emendation is unnecessary since
'lining' is a common sixteenth-century term for any material used to line or
back another. The sorting and repair of what are presumably old garments
for the relief of the poor present a sharp contrast to Cheney's report of
Richard's divising of extravagant fashion later in the scene.
2. types] patterns.

Duchess of Gloucester. Madam, 'tis true. No sooner had he
    claimed   5
The full possession of his government
But my dear husband and his noble brethren
Were all dismissèd from the council table,
Banished the court, and, even before their faces,
Their offices bestowed on several grooms.
Duchess of Ireland. My husband Ireland, that unloving lord   10
—God pardon his amiss, he now is dead—
King Richard was the cause he left my bed.
Queen Anne. No more, good cousin. Could I work the means,
He should not so disgrace his dearest friends.
Alack the day! Though I am England's queen   15
I meet sad hours and wake when others sleep.
He meets content, but care with me must keep.
Distressèd poverty o'erspreads the kingdom:
In Essex, Surrey, Kent and Middlesex
Are seventeen thousand poor and indigent   20
Which I have numbered; and to help their wants
My jewels and my plate are turned to coin
And shared amongst them. O riotous Richard,
A heavy blame is thine for this distress

---

9. *grooms*] servants; the term is used here in a derogatory sense to
describe Richard's minions.

10–11. *Ireland . . . dead*] Holinshed gives the date of the death of Robert
Vere, Duke of Ireland, as 1392. Exiled by Woodstock's faction, he died acci-
dentally during a boar hunt near Louvain.

12. *King . . . bed*] The Duchess's charge of homosexuality against
Richard parallels Bolingbroke's accusation against Bushy and Greene in *R2*,
3.1.11–15. Although Robert Vere was one of Richard's early favourites there
is no specific evidence of his homosexual relationship with the King. Such
charges may be drawn from Holinshed's general comment on Richard's
reign: 'Furthermore, there reigned abundantlie the filthie sinne of leacherie
and fornication, with abhominable adulterie, speciallie in the king' (p. 508).

16. *meet*] experience.

18–23. *Distressèd . . . them*] Although the specific claims made here for the
Queen's charitable nature are unsupported historically, there is evidence for
her conciliatory influence in Richard's quarrel with the City of London,
when in 1392 the Mayor and the Sheriffs were imprisoned because of their
refusal to grant the king's request for £1,000, and, in addition, London's liberties were cancelled.

23. *riotous*] wanton, dissolute, perhaps also suggesting sexual as well as
other forms of debasement; cf. *Lear* (*Tragedy*), 4.5.120–1, 'The fitchew nor
the soiled horse goes to't / With a more riotous appetite'.

That dost allow thy polling flatterers   25
To gild themselves with others' miseries.
Duchess of Gloucester. Wrong not yourself with sorrow,
    gentle Queen,
Unless that sorrow were a helping means
To cure the malady you sorrow for.
Queen Anne. The sighs I vent are not mine own, dear aunt,   30
I do not sorrow in mine own behalf,
Nor now repent with peevish frowardness
And wish I ne'er had seen this English shore,
But think me happy in King Richard's love.
No, no, good aunt, this troubles not my soul: 35
'Tis England's subjects' sorrow I sustain,
I fear they grudge against their sovereign.
Duchess of Gloucester. Fear not that, madam, England's not
    mutinous:
'Tis peopled all with subjects, not with outlaws.
Though Richard, much misled by flatterers,   40
Neglects and throws his sceptre carelessly,
Yet none dares rob him of his kingly rule.
Duchess of Ireland. Besides, your virtuous charity, fair
    Queen,
So graciously hath won the commons' love
As only you have power to stay their rigour.   45
Queen Anne. The wealth I have shall be the poor's revènue

---

25. polling] *Frijlinck;* pooleing *MS;* paleing *Halliwell, Keller.* 27–69.]
*marked for omission in MS and lacking speech prefixes, here supplied by
Rossiter.* 43. Duchess of Ireland] *conj. Frijlinck; no speech prefix in MS.*
45. rigour] Rigo<r *MS;* rage *Halliwell, Keller.*

---

25. *polling*] shaving, fleecing; Frijlinck notes that previous editors' misreading of the MS as 'paleing' has led to an interpretation which has found
its way as a solitary example into *OED* (repeated in the latest edition) as a
participial adjective from the verb to 'pale' or surround. Rossiter notes that
there may be an allusion to the poll-tax here and also a pun on Lapoole.
Stow quotes Gower's *Vox Clamantis* in his treatment of Richard II: 'The
people also whom hee polde, against him did rebel'.
    27–69.] These lines, marked for omission in the MS, may have been cut
by the players for fear of giving offence to the authorities. See 'Censorship'
section in Introduction. This passage marks a significant addition by the
dramatist to his source, Holinshed.
    32. *frowardness*] perverseness, discontent.
    41. *throws . . . carelessly*] wields his sceptre, i.e. his power, carelessly.

As sure as 'twere confirmed by parliament.
This mine own industry—and sixty more
I daily keep at work—is all their own.
The coin I have I send them. Would 'twere more!   50
To satisfy my fears or pay those sums
My wanton lord hath forced from needy subjects
I'd want myself. Go, let those trunks be filled
With those our labours to relieve the poor.
Let them be carefully distributed.   55

Enter CHENEY.

For those that now shall want, we'll work again
And tell them ere two days we shall be furnishèd.
Cheney. What is the court removing? Whither goes that
    trunk?
Maid. 'Tis the Queen's charity, sir, of needful clothing
    To be distributed amongst the poor.   60
                              [*Exeunt* Maids *with trunks.*]
Cheney. [*Aside*] Why, there's one blessing yet, that England
    hath
    A virtuous queen, although a wanton king—
    Good health, sweet princess. Believe me, madam,
    You have quick utterance for your housewifery.
    Your grace affords good pennyworths sure, ye sell so fast!   65

55.1. Enter CHENEY] *Positioned in the margin at l. 55 and deleted in MS.*
57.] 'woodstocke' *written in left-hand margin of MS.*   59. Maid] *Rossiter; D.*
Ire. Armstrong.   61. SD] *conj. Rossiter.*

55.1. Enter CHENEY] Cheney's entry is deleted in the MS because of the
cutting of ll. 27–69; see note to l. 69.

56. *want*] suffer want.

57.] The insertion in the margin of the manuscript of Woodstock's
name may indicate a state of the text in which he rather than Cheney was
given the lines to the Queen, 'Why there's . . . swift return' (ll. 61–6). These
lines seem in their bluff directness and open criticism of the King more
appropriate to Woodstock than Cheney, but Woodstock's presence here is
precluded by ll. 70–2.

59. Maid] Rossiter's attribution of these lines to an anonymous court lady
rather than one of the duchesses is plausible because of the speaker's respectful tone to Cheney.

64. *quick utterance*] i.e. good business.

65. *Your grace . . . fast*] possibly proverbial; more akin to Woodstock's ban-
tering turn of phrase than to Cheney's manner of speaking; see note to l. 57 above.

Pray Heaven your gettings quit your swift return!
Queen Anne. Amen, for 'tis from Heaven I look for
   recompense.
Cheney. No doubt, fair queen, the righteous powers will
   quit you
For these religious deeds of charity.
But to my message. [*To Duchess of Gloucester*] Madam, my
   lord the Duke   70
Entreats your grace prepare with him to horse:
He will this night ride home to Plashy House.
Duchess of Gloucester. Madam, ye hear I'm sent for.
Queen Anne.   Then begone.
Leave me alone in desolation.
Duchess of Ireland. [*To Duchess of Gloucester*] Adieu, good
   aunt, I'll see ye shortly there: 75
King Richard's kindred are not welcome here.
Queen Anne. Will ye all leave me then? O woe is me,
I now am crowned a queen of misery.
Duchess of Gloucester. Where didst thou leave my husband,
   Cheney? Speak.
Cheney. Accompanied with the dukes of York and Lancaster   80
Who, as I guess, intends to ride with him,
For which he wished me haste your grace's presence.
Duchess of Gloucester. [*Aside to Cheney*] Thou seest the
   passions of the Queen are such
I may not too abruptly leave her highness;
But tell my lord I'll see him presently.   85
Queen Anne. Sawst thou King Richard, Cheney? Prithee tell
   me,
What revels keeps his flattering minions?

69.] *Enter Cheny in left margin in MS, with* Health to yor matie *added in text between this line and the next.* 70. SD] *Rossiter.* 75. SD] *This ed.* 83. SD] *This ed.*

---

  66. *gettings*] gains, earnings.
  quit] reward, repay.
  69.] The cutting of ll. 27–69 in the MS required a fresh entry for Cheney and the addition of the otherwise redundant phrase 'Health to yor matie' written in the same ink as 'Enter Cheney' and the surrounding speech prefixes. This alteration was necessary in order to accommodate the cut, introducing Cheney at an appropriate point in the action.

Cheney. They sit in council to devise strange fashions,
       And suit themselves in wild and antic habits
       Such as this kingdom never yet beheld: 90
       French hose, Italian cloaks and Spanish hats,
       Polonian shoes with peaks a handful long,
       Tied to their knees with chains of pearl and gold.
       Their pluméd tops fly waving in the air
       A cubit high above their wanton heads.   95
       Tresilian with King Richard likewise sits,
       Devising taxes and strange shifts for money
       To build again the hall at Westminster
       To feast and revel in; and when abroad they come
       Four hundred archers in a guard attends them.   100
Queen Anne. O certain ruin of this famous kingdom!
       Fond Richard, thou buildst a hall to feast in
       And starvest thy wretched subjects to erect it.
       Woe to those men that thus incline thy soul
       To these remorseless acts and deeds so foul.   105
                                                A flourish [within].
Duchess of Gloucester. The trumpets tell us that King
       Richard's coming.

---

99. and revel] *deleted in MS.* 105.1. SD] A Florish *in left-hand margin at l.
104 in MS.* 106. *Duchess of Gloucester.* The] *Halliwell; MS eroded.*

88–95. *They sit . . . heads]* References to excessive expenditure on fashionable clothes are found in the Chronicles and also reflect Elizabethan and
Jacobean indictments of enthusiasm for bizarre foreign fashions; cf.
Marlowe, *Edward*, 1.4.401–17 and *MerV.*, 1.2.65–73. Historically, from the
early years of Richard's rule magnificent court dress became *de rigueur*; see
Mathew, pp. 26–9.
   92. *Polonian]* Polish. Other dramatists comment on flamboyant Polish
footwear; Dekker in *Seven Deadly Sins* says of the English fashionable man,
'Palonia gave him the boots'. Rowlands in *More Knaves Yet?* (1613) talks of
'Palonion heels' and in *Martin Mark-all* (1610) of 'a Palony shoe with a bell'
(Sugden). Stow blames, in part, the Bohemian attendants of the Queen for
some of the excesses in fashion.
   handful] i.e. the span of a hand.
   94. *tops]* hats.
   95. *cubit]* a measure derived from the forearm; usually about 18–22 in.
   97. *shifts]* tricks, devices.
   99. *To . . . in]* Frijlinck conjectures that 'Feast &' should have been
deleted in the MS instead of '& revel'. Although this rearrangement of the
manuscript's deletion produces a metrically regular line, both Frijlinck's
deletion and that of the MS weaken the emphasis of Cheney's criticism.
   102. *Fond]* foolish, irresponsible.

I'll take my leave, fair Queen; but, credit me,
Ere many days again I'll visit ye.   [*Exit with* CHENEY.]
Duchess of Ireland. I'll home to Langley with my Uncle York,
    And there lament alone my wretched state.   [*Exit.*]   110
Queen Anne. Blest Heaven conduct ye both. Queen Anne
    alone
For Richard's follies still must sigh and groan.
                                        Exit QUEEN [ANNE].

---

108 & 110. SDs] *This ed.; Exeunt both the Duchesses at l. 110 in MS.*

109. *Langley*] King's Langley, a village in west Hertfordshire about twenty
miles from London.

Act 3

Sound a sennet. Enter KING RICHARD, BAGOT,
BUSHY, GREENE *and* SCROOP, *very richly attired in
new fashions, and* TRESILIAN [*with blank charters*]
whispering with the King. A guard of archers after them.

King Richard. Come, my Tresilian.
　　Thus like an emperor shall King Richard reign
　　And you so many kings attendant on him.
　　Our guard of archers, keep the doors, I charge ye;
　　Let, no man enter to disturb our pleasures!　　　　　5
　　Thou toldst me, kind Tresilian, thou'dst devised
　　Blank charters, to fill up our treasury,
　　Opening the chests of hoarding cormorants
　　That laugh to see their kingly sovereign lack.
　　Let's know the means we may applaud thy wit.　　　10
Tresilian. See here, my lord, only with parchment, innocent
　　sheepskins. Yet see here's no fraud, no clause, no deceit
　　in the writing.
All. Why, there's nothing writ!
Tresilian.　　　　　　　　　　There's the trick on't.

3.1.5.] Blankes *in left-hand margin in MS.*

3.1.2–3. *Thus . . . him*] Whilst this is an index of Richard's extravagance,
it may also reflect the historical possibility in 1397 of his being elected
Holy Roman Emperor as part of the settlement of the Schism of the Popes.
Richard is reported as saying, 'I am entire Emperor of my Realm'. See
Hutchison, p. 199.
　　5.] The marginal note 'Blankes' is probably the book-keeper's reminder
to provide the blank charters which Tresilian shows King Richard at l. 11.
　　7. *Blank charters*] Historically, signed blank charters (blank cheques), in
which the King might write any figure he chose, were imposed on rich citizens for unknown crimes in 1398–9, some ten years after Tresilian's execution. See Hutchison, pp. 203–4.
　　8. *cormorants*] The rapacious sea bird, the cormorant, was frequently
invoked in Elizabethan literature to represent a type of voracious glutton.
　　10. *means we*] either 'measures for which we' or 'means so that we'.

These blank charters shall be forthwith sent   15
To every shrieve through all the shires of England,
With charge to call before them presently
All landed men, freeholders, farmers, graziers,
Or any else that have ability.
Then in your highness' name they shall be charged   20
To set their names and forthwith seal these blanks;
That done, these shall return to court again,
But cartloads of money soon shall follow them.
Scroop. Excellent Tresilian!
Bushy.   Noble Lord Chief Justice!
Bagot. Where should his grace get such a councillor?   25
Greene. Not if his beard were off! Prithee, Tresilian, off
    with it.
    'Sfoot, thou seest we have not a beard amongst us.
    Thou sendst out barbers there to poll the whole
        country,
    'Sfoot, let some shave thee.
Bushy. 'Twould become thee better i'faith, and make thee   30
    look more grim when thou sit'st in judgement.
Tresilian. I tell ye, gallants, I will not lose a hair of my lord-
    ship and King Richard's favour for the Pope's revènues.

                Enter the QUEEN [ANNE].

Greene. By your leave there. Give way to th'Queen.
King Richard. Now, Anne o' Beame, how cheers my dearest
        Queen?   35
    Is't holiday, my love? Believe me, lords,
    'Tis strange to take her from her sempstery:

---

24. *Scroop*] all *deleted before* 'Scroo:' *MS; All:* Halliwell; *All Sirres* Keller.
28.] *a word, possibly* growe, *written in the left-hand margin of MS.* out] *MS;*
our *Rossiter.* 32–3.] *as verse in* Rossiter.

---

19. *have ability*] i.e. have the capacity to pay.
26. *beard were off*] From the stage entry for the scene it would appear that
Tresilian has yet to catch up with the new fashions; he has also retained his
beard whilst the King and his favourites are clean-shaven.
28. *poll*] shave, i.e. tax and sequester.
33. *Pope's revènues*] Tresilian extends the pun on shaving to hint at the
wealth, surpassing the Pope's revenues, which he no doubt hopes to accrue
from the exploitation of his office.
35. *how cheers*] how is it with you.
37. *'Tis . . . sempstery*] i.e. 'It is unusual to catch her away from her
sewing'.

She and her maids are all for houswif'ry.
Shalt work no more, sweet Nan, now Richard's king,
And peer, and people all shall stoop to him.   40
We'll have no more protecting uncles, trust me.
Prithee, look smooth and bid these nobles welcome.
Queen Anne. Whom my lord favours must to me be
    welcome.
King Richard. These are our councillors, I tell ye, lady,
And these shall better grace King Richard's court   45
Than all the doting heads that late controllèd us.
Thou seest already we begin to alter
The vulgar fashions of our homespun kingdom.
I tell thee, Nan, the states of Christendom
Shall wonder at our English royalty.   50
We held a council to devise these suits.
Sir Henry Greene devised this fashion shoe;
Bushy this peak; Bagot and Scroop set forth
This kind coherence 'twixt the toe and knee
To have them chained together lovingly;   55
And we as sovereign did confirm them all.
Suit they not quaintly, Nan? Sweet Queen, resolve me.
Queen Anne. I see no fault that I dare call a fault,
But would your grace consider, with advice,
What you have done unto your reverend uncles—   60
My fears provoke me to be bold, my lord,
They are your noble kinsmen—to revoke
The sentence were—
King Richard.   An act of folly, Nan.

---

40. peer] peere *MS;* peers *Rossiter.*   62–5.] *This ed.;* They . . . weare / an
. . . lawes / if . . . lawe / no . . . queene *MS.*

41. *protecting*] i.e. governing the realm on Richard's behalf.
42. *smooth*] pleasant, affable.
48. *vulgar*] common or unsophisticated.
homespun] alluding in particular to the homely and unpretentious dress of
Woodstock.
51. *We . . . suits*] There is no historical authority for such a council but
the dramatist's invention emphasises the King's irresponsibility in devoting
a council meeting to such trivial issues. Rossiter contrasts these activities
with Richard's original aspirations (2.1.93–6).
53. *peak*] projecting toe of a shoe; see 3.2.210.
54. *kind coherence*] natural linkage; Richard refers to the decorative chains
which link the toe of the shoe to the knee.
57. *quaintly*] elegantly.

King's words are laws. If we infringe our word
We break our law. No more of them, sweet Queen.   65
Tresilian. Madam, what's done was with advice enough.
The King is now at years and hath shook off
The servile yoke of mean Protectorship.
Bushy. His highness can direct himself sufficient.
Why should his pleasures then be curbed by any   70
As if he did not understand his state?
King Richard. They tell thee true, sweet love. Come ride
    with me
And see today my hall at Westminster
Which we have builded new to feast our friends.
Greene. Do, do, good madam. Prithee, sweet king, let's ride   75
somewhither and it be but to show ourselves. 'Sfoot, our
devices here are like jewels kept in caskets, or good faces
in masks that grace not the owners because they're
obscured. If our fashions be not published, what glory's
in the wearing?   80
King Richard. We'll ride through London only to be gazed at.
Fair Anne o' Beame, you shall along with us;
At Westminster shalt see my sumptuous hall,
My royal tables richly furnishèd
Where every day I feast ten thousand men,   85
To furnish out which feast I daily spend
Thirty fat oxen and three hundred sheep,

---

74. new] *This ed.;* now *MS.*   85. ten thousand] 10000 *MS* (1 *altered from* 4).

---

64. *King's words are laws*] proverbial, 'What the King wills, that the law
wills' (Tilley K72).

67. *at years*] of legal age.

68. *mean*] demeaning.

71. *state*] high rank, status.

74. *new*] The emendation seems appropriate since Richard rebuilt
Westminster Hall; see note to 2.2.195–7.

79. *published*] displayed in public.

81. *We'll . . . gazed at*] Cf. *1H4* where Bolingbroke describes Richard as
'the skipping King, he ambled up and down . . . grew a companion to the
common streets, / Enfeoffed himself to popularity' (3.2.60–9).

86. *spend*] consume.

87–8. *Thirty . . . numberless*] Richard II's feasting was certainly lavish, and
it is not necessarily the case that the Chroniclers grossly exaggerate the number
of guests he entertained and the extravagance of the dishes which he provided.
It seems that his household did not fall far short of ten thousand people and

With fish and fowl in numbers numberless.
Not all our chronicles shall point a king
To match our bounty, state and royalty;   90
Or let our successors yet to come
Strive to exceed me; and if they forbid it,
Let records say, 'Only King Richard did it'.
Queen Anne. O but, my lord, 'twill tire your revènues
To keep this festival a year together.   95
King Richard. As many days as I write England's king
We will maintain that bounteous festival.
Tresilian, look to your blank charters speedily,
Send them abroad with trusty officers.
And, Bagot, see a messenger be sent   100
To call our Uncle Woodstock home to th'court;
Not that we love his meddling company,
But that the ragged commons loves his plainness
And should grow, mutinous about these blanks,
We'll have him near us. Within his arrow's length   105
We stand secure. We can restrain his strength.
See it be done. Come, Anne, to our great hall

---

91. successors] successessors *MS (owing to faulty correction—succe being
interlined by another hand in darker ink above predi which is deleted).*
103. ragged] *Rossiter, Armstrong;* raged *MS, Parfitt.*

---

that as many as three hundred cooks were employed to cater for their needs.
The provisions gathered for a great feast co-hosted by Richard and (ironically,
given the text's treatment of events) the Duke of Lancaster in September 1387
included '14 oxen lying in salte, 2 oxen ffreyssh, 120 carcas of shepe fressh, 12
bores, 14 calvys, 140 pigges, 3 ton of salt veneson, 50 swannes, 210 gees, 60
dozen hennes, 400 conygges [large rabbits], 100 dozen peions [pigeons] and 11
thousand egges' (Sass, pp. 19–20). Richard was the first English monarch to
commission a cookery-book, *The Forme of Cury*, i.e. 'the (proper) method of
cookery' which was 'compiled of the chef Maister Cokes of kyng Richard the
Se[cu]nde kyng of [En]glond aftir the conquest . . . the which was accounted
[th]e best and ryallist vyand[ier] of alle cristen [k]ynges', *Curye on Inglysch*,
EETS (1985), eds Constance B. Hieatt and Sharon Butler, p. 20.
    89. *point*] point out, depict.
    96. *write*] call myself.
    103. *ragged*] Parfitt supports MS's reading 'raged' on the grounds that the
commons are more often seen as angry than as 'ragged', but in view of the
importance of clothing in this play the latter reading seems in context to be
peculiarly appropriate, allowing Richard an added jibe at Woodstock's plainness of dress.
    104. *And should grow*] in case they grow.

Where Richard keeps his gorgeous festival.
> [*Trumpets*] *sound. Exeunt. Manet* TRESILIAN.
Tresilian. Within there, ho!

> *Enter* CROSBY *and* FLEMING.

Crosby. Your lordship's pleasure?   110
Tresilian. What, are those blanks despatched?
Fleming. They're all trussed up, my lord, in several packets.
Where's Nimble? Where's that varlet?

> *Enter* NIMBLE [*in peaked shoes with knee-chains*].

Nimble. As nimble as a morris-dancer now my bells are on.
How do ye like the rattling of my chains, my lord?   115
Tresilian. O villain! Thou wilt hang in chains for this.
Art thou crept into the court fashion, knave?
Nimble. Alas, my lord, ye know I have followed your lordship
without e'er a rag since ye run away from the court once;
and I pray let me follow the fashion a little to show myself   120
a courtier.
Tresilian. Go spread those several blanks throughout the
kingdom,
And here's commission with the Council's hands
With charge to every shrieve and officer
T'assist and aid you; and when they're sealed and
signed   125
See ye note well such men's ability
As set their hands to them. Inquire what rents,
What lands, or what revènues they spend by th'year,
And let me straight receive intelligence.
Besides, I'd have you use yourselves so cunningly   130
To mark who grudges or but speaks amiss
Of good King Richard, myself, or any of his new
councillors.

108.1. SD] *Add. Rossiter.*

---

114. *morris-dancer . . . on*] Morris-dancers attached bells to their legs to
enhance the effect of their performance; cf. *The Witch of Edmonton*, 'Young
Banks. And forget not five leash of new bells/First Dancer. Double bells!'
(Dekker, *Witch*, 2.1.37–8).
  123. *with . . . hands*] i.e. signed by the members of the Council.
  126. *ability*] wealth, means.
  130. *use*] employ.
  131. *grudges*] grumbles.

Attach them all for privy whisperers,
And send them up. I have a trick in law
Shall make King Richard seize into his hands   135
The forfeiture of all their goods and lands.
Nimble, take thou these blanks and see you take
especial note of them.
Nimble. I'll take the ditty, sir, but you shall set a note to't; for
if any man shall speak but an ill word of anything that's   140
written here—
Tresilian. Why, ass, there's nothing.
Nimble. And would ye have them speak ill of nothing? That's
strange. But I mean, my lord, if they should but give this
paper an ill word, as to say, 'I will tear this paper', or   145
worse, 'I will rend this paper', or fouler words than that,
as to say, 'I will bumfiddle, your paper'; if there be any
such, I have a black book, for them, my lord, I warrant
ye.
Tresilian. Be it your greatest care to be severe.   150
Crosby and Fleming, pray be diligent.
Crosby. We shall, my lord.
Nimble. But how if we meet with some ignoramus fellows, my
lord, that cannot write their minds, what shall they do?
Tresilian. If they but set to their marks, 'tis good.   155
Nimble. We shall meddle with no women in the blanks, shall
we?
Tresilian. Rich widows, none else; for a widow is as much as
man and wife.

136–7. The . . . lands / Nimble] *Rossiter; as one line in MS.*   145. tear] teare
MS; treat *Armstrong.*

---

133. *Attach*] arrest.
134. *send them up*] i.e. commit them for trial in London.
139. *I'll . . . to't*] i.e. I will deliver the words (with a pun on 'dittay', a term
in Scottish law meaning an indictment) whilst you shall compose the melody,
i.e. legally entrap them.
147. *bumfiddle*] use as lavatory paper. *OED* cites this example.
148. *black book*] commonly used for lists of rogues and villains; see
Webster, 4.1.33.
156. *meddle . . . blanks*] bawdy quibble; 'meddle' in the sense of copu-
late with (Williams, *Glossary*). The blank is the bull's eye of the archery
butt.
158–9. *for . . . wife*] referring to the fact that widows were accorded 'male'
rights over money, property, etc. Cf. the proverb, 'Widows are always rich'
(Tilley w342).

Nimble. Then a widow's a hermaphrodite, both cut and long-   160
tail. And if she cannot write, she shall set her mark to it.
Tresilian. What else, sir?
Nimble. But if she have a daughter, she shall set her mother's
mark to't?
Tresilian. Meddle with none but men and widows, sir, I charge   165
ye.
Nimble. Well, sir, I shall see a widow's mark then; I ne'er saw
none yet!
Tresilian. You have your lessons perfect. Now begone;
Be bold and swift in execution.   *Exit* TRESILIAN.   170
Nimble. God buy ye, my lord. We will domineer over the
vulgar like so many Saint Georges over the poor dragons.
Come, sirs; we are like to have a flourishing common-
wealth, i'faith!   *Exeunt.*

[3.2]

        Enter WOODSTOCK, LANCASTER *and* YORK *at Plashy.*

Woodstock. Come, my good brothers, here at Plashy House
I'll bid you welcome with as true a heart

171. God buy ye] *This ed.;* God be'ye *Parfitt;* god boy *MS.*

3.2.2. heart] *Halliwell;* <har>te *MS (the first three letters obscured by the* y *of* Plashy *above).*

160–1. *cut and longtail*] docked and undocked, with bawdy reference to female and male genitalia.
    161. *mark*] Nimble pursues an extended bawdy quibble on 'mark', 'a target in archery hence that sexual mark or target at which a man sexually aims' (Partridge). For the bawdy implicatons of Nimble's name see note on *Dramatis Personae*. Rossiter also glosses 'a widow's mark' (l. 167) as a parallel to 'the widow's mite', a mark being equivalent to 13*s* 4*d*.
    171. *God buy ye*] Either 'Good-bye' or perhaps ironically, given Tresilian's schemes, 'God redeem you'. For the confusion of this phrase with 'God be with ye' see G. R. Hibbard's note on *Ham.*, 2.1.68 (Oxford, 1987).
    172. *Saint Georges . . . dragons*] Saint George's exploits were a popular feature of folk plays and morris-dances; see Chambers, MS, I, pp. 196–7 and 218.

3.2.0.1. Plashy] see note to ll. 9–14 below.
    1–4. *Come . . . court*] Woodstock's honest and homely greeting hints at a concept of hospitality which sharply contrasts with the King's lavish conspicuous consumption.

As Richard with a false, and mind corrupt,
Disgraced our names and thrust us from his court.
Lancaster. Beshrew him that repines, my lord. For me,   5
I lived with care at court, I now am free.
York. Come, come, let's find some other talk—I think not
    on it;
I ne'er slept soundly when I was amongst them,
So let them go. This house of Plashy, brother,
Stands in a sweet and pleasant air, i'faith: 10
'Tis near the Thames and circled round with trees
That in the summer serve for pleasant fans
To cool ye, and in winter strongly break
The stormy winds that else would nip ye too.
Woodstock. And in faith, old York,   15
We have all need of some kind wintering:
We are beset, heaven shield, with many storms.
And yet these trees at length will prove to me
Like Richard and his riotous minions:
Their wanton heads so oft play with the winds,   20
Throwing their leaves so prodigally down
They'll leave me cold at last; and so will they
Make England wretched and, i'th' end, themselves.
Lancaster. If Westminster Hall devour as it has begun,
'Twere better it were ruined, lime and stone.   25
Woodstock. Afore my God, I late was certified
That at one feast was served ten thousand dishes.
York. He daily feasts, they say, ten thousand men,
And every man must have his dish at least.

---

5. lord. For me,] *This ed.;* lord, for me: *Rossiter;* lord for me *MS.*

5. *Beshrew . . . repines*] i.e. 'the devil take he who is discontent'.
6. *care*] worry, apprehension.
9–14. *Plashy . . . nip ye too*] Plashy (modern-day Pleshey in Essex) is in fact some considerable distance from the Thames, but the dramatist is representing Woodstock's seat as an idealised icon of rural peace and harmony in contrast to the strained artifice of Richard's court. Cf. Jonson's poem on Sir Philip Sidney's estate, *To Penshurst.*
16. *wintering*] winter shelter for farm animals. Woodstock evokes the metaphor of the traditional country estate to articulate the King's neglect of communal care and responsibility.
26. *certified*] assured.
27. *dishes*] dishfulls, helpings.
27–32. *at one feast . . . guard*] see 3.1.87–8 n.

Woodstock. Thirty fat oxen and three hundred sheep   30
   Serve but one day's expenses.
Lancaster. A hundred scarcely can suffice his guard:
   A camp of soldiers feeds not like those bowmen.
Woodstock. But how will these expenses be maintained?
York. Oh they say there are strange tricks come forth   35
   To fetch in money; what they are I know not.
Woodstock. You've heard of the fantastic suits they wear?
   Never was English king so habited.
Lancaster. We could allow his clothing, brother Woodstock,
   But we have four kings more are equalled with him.   40
   There's Bagot, Bushy, wanton Greene and Scroop,
   In state and fashion without difference.
York. Indeed, they're more than kings, for they rule him.
Woodstock. Come, come, our breaths reverberate the wind.
   We talk like good divines, but cannot cure   45
   The grossness of the sin; or shall we speak
   Like all-commanding wise astronomers,
   And flatly say, such a day shall be fair,
   And yet it rains, whether he will or no?
   So may we talk, but thus will Richard do.   50

       Enter CHENEY *with blanks.*

Lancaster. How now, Cheney, what drives thee on so fast?
Cheney. If I durst, I would say my Lord
   Tresilian drives me. One half as ill,

30–1. Thirty . . . expenses] *Rossiter; as prose MS.* 53. One half as ill] *MS;*
on behalf so ill *Rossiter.*

---

40. *four kings*] an ironic inversion of Edward III's triumph recounted by
his ghost at 5.1.94.

42. *difference*] An heraldic term, 'the alteration in or addition to a coat of
arms to distinguish a younger or lateral branch of the family from the chief
line'. However, in a more general sense the fact that the dress of the King's
followers is indistinguishable from that of the King himself is shocking in
that Elizabethan sumptuary laws, although frequently transgressed, prescribed strict clothing codes for various strata of society.

44. *our . . . wind*] i.e. 'our words are as empty as the wind'.

47. *astronomers*] astrologers.

53–4. *One . . . news*] Parfitt justifies MS's reading, paraphrasing: 'Already
partly unfortunate (since the contemptible Tresilian drives me) on top of this
I bring bad news', or perhaps the meaning is simply 'I'm half as bad as he
is since I'm the herald of bad news'.

I'm still the pursuivant of unhappy news.
Here's blank charters, my lord—I pray behold them!—   55
Sent from King Richard and his councillors.
Woodstock. Thou mak'st me blank at very sight of them!
What must these?
Lancaster. They appear in shape of obligations.
Cheney. They are no less: the country's full of them.   60
Commissions are come down to every shrieve
To force the richest subjects of the land
To set their hands and forthwith seal these blanks
That shall confirm a due debt to the king,
And then the bond must afterwards be paid,   65
As much or little as they please to 'point it.
Lancaster. O strange, unheard-of vile taxation!
Woodstock. Who is't can help my memory a little?
Has not this e'er been held a principle:
'There's nothing spoke or done that has not been?'   70
York. It was a maxim ere I had a beard.
Woodstock. 'Tis now found false, an open heresy.
This is a thing was never spoke nor done.
Blank charters call ye them? If any age
Keep but a record of this policy,   75
I phrase it too, too well—flat, villainy!—
Let me be chronicled Apostata,

57–8. Thou . . . these] *one line in MS.* 63–6.] *This ed.;* To . . . blanks / And
. . . paid / That . . . king / As . . . itt *MS.* 65. paid] *Frijlinck (MS obscured);*
seald *Keller;* kept *conj. Rossiter.*

54. *pursuivant*] herald.
57. *blank*] blanch, pale.
63–6.] The scribe appears inadvertently to have copied ll. 64 and 65 in
reverse order since it is the blanks which confirm the debt, the bonds being
paid subsequently.
66. *'point*] appoint, nominate.
70. *There's . . . been*] i.e. there has been no legislation decided on or put
into effect for which there was no precedent. Woodstock appears to be object-
ing to more than the novelty of this new taxation; he may be appealing to
the customary importance of precedence in English law and/or to this new
tax's apparently retrospective character.
75. *policy*] Parfitt suggests that a play on 'poll' (i.e. 'shaving') is indicated
by MS's spelling 'pollysye'.
76. *flat*] downright.
77. *Apostata*] i.e. apostate; one who rebels against religious or moral
authority.

Rebellious to my God and country both.
Lancaster. How do the people entertain these blanks?
Cheney. With much dislike, yet some for fear have signed
    them;   80
Others there be refuse and murmur strangely.
Woodstock. Afore my God, I cannot blame them for it.
He might as well have sent defiance to them.
O vulture England, wilt thou eat thine own?
Can they be rebels called that now turn head?   85
I speak but what I fear, not what I wish.
This foul oppression will withdraw all duty
And in the commons' hearts hot rancours breed
To make our country's bosom shortly bleed.
Lancaster. What shall we do to seek for remedy?   90
York. Let each man hie him to his several home
Before the people rise in mutiny,
And, in the mildest part of lenity,
Seek to restrain them from rebellion—
For what can else be looked for? Promise redress: 95
That eloquence is best in this distress.
Lancaster. York counsels well. Let's haste away.
The time is sick; we must not use delay.
York. Let's still confer by letters.
Woodstock.   Content, content:
So friends may parley even in banishment.   100
Farewell, good brothers. Cheney, conduct them forth.
                Exeunt all but WOODSTOCK.
Adieu, good York and Gaunt, farewell for ever.
I have a sad presage comes suddenly
That I shall never see these brothers more;

---

81. strangely] *Parfitt*; strangly *MS;* strongly *Rossiter.*   82. Afore my God]
crossed out in MS.

79. *entertain*] receive.
81. *murmur*] grumble, agitate.
strangely] violently.
83. *defiance*] a challenge to combat, a declaration of aversion.
85. *turn head*] a hunting term meaning turn and face the enemy.
88. *commons'*] the common people generally rather than, as Rossiter's text
('Commons') seems to imply, the members of the House of Commons.
98. *The . . . delay*] Cf. the proverb, 'Delay breeds danger' (Tilley D195).
99. *still*] constantly.

On earth, I fear, we never more shall meet.   105
Of Edward the Third's seven sons we three are left
To see our father's kingdom ruinate.
I would my death might end the misery
My fear presageth to my wretched country.
The commons will rebel without all question,   110
And, 'fore my God, I have no eloquence
To stay this uproar. I must tell them plain:
We all are struck but must not strike again.

Enter a Servant.

How now? What news?
Servant. There's a horseman at the gate, my lord.   115
    He comes from the king, he says, to see your grace.
Woodstock. To see me, sayst thou? A God's name, let him
        come
    So he brings no blank charters with him.
    Prithee bid him 'light and enter.
Servant. I think he dares not for fouling on his feet, my lord.   120

---

105. On . . . meet] *crossed out in MS.*   109.] George *in left-hand margin of MS.*   115. *Servant*] ser. MS *(altered from* Che).   117–18. come / So he] *Rossiter;* com, / he *MS.*   117–19. To . . . enter] *MS; as prose in Parfitt.*

---

105. *On . . . meet*] Although the line has been cancelled in the MS, as perhaps being repetitive, none the less it acts as a useful intensifier of the gravity of Woodstock's emotion.

106. *Edward . . . left*] Two of Edward III's sons died in infancy and Edward, the Black Prince, and Lionel, Duke of Clarence, were dead before the events depicted here. Edward's sons are listed by York in *Contention*, 2.2.10–17 (see also *Dramatis Personae*, l. 1 n.). Such a talismanic reference to Edward's seven sons is also to be found in *R2*, 1.2.11–21; 'seven' is perhaps significant in that it recalls Jesse, the father of David, who also had seven sons and was the progenitor of the line which ended with Christ.

109.] The marginal name 'George' may possibly be the name of the actor playing the servant for a revival of the text. Two Caroline actors have been suggested as possible candidates, George Stutfield and George Willans or Williams (see Bentley, II), but George is a sufficiently common name for identification to be difficult.

113. *We . . . again*] i.e. 'we are all wounded by the King's actions yet we must not retaliate by rebelling.'

118. *So*] provided that. Rossiter's addition is necessary since Woodstock is in no position to know whether or not the King's messenger is carrying blank charters.

119. *'light*] alight.

I would have had him 'light but he swears as he's a
courtier he will not off on's horseback till the inner gate
be open.
Woodstock. Passion of me, that's strange. I prithee give him
satisfaction. Open the inner gate. What might this fellow   125
be?
Servant. Some fine fool. He's attired very fantastically, and
talks as foolishly.
Woodstock. Go let him in, and when you have done, bid
Cheney come and speak with me.   130
Servant. I will, my lord.

Enter a spruce Courtier *a-horseback.*

Servant. Come on, sir, ye may ride into my lord's cellar now
and ye will, sir.
Courtier. Prithee, fellow, stay and take my horse.
Servant. I have business for my lord, sir, I cannot.   135
                                                  Exit Servant.
Courtier. A rude swain, by heaven; but stay, here walks
another. Hearst-ta? Thou! Fellow! Is this Plashy House?
Woodstock. Ye should have asked that question before ye came
in, sir. But this is it.
Courtier. [*Aside*] The hinds are all most rude and gross.—   140
I prithee walk my horse.
Woodstock. I have a little business, sir.

127–8.] *Rossiter;* Some . . . fantastically / & . . . foolishly *MS.* 137. Thou!
Fellow!] *This ed.;* thou: fellow *MS.;* thou! fellow *Rossiter;* Thou fellow! *Parfitt.*
140. [*Aside*]] *This ed.*

131.1. spruce *Courtier*] Hibbard notes (New Cambridge edition of
Hamlet) that the encounter between Woodstock and the spruce Courtier fore-
shadows that between Hamlet and Osric.
   a-horseback] The text demands the entrance of the Courtier on horseback and the horse to remain 'on stage' in Woodstock's charge. It is most
likely that the horseman entered into the playhouse yard thus providing the
actor playing Woodstock with the opportunity for a close actor/audience
engagement as he walked the horse. This is one of the three uncontested
examples of the entrance of a horse in Elizabethan and Jacobean drama (see
Dessen and Thomson), although *The Famous Victories of Henry V* may also
call for such a practice. See the discussion of this point in *The Oldcastle Controversy*, ed. Corbin and Sedge (1991), p. 148, and Hattaway, p. 88.
   140. *hinds*] servants, a disimissive term with associations of rusticity or
boorishness; a response to Woodstock's plainness of dress.

Courtier. Thou shalt not lose by't. I'll give thee a tester for thy
pains.

Woodstock. I shall be glad to earn money, sir.   145

Courtier. Prithee do, and know thy duty. Thy head's too saucy.

Woodstock. Cry ye mercy, I did not understand your worship's
calling.

Courtier. The Duke of Gloucester lies here, does he not?

Woodstock. Marry, does he, sir.   150

Courtier. Is he within?

Woodstock. He's not far off, sir. He was here even now.

Courtier. Ah, very good; walk my horse well, I prithee, h'as
travelled hard and he's hot i'faith. I'll in and speak with
the duke and pay thee presently.   *Exit* Courtier.   155

Woodstock. I make no doubt, sir. O strange metamorphosis!
Is't possible that this fellow that's all made of fashions
should be an Englishman? No marvel if he know not me,
being so brave and I so beggarly. Well, I shall earn money
to enrich me now and 'tis the first I earned, by th'rood,   160
this forty year. Come on, sir, you have sweat hard about
this haste, yet I think you know little of the business.
[*Walks the horse.*] Why so, I say? You're a very indifferent
beast; you'll follow any man that will lead you. Now truly,
sir, you look but e'en leanly on't. You feed not in West-   165
minster Hall a-days where so many sheep and oxen are
devoured. I'm afraid they'll eat you shortly if you tarry
amongst them. You're pricked more with the spur than
the provender, I see that. I think your dwelling be at
Hackney when you're at home, is't not? You know not the   170
Duke neither, no more than your master, and yet I think

158–9. No marvel . . . beggarly] *This ed.;* No . . . me / Being . . . beggarly
Parfitt; should . . . me / being . . . beggerly *MS.*   163. SD] *This ed.*

143. *tester*] sixpence, i.e. $2^{1}/_{2}$p.

146. *Thy . . . saucy*] The courtier's rebuke refers to Woodstock's failure to
show appropriate deference by bowing his head.

148. *calling*] rank, status.

156–232.] The MS is indeterminate in its layout in this sequence, sometimes seeming to indicate rather unconvincing verse.

168–9. *pricked . . . provender*] i.e. made lively by the use of the spur rather
than by being well foddered.

170. *Hackney*] play on the place Hackney in London and the idea of a
mediocre horse ('hack').

you have as much wit as he. Faith, say a man should steal
ye and feed ye fatter, could ye run away with him lustily?
Ah, your silence argues a consent, I see. By th' Mass, here
comes company. We had been both taken if we had, I see.   175

Enter CHENEY, Courtier *and* Servant.

Cheney. Saw ye not my lord at the gate, say ye?
    Why I left him there but now.
Courtier. In sooth I saw no creature, sir, only an old groom
    I got to walk my horse.
Cheney. A groom, say ye? 'Sfoot, 'tis my lord the Duke. What   180
    have ye done? This is somewhat too coarse your grace
    should be an ostler to this fellow!
Courtier. I do beseech your grace's pardon. The error was in
    the mistake. Your plainness did deceive me. Please it your
    grace to redeliver—   185
Woodstock. No, by my faith, I'll have my money first. Promise
    is a debt.
Courtier. I know your grace's goodness will refuse it.
Woodstock. Think not so nicely of me; indeed I will not.
Courtier. If so you please, there is your tester.   190
Woodstock. If so you please, there is your horse, sir.
    Now, pray you, tell me, is your haste to me?
Courtier. Most swift and serious from his majesty.
Woodstock. What, from King Richard, my dear lord and
    kinsman? Go, sirrah, take you his horse, lead him to the   195

---

173. lustily] *Keller conj.;* luste< *MS.* 174–5. By . . . see] *MS;* By . . .
company / We . . . see *Parfitt.* 175.1. Servant] *This ed.;* servants *MS.*
178–9. In . . . horse] *Rossiter;* In . . . groom / I . . . horse *MS.* 182. fellow]
Halliwell; f< *Frijlinck; MS obliterated.* 183. *Courtier*] *Halliwell; no speech prefix
in MS.* 184. mistake] mistake< *MS;* mistake that *Rossiter.* 185. redeliver—] redeliver < *MS.* 187. is a debt] *Carpenter conj.;* is a promise *Halliwell, Keller;* is a< *MS.* 195. sirrah] sirra < *MS;* for[ward] *Halliwell, Keller.*

---

175. *We . . . see*] The reference appears to be to the idea of running away.
175.1. *Servant*] MS indicates more than one servant; this is unnecessary.
The scene's comedic effect is enhanced if the servant is the same as the one
at l. 115 above.
184. *mistake*] misidentification.
186–7. *Promise . . . debt*] Carpenter's conjecture seems preferable to that
of Keller since Woodstock demands payment and also because of the cur-
rency of the proverb 'Promise is debt' (Tilley P603).
189. *nicely*] daintily, politely.

stable, meat him well. I'll double his reward: there's
twelve pence for ye.

Servant. I thank your grace.   *Exit* Servant *with the horse.*

Woodstock. Now, sir, your business.

Courtier. His majesty commends him to your grace.   200

Woodstock. This same's a rare fashion you have got at court.
Of whose devising was't, I pray?

Courtier. I assure your grace, the King his council sat three
days about it.

Woodstock. By my faith, their wisdoms took great pains,   205
I assure ye. The state was well employed the whiles, by
th'rood! Then this at court is all the fashion now?

Courtier. The King himself doth wear it, whose most gracious
majesty sent me in haste—

Woodstock. This peak doth strangely well become the foot.   210

Courtier. This peak the King doth likewise wear, being a
Polonian peak; and me did his highness pick from forth
the rest—

Woodstock. He could not have picked out such another,
I assure ye.   215

Courtier. I thank your grace that picks me out so well.
But, as I said, his highness would request—

Woodstock. But this most fashionable chain, that links as it
were the toe and knee together—

Courtier. In a most kind coherence, so it like your grace. For   220
these two parts being in operation and quality different,
as for example: the toe a disdainer or spurner; the knee
a dutiful and most humble orator; this chain doth, as it
were, so toeify the knee and so kneeify the toe that
between both it makes a most methodical coherence or   225
coherent method.

---

203. the King his council] ye king Richards his Counsell (Richards *crossed
out*) MS; King Richard's council *Halliwell, Keller.*

196. *meat*] feed.

212. *Polonian*] see 2.3.92 n.

220. *coherence*] agreement.

222–3. *toe . . . orator*] This would appear to be an internal stage direction for the Courtier who might mime disdaining or spurning with the
toe of his shoe and humble advocacy by making obeisance with his
knee.

Woodstock. 'Tis most excellent, sir, and full of art. Please ye
    walk in.
Courtier. My message tendered, I will tend your grace.
Woodstock. Cry ye mercy, have you a message to me?   230
Courtier. His majesty, most affectionately, and like a royal
    kinsman,
    Entreats your grace's presence at the court.
Woodstock. Is that your message, sir? I must refuse it then.
    My English plainness will not suit that place;
    The court's too fine for me. My service here   235
    Will stand in better stead to quench the fire
    Those blanks have made—I would they were all burnt
    Or he were hanged that first devised them, sir,
    They stir the country so. I dare not come,
    And so excuse me, sir. If the King think it ill   240
    He thinks amiss. I am Plain Thomas still.
    The rest I'll tell ye as ye sit at meat.
    Furnish a table, Cheney, call for wine.   [*Exit* CHENEY.]
    Come, sir, ye shall commend me to the King:
    Tell him I'll keep these parts in peace to him.   245
                         Exeunt omnes.

[3.3]

    Enter Master IGNORANCE *the Baily of Dunstable,*
      CROSBY, FLEMING *and* NIMBLE *with blanks.*
       [Officers *with bills in attendance.*]

Crosby. Despatch, good Master Baily, the market's almost
    done you see. 'Tis rumoured that the blanks are come,
    and the rich chuffs begin to flock out o'th' town already.

3.3.0.3. SD] *addition Rossiter.*

  229. *tend*] wait or attend upon.
  234–41. *My English . . . still*] The plainness of Woodstock's discourse
matches the plainness of his dress and contrasts with the courtier's exaggerated over-ornamented style.

   3.3.0.1. Baily] bailiff, a sheriff's deputy who executes writs, destrains and
arrests.
  0.3. bills] axe-like weapons carried by watchmen.
   3. *chuffs*] misers, probably by association with 'choughs', birds of the crow
family, especially jackdaws which had a reputation for hoarding; cf. *1H4*, 2.2.72.

You have seen the high shrieve's warrant and the council's
commission, and therefore I charge ye, in the king's   5
name, be ready to assist us.

Ignorance. Nay, look ye, sir. Be not too pestiferous, I beseech
ye, I have begun myself and sealed one of your blanks
already, and by my example there's more shall follow. I
know my place and calling. My name is Ignorance and I   10
am Baily of Dunstable. I cannot write nor read, I confess
it, no more could my father, nor his father, nor none of
the Ignorants this hundred year, I assure ye.

Nimble. Your name proclaims no less, sir, and it has been a
most learned generation.   15

Ignorance. Though I cannot write, I have set my mark—*ecce
signum.* Read it, I beseech ye.

Nimble. The mark of Simon Ignorance, the Baily of Dunstable, being a sheephook with a tarbox at end on't.

Ignorance. Very right. It was my mark ever since I was an inno-   20
cent; and therefore, as I say, I have begun and will assist
ye; for here be rich whoresons i'th' town, I can tell ye,
that will give ye the slip and ye look not to it.

Fleming. We therefore presently will divide ourselves: you two
shall stay here whiles we, Master Ignorance, with some   25
of your brethren, the men of Dunstable, walk through the
town noting the carriage of the people. They say there are
strange songs and libels, cast about the marketplace
against my Lord Tresilian and the rest of the King's young

---

6. assist us] *Frijlinck; MS obscure because of a tear at this point;* fill them
vpp *Halliwell.* 7. *Ignorance] This ed.; Bayley or Bayl throughout the scene MS.*

---

7. *pestiferous]* pestilential; this becomes the Baily's catchword which
steadily loses any meaning with its increasing use.

11. *Dunstable]* a pun on 'dunce'. Dunstable, a town in southern Bedfordshire 33 miles from London, had a proverbial reputation for plainness
and simplicity: 'As plain as Dunstable Highway' (Tilley D646).

16–17. ecce signum] behold my mark. Ironically Ignorance uses the Latin
correctly although he may be ignorant of its significance.

19. *sheephook . . . tarbox]* Shepherd's tools which perhaps denote the
Baily's humble origins; the tarbox contained the tar which was used in the
surgery of sheep, cf. *AYL*, 3.2.60–1.

20–1. *innocent]* a child, but also a half-wit or fool.

22. *whoresons]* fellows.

27. *carriage]* conduct, behaviour.

28. *libels]* pamphlets.

councillors. If such there be, we'll have some aid and   30
attach them speedily.

Ignorance. Ye shall do well, sir, and for your better aiding, if
you can but find out my brother, Master Ignoramus, he
will be most pestiferous unto ye, I assure ye.

Crosby. I'm afraid he will not be found, sir, but we'll inquire.   35
Come, fellow Fleming; and, Nimble, look to the whis-
perers, I charge ye.   *Ex[eun]t* CROSBY *and* FLEMING.

Nimble. I warrant ye. Come, Master Baily, let your billmen
retire till we call them. [*Officers with bills retire.*] And you
and I will here shadow ourselves and write down their   40
speeches.

Ignorance. Nay, you shall write and I will mark, sir.

> *Enter* a Farmer, *a* Butcher *and* [COWTAIL]
> *a* Grazier *very hastily.*

Ignorance. And see, see, here comes some already, all rich
chubs, by the Mass, I know them all, sir.

Farmer. Tarry, tarry, good neighbours; take a knave with ye.   45
What a murrain! Is there a bear broke loose i'th' town
that ye make such haste from the market?

Cowtail. A bear? No, nor a lion baited neither. I tell ye, neighbour, I am more afraid of the bee than the bear: there's
wax to be used today and I have no seal about me. I may   50
tell you in secret here's a dangerous world towards.
Neighbour, you're a farmer, and I hope here's none but
God and good company. We live in such a state, I am e'en
almost weary of all, I assure ye. Here's my other neighbour, the butcher that dwells at Hockley, has heard his   55

---

39. SD] *This ed.*

31. *attach them*] arrest them, i.e. the perpetrators.
40. *shadow*] conceal.
42. *mark*] i.e. watch, with ironic pun, in view of Ignorance's illiteracy, on 'making a mark'.
44. *chubs*] lads, chaps, but also dolts, fools.
45. *take a knave with ye*] i.e. wait for me.
46. *What a murrain!*] 'What a plague!'
50. *wax . . . today*] i.e. in sealing up the blank charters.
55. *Hockley*] Rossiter suggests Hockliffe in Essex, but it is more likely to refer to Hockley in the Hole, a village between Dunstable and Fenny Stratford which had a reputation for highway robbery.

landlord tell strange tidings. We shall be all hoisted and
we tarry here, I can tell ye.

Nimble. They begin to murmur. I'll put them down all for
whisperers. Master Baily, what's he that talks so?

Ignorance. His name is Cowtail, a rich grazier, and dwells here   60
hard by at Leighton Buzzard.

Nimble. [*Writing*] Cowtail, a grazier, dwelling at Leighton—
Buzzard, Master Baily?

Ignorance. Right, sir. Listen again, sir.

Farmer. Ah, sirrah, and what said the good knight your land-   65
lord, neighbour?

Butcher. Marry, he said—but I'll not stand to anything, I tell
ye that aforehand; he said that King Richard's new councillors—God amend them—had crept into honester
men's places than themselves were; and that the King's   70
uncles and the old lords were all banished the court; and
he said flatly we should never have a merry world as long
as it was so.

Nimble. [*Aside*] Butcher, you and your landlord will be both
hanged for't.   75

Butcher. And then he said that there's one Tresilian, a lawyer,
that has crept in amongst them and is now a lord,
forsooth, and he has sent down into every country of
England a sort of black chapters.

Farmer. Black chapters? A God's name, neighbour, out of   80
what black book were they taken?

Cowtail. Come, come, they are blank charters, neighbours. I
heard of them afore, and therefore I made such haste

62. SD] *Rossiter.*   74. SD] *This ed.*

56. *hoisted*] overtaxed, surcharged (*OED* v. 4; *OED* first records the usage
in 1607 in Middleton's *Michaelmas Term*).

61. *Leighton Buzzard*] a town in Bedfordshire, 18 miles south-west of
Bedford and 5 miles west of Hocliffe (Hockley). *Buzzard* was often used for
a fool or blockhead. MS's punctuation implies that Nimble plays on this
meaning in l. 63 when writing out the name of the place.

67. *stand to*] testify to.

72. *we . . . world*] A common expression meaning 'things will never be
right'; cf. *Meas.*, 3.1.275, 'Twas never merry world since . . .'.

78. *country*] district, region.

79. *black chapters*] i.e. blank charters; the malapropism emphasises the
Butcher's rusticity, provides a feed for the joke on 'black book' and points up
the novelty of the new tax since he can find no adequate way to describe it.

away. They're sent down to the high shrieve with special
charge that every man that is of any credit or worship i'th'   85
country must set their hands and seal to them, for what
intent I know not. I say no more. I smell something.

Farmer. Well, well, my masters, let's be wise. We are not all
one man's sons. They say there are whispering knaves
abroad; let's hie us home for, I assure ye, 'twas told me   90
where I broke my fast this afternoon that there were
above three score gentlemen in our shire that had set their
hands and seals to those blank charters already.

Cowtail. Now God amend them for it, they have given an ill
example we shall be forced to follow.   95

Butcher. I would my wife and children were at Jerusalem, with
all the wealth! I'd make shift for one, I warrant them.
Come, neighbours, let's begone.

Nimble. Step forward with your bills, Master Baily. Not too
fast, sirs! I charge ye, i'th' King's name, to stand till we   100
have done with ye.

Omnes. Saint Benedicite!, What must we do now, trow?

Ignorance. Be not so pestiferous, my good friends and neighbours. You are men of wealth and credit in the country;
and therefore as I myself and others have begun, I charge   105
ye in his highness' name presently to set your hands and
seals to these blank charters.

---

85. credit] *conj. Frijlinck;* c< *Frijlinck; MS now obliterated;* [state] *Halliwell;*
st[ate] *Keller.* 87. something] *Halliwell; MS illegible because of tear.*
88–9. Well . . . sons] *as one line and crossed out in darker ink in MS.*
89. sons] *conj. Frijlinck;* <s *Frijlinck (MS now obliterated);* family *Halliwell;*
f[amily] *Keller.* 90. for, I assure ye] *deleted in MS.* 91. afternoon]
after[noon] *Halliwell;* afte[rnoon] *Keller;* after< *MS.* 98. begone] *MS;* be
off *Halliwell;* be of[f] *Keller.*

---

85. *worship*] honour, distinction.

88–9. *We . . . sons*] Although deleted in MS, the Farmer's response relates
directly to Cowtail's scepticism. Rossiter glosses 'Even if one of us is a born
fool, the rest needn't be'.

96–7. *Jerusalem . . . wealth*] Parfitt detects two strands of association here:
(1) Jerusalem as the place of final peace; (2) Jerusalem as home of the Jews
('with all the wealth').

99. *bills*] i.e. the officers carrying bills.

102. *Saint Benedicite*] An exclamation which conflates a call upon Saint
Benedict and the traditional blessing 'Benedicte'.

Cowtail. Jesu receive my soul, I'm departed!

Farmer. I'm e'en stern at heart too.

Butcher. Alas, sir, we are poor men, what should our hands   110
do?

Ignoranace. There is no harm, I warrant ye; what need you
fear when ye see Baily Ignorance has sealed before ye?

Cowtail. I pray ye, let's see them, sir.

Nimble. Here, ye bacon-fed pudding eaters, are ye afraid of a   115
sheep-skin?

Cowtail. Mass, 'tis somewhat darkly written.

Farmer. Ay, ay, 'twas done i'th' night, sure.

Cowtail. Mass, neighbours, here's nothing that I see.

Butcher. And can it be any harm, think ye, to set your hands   120
to nothing? These blank charters are but little pieces of
parchment. Let's set our marks to them and be rid of a
knave's company.

Farmer. As good at first as last; we can be but undone.

Cowtail. Ay, and our own hands undoes us, that's the worst   125
on't. Lend's your pen, sir.

Butcher. We must all venture, neighbours, there's no remedy.

Nimble. [*Aside*] They grumble as they do it. I must put them
down for whisperers and grumblers.—Come, have you
done yet?   130

Cowtail. Ay, sir. [*Aside*] Would you and they were sodden for
my swine!

---

109. stern] *This ed.;* stirne *MS (altered reading);* stroke to *MS (original
reading);* struck to *conj. Frijlinck;* stroke thro *conj. Rossiter;* sticket *Halliwell;*
stirne *Keller.* 120. set] *Rossiter;* sott *MS.* 128. SD] *This ed.* 131. SD]
Rossiter.

---

108. *departed*] killed, dead.

109 *stern*] cast down (*OED* v2, only one citation, 1599); Frijlinck's
conjecture 'struck to' is a plausible reading of MS's original state 'stroke
to'.

110. *our hands*] The stress should be on 'our' rather than 'hands'.

115. *bacon-fed . . . eaters*] Bacon was regarded as an appropriate diet for
such lower-class workers as ploughmen and carters; see Tudor physician
Andrew Boorde, p. 273.

117. *darkly*] obscurely.

124. *As . . . last*] Cf. the proverb, 'As good do it at first as at last' (Tilley
F294).

131. *sodden*] boiled feed.

Nimble. Here's wax then. I'll seal them for ye, and you shall
severally take them off and then deliver them as your
deeds.   [*They*] *seal them.*   135
Come, you boar's grease, take off this seal here. So; this
is your deed?

Farmer. Faith, sir, in some respect it is and it is not.

Nimble. And this is yours?

Cowtail. Ay, sir, against my will, I swear.   140

Nimble. Ox-jaw, take off this seal. You'll deliver your deed with
a good conscience?

Butcher. There 'tis, sir, against my conscience, God's my
witness. I hope ye have done with us now, sir.

Nimble. No, ye caterpillars, we have worse matters against   145
ye yet. Sirrah, you know what your landlord told ye
concerning my Lord Tresilian and King Richard's new
favourites; and, more than that, you know your own
speeches and therefore, Master Baily, let some of your
billmen away with them to the high shrieve's presently,   150
either to put in bail or be sent up to th'court for privy
whisperers.

Ignorance. Their offences are most pestiferous. Away with
them.

134.] 3:B *written in the left-hand margin of MS (the B is not entirely clear).*
140. *Cowtail*] Gray MS *(altered from Butcher).*

133–42. *Here's wax . . . conscience*] The precise nature of the procedure
here seems to be that Nimble seals the charters after they have been signed
and returns them to the signatories for delivery to the County Sheriff; see
ll. 276–8 below.

134.] Frijlinck suggests that the marginal note '3:B' relates either to the
'three blanks' or possibly to the 'three billmen' who are required to take
the prisoners in charge. Rossiter notes that since the 'billmen' have
already been mentioned at l. 99 it is unlikely that the marginal note
refers to them; however, if Long's view of the marginalia for this manuscript is correct, the note is not so much a prompter's cue as a reminder
of a property or staging requirement for this scene; see Long, *Bed*, pp.
96–107.

severally take them off] Each individual is required to set his seal in the
wax provided by Nimble. It would seem that they make an impression in the
wax with their thumb or possibly a ring.

deliver] return or surrender.

141. *Ox-jaw*] an insulting phrase appropriate to the Butcher's trade.

145. *caterpillars*] rapacious, greedy individuals; cf. *R2*, 2.3.165–6.

151. *privy*] secret.

Omnes. Now out alas, we shall all to hanging, sure!   155
                    Exeunt Officers *with the three men.*
Nimble. Hanging? Nay that's the least on't, ye shall tell me
    that a twelvemonth hence else. Stand close, Master Baily;
    we shall catch more of these traitors presently.
Ignorance. You shall find me most pestiferous to assist ye; and
    so, I pray ye, commend my service to your good lord and   160
    master. Come, sir, stand close; I see—

            Enter a Schoolmaster *and a* Serving-man.

Serving-man. Nay, sweet Master Schoolmaster, let's hear't
    again, I beseech ye.
Schoolmaster. Patientia! You're a serving-man, I'm a scholar. I
    have shown art and learning in these verses, I assure ye;   165
    and yet if they were well searched they're little better than
    libels; but the carriage of a thing is all, sir: I have covered
    them rarely.
Serving-man. 'Sfoot, the country's so full of intelligencers that
    two men can scarce walk together but they're attached   170
    for whisperers.
Schoolmaster. This paper shall wipe their noses and they shall
    not boo to a goose for't; for I'll have these verses sung to
    their faces by one of my schoolboys, wherein I'll tickle
    them all i'faith. Shalt hear else. But first let's look there   175
    be no pitchers with ears, nor needles with eyes about us.
Serving-man. Come, come, all's safe, I warrant ye.

---

155. sure] Sure *MS (or* Sire*);* sire *Halliwell;* Sire *Keller.*   155.1. *the three*]
Rossiter; them (3) *MS.*   156. on't] ont *Halliwell;* ant *MS.*   161. I see] I see
h< *Frijlinck ('the tail of a long letter is visible after the "h" in MS'); the whole
phrase is now obliterated by a tear in MS.*   173. boo] *Rossiter;* boe *MS;* bo
Halliwell; be *Keller;* say bo *conj. Carpenter.*

---

164. *Patientia*] Be patient, calm yourself.
167. *carriage*] handling, execution.
167-8. *covered them rarely*] disguised them with great skill.
172. *wipe . . . noses*] cheat or defraud them (*OED* 10b).
172-3. *they . . . goose*] proverbial; cf. 'He cannot say Bo to a goose' (Tilley
B481).
174. *tickle*] irritate, nettle; or perhaps, in view of the Schoolmaster's
calling, 'thrash'.
176. *pitchers with ears*] i.e. eavesdroppers; proverbial, 'Small (Little)
Pitchers have wide ears' (Tilley P363).
needles with eyes] i.e. observers.

Schoolmaster. Mark then. Here I come over them for their
　　blank charters; shalt hear else:
　　　　　　Will ye buy any parchment knives?　　　　　　180
　　　　　　We sell for little gain:
　　　　　　Whoe'er are weary of their lives
　　　　　　They'll rid them of their pain.

　　　　　　Blank charters they are called
　　　　　　A vengeance on the villain,　　　　　　185
　　　　　　I would he were both flayed and balled
　　　　　　God bless my Lord Tresilian.
　　Is't not rare?
Nimble. [*Aside*] O rascals! They're damned three hundred
　　fathom deep already.　　　　　　190
Schoolmaster. Nay, look ye, sir, there can be no exceptions
　　taken, for this last line helps all, wherein with a kind of
　　equivocation I say 'God bless my Lord Tresilian'. Do ye
　　mark, sir? Now here in the next verse I run o'er all the
　　flatterers i'th' court by name. Ye shall see else:　　　　　　195
　　　　　　A poison may be Greene,
　　　　　　But Bushy can be no faggot:
　　　　　　God mend the king and bless the queen,
　　　　　　And 'tis no matter for Bagot.

　　　　　　For Scroop, he does no good;　　　　　　200
　　　　　　But if you'll know the villain,
　　　　　　His name is now to be understood:
　　　　　　God bless my Lord Tresilian.
　　How like ye this, sir?
Serving-man. Most excellent i'faith, sir.　　　　　　205

186. flayed] *Rossiter;* flead *MS.* balled] *Parfitt;* bald *Rossiter;* bauld *MS.*
188. Is't not rare] *crossed out in MS.*

---

178. *come over*] taunt, satirise.
186. *balled*] a pun on 'to ball': to strike bald; the dramatist has taken a
hint from the verses of John Ball who circulated a riddling letter full of dark
sentences among the Essex peasants at the time of the Peasants' Revolt.
187. *bless*] Ambiguous because 'bless' was often used ironically to mean
'curse' or 'damn' (see *OED* 11).
197. *But . . . faggot*] Bushy's name suggests the opposite of a faggot (a
straight-cut and debarked stave); 'faggot' may allude to the punishment of
heretics by being burned alive (*OED* 2). 'Faggot' as an abusive term for a
homosexual is not recorded by *OED* before 1914.

Nimble. O traitors! Master Baily, do your authority.

Ignorance. Two most pestiferous traitors. Lay hold of them, I charge ye.

Serving-man. What mean ye, sir?

Nimble. Nay, talk not; for if ye had a hundred lives they　210
were all hanged. Ye have spoken treason in the ninth
degree.

Schoolmaster. Treason? *Patientia,* good sir. We spoke not a
word.

Ignorance. Be not so pestiferous. Mine ears have heard your　215
examinations, wherein you uttered most shameful
treason, for ye said, 'God bless my Lord Tresilian'.

Schoolmaster. I hope there's no treason in that, sir.

Nimble. That shall be tried. Come, Master Baily, their hands
shall be bound under a horse's belly and sent up to him　220
presently. They'll both be hanged, I warrant them.

Serving-man. Well, sir, if we be, we'll speak more ere we be
hanged in spite of ye.

Nimble. Ay, ay, when you're hanged speak what you will, we
care not. Away with them.　225

　　　　Exeunt the Schoolmaster *and*
　　　　Serving-man [*with* Officer].

Ye see, Master Baily, what knaves are abroad now you are
here. 'Tis time to look about, ye see.

Ignorance. I see there are knaves abroad indeed, sir. I peek for
mine own part. I will do my best to reform the pestifer-
ousness of the time, and as for example I have set my　230
mark to the charters, so will I set mine eyes to observe
these dangerous cases.

　　　　Enter one a-whistling.

---

223. ye] *Halliwell;* y< *MS.*　228. peek] peake *MS;* pick *Rossiter;* speak
Parfitt.　229. part] *Halliwell, Keller;* p< *MS.*　230. time] time< *MS;* times
Halliwell, Keller.

211–12. *in . . . degree*] a measure of the seriousness of the crime. Nimble
is seeking to impress rather than offering any legitimate legal definition.

219–20. *hands . . . belly*] i.e. lying on top of the horse with their hands
tied around its belly.

228. *peek*] observe. Parfitt's emendation is plausible but unnecessary,
since 'peek' reinforces the sense of spying.

Nimble. Close again, Master Baily, here comes another whis-
    perer I see by some—O villain, he whistles treason! I'll
    lay hold of him myself.   235
Whistler. Out alas, what do ye mean, sir?
Nimble. A rank traitor, Master Baily. Lay hold on him, for he
    has most erroneously and rebelliously whistled treason.
Whistler. Whistled treason? Alas, sir, how can that be?
Nimble. Very easily, sir. There's a piece of treason that flies up   240
    and down the country in the likeness of a ballad, and this
    being the very tune of it, thou hast whistled treason.
Whistler. Alas, sir, ye know I spake not a word.
Nimble. That's all one; if any man whistle treason, 'tis as ill
    as speaking it. Mark me, Master Baily; the bird whistles   245
    that cannot speak, and yet there be birds in a manner that
    can speak too: your raven will call ye rascal, your crow
    will call ye knave, Master Baily; *ergo*, he that can whistle
    can speak, and therefore this fellow hath both spoke and
    whistled treason. How say you, Baily Ignorance?   250
Ignorance. Ye have argued well, sir; but ye shall hear me sift
    him nearer for I do not think but there are greater heads
    in this matter, and therefore, my good fellow, be not pes-
    tiferous but say and tell the truth. Who did set you a-
    work? Or who was the cause of your whistling? Or did   255
    any man say to you, 'Go whistle'?
Whistler. Not any man, woman or child, truly, sir.
Ignorance. No? How durst you whistle then? Or what cause
    had ye to do so?
Whistler. The truth is, sir, I had lost two calves out of my   260
    pasture, and being in search for them, from the top of the
    hill I might spy you two i'th' bottom here, and took ye
    for my calves, sir; and that made me come whistling down
    for joy in hope I had found them.

---

234. some] *Rossiter;* his [looks] *Halliwell, Keller;* som< MS *(the last letter
seems to be* m *but only two minims remain).*   240. Nimble] *Keller;* Bayl: *MS.*
242. whistled treason] *Halliwell;* whis< / trea< MS *(spread over the end of two
lines and partly obliterated).*   245. speaking it] *Halliwell;* speaking< it *Frijlinck (MS obscure).*   247. call ye rascal] *Keller;* call ye< MS.   252-3.
greater heads in this matter] *conj. Frijlinck;* greater heads *(lacuna)* MS; great
up-heads [ith country] *Keller.*   263. calves] *Rossiter;* caves MS.

---

240. Nimble] Keller's attribution of this speech to Nimble seems appropriate to the context and the sharpness of the dialogue.
    248. ergo] therefore.

Nimble. More treason yet! He take a courtier and a baily for   265
two calves? To limbo, with him; he shall be quartered and
then hanged.

Whistler. Good Master Baily, be pitiful.

Ignorance. Why law ye, sir, he makes a pitiful fellow of a baily
too! Away with him! Yet stay awhile; here comes your   270
fellows, sir.

Enter CROSBY *and* FLEMING.

Crosby. Now, Master Baily, are your blanks sealed yet?

Ignorance. They are, sir, and we have done this day most
strange and pestiferous service, I assure ye, sir.

Fleming. Your care shall be rewarded. Come, fellow Nimble,   275
we must to court about other employments. There are
already thirteen thousand blanks signed and returned to
the shrieves and seven hundred sent up to th'court for
whisperers, out of all which my lord will fetch a round
sum, I doubt it not. Come, let's away.   280

Nimble. Ay, ay, we'll follow. Come, ye sheep-biter. Here's a
traitor of all traitors that not only speaks, but has whistled treason. Come, come, sir. I'll spoil your whistle, I
warrant ye.   *Exeunt omnes.*

---

272. *Crosby*] *Halliwell, Keller; not in MS.*

266. *calves*] idiots, dolts. Nimble wilfully misunderstands the Whistler.
limbo] prison (*OED* 2).
266–7. *quartered . . . hanged*] The standard procedure was hanging,
drawing and quartering. Nimble's misunderstanding of the ordering of execution, which would require the hanging of a corpse, is in the context of the
scene both comic and grotesque.
269. *Why law ye*] An exclamation; 'law' is perhaps a corruption of 'la'; cf.
LLL, 5.2.44.
281. *sheep-biter*] shifty, sneaking fellow.

Act 4

[4.1]

Enter TRESILIAN *with writings and a* [Servant]
with bags of money.

Tresilian. Sirrah, are the bags sealed?
Servant. Yes, my lord.
Tresilian. Then take my keys and lock the money in my
study; safe bar and make sure, I charge ye. So, begone.
Servant. I will, my lord.   *Exit* Servant.
Tresilian.   So, seven thousand pounds   5
From Bedford, Buckingham and Oxford shires,
These blanks already have returned the king.
So then there's four for me and three for him:
Our pains in this must needs be satisfied.
Good husbands will make hay while the sun shines   10
And so must we, for thus conclude these times:
So men be rich enough, they're good enough.
Let fools make conscience how they get their coin,
I'll please the King and keep me in his grace,
For prince's favours purchase land apace.   15
These blanks that I have scattered in the realm
Shall double his revènues to the crown.

Enter BUSHY *and* SCROOP.

4.1.0.1 [Servant]] *This ed.;* man *MS.*   5–6. So . . . shires] *one line in MS.*
9. satisfied] *Keller;* satisfye *MS (final e may be a lower-case* d*).*

4.1.0.1–2. SD] Before a word is spoke the stage image graphically conveys
the link between Tresilian's legal trade and his greedy rapacity. Cf. Marlowe, *Jew*,
1.1.0.1–2. 'Enter BARABAS in his counting-house, with heaps of gold before him'.
   4. *safe bar*] fasten securely.
   10. *husbands*] farmers.
   make hay . . . shines] Cf. the proverb, 'Make Hay while the sun shines'
(Tilley H235).
   11–12. *for thus . . . enough*] i.e. the conclusion of these times is that wealth
ensures merit.
   15. *prince's favours*] i.e. the favours of a monarch.

130

Scroop. Now, Lord Tresilian, is this coin come yet?
Bushy. King Richard wants money, you're too slack,
    Tresilian.
Tresilian. Some shires have sent, and more, my lords, will
    follow.   20
    These sealèd blanks I now have turned to bonds
    And these shall down to Norfolk presently.
    The chuffs with much ado have signed and sealed,
    And here's a secret note my men have sent
    Of all their yearly states amounts unto,   25
    And by this note I justly tax their bonds.
    Here's a fat whoreson in his russet slops
    And yet may spend three hundred pounds by th'year,
    The third of which the hogsface owes the King;
    Here's his bond for't with his hand and seal.   30
    And so by this I'll sort each several sum:
    The thirds of all shall to King Richard come.
    How like you this, my lords?
Scroop. Most rare, Tresilian! Hang 'um, codsheads,
    Shall they spend money and King Richard lack it?   35
Bushy. Are not their lives and lands and livings his?
    Then rack them thoroughly.
Tresilian. O my lords, I have set a trick afoot for ye, and ye
    follow it hard and get the king to sign it, you'll be all kings
    by it.   40
Bushy. The farming out the kingdom? Tush, Tresilian, 'tis half
    granted already and had been fully concluded had not
    the messenger returned so unluckily from the Duke of
    Gloucester, which a little moved the King at his uncle's

---

    19. wants] needs, lacks.
    21. *These . . . bonds*] i.e. the blank charters have been filled in and can
now be used to extract money from their signitaries.
    25. *states*] properties, estates.
    27. *slops*] loose, knee-length breeches.
    36. *Are not . . . his*] A reflection of Article 23 in Richard's indictment of
1399, 'Item, he most tyrannouslie said, that the lives and goods of his subjects were in his hands and at his disposition' (Holinshed, p. 503).
    37. *rack*] extort financially, with a play on the sense of 'torture'.
    41. *The farming . . . kingdom*] See Holinshed: 'The common brute
[rumour] ran, that the king had set to farme the realme of England, unto
Sir William Scroope earle of Wiltshire, and then treasuror of England, to
sir John Bushie, sir John Bagot and sir Henrie Greene knights' (p. 496).

stubbornness. But to make all whole we have left that   45
smooth-faced flattering Greene to follow him close, and
he'll never leave till he has done it, I warrant ye.

Scroop. There's no question on't. King Richard will betake
himself to a yearly stipend and we four by lease must rent
the kingdom.   50

Bushy. Rent it, ay, and rack it too, ere we forfeit our leases,
and we had them once.

Enter BAGOT.

How now, Bagot, what news?

Bagot. All rich and rare! The realm must be divided presently,
and we four must farm it. The leases are a-making, and   55
for £7,000 a month the kingdom is our own, boys.

Bushy. 'Sfoot, let's differ for no price, and it were £70,000 a
month, we'll make somebody pay for't.

Scroop. Where is his highness?

Bagot. He will be here presently to seal the writings. He's a   60
little angry that the Duke comes not, but that will vanish
quickly. On with your soothest faces, ye wenching rascals.
Humour him finely and you're all made by it.

Sound [trumpets]. Enter KING RICHARD,
GREENE *and others.*

Bushy. See, see, he comes, and that flattering hound,
Greene, close at's elbow.   65

Scroop. Come, come, we must all flatter if we mean to live by
it.

King Richard. Our uncle will not come then?

Greene. That was his answer, flat and resolute.

King Richard. Was ever subject so audacious?   70

---

62. soothest] *MS;* smoothest *conj. Rossiter.*   63.1. SD] sound *deleted in left
margin in MS.*

---

56. *£7,000 . . . month*] £84,000 a year would have been a very considerable income both in King Richard's reign and in the 1590s. Stone, p. 762,
gives the mean net income for a range of peers as £2,930 for the year 1602.
Tresilian's mention at ll. 5–6 above of having already raised £7,000 from
three shires indicates the level of profit available to the flatterers.

57. *differ for*] dispute or quarrel over.

62. *soothest*] presumably 'most truthful looking' (i.e. to deceive Richard);
but possibly MS's 'soothest' is a slip for 'smoothest'.

Bagot. And can your grace, my lord, digest these wrongs?
King Richard. Yes, as a mother that beholds her child
  Dismembered by a bloody tyrant's sword.
  I tell thee, Bagot, in my heart remains
  Such deep impressions of his churlish taunts   75
  As nothing can remove the gall thereof
  Till with his blood mine eyes be satisfied.
Greene. 'Sfoot, raise powers, my lord, and fetch him thence
  perforce.
King Richard. I dare not, Greene, for whiles he keeps i'th'
  country   80
  There is no meddling; he's so well beloved
  As all the realm will rise in arms with him.
Tresilian. 'Sfoot, my lord, and you'd fain have him, I have a
  trick shall fetch him from his house at Plashy in spite of
  all his favourites.   85
Greene. Let's ha't, Tresilian; thy wit must help or all's dashed
  else.
Tresilian. Then thus, my lord: whiles the Duke securely revels
  i'th' country, we'll have some trusty friends disguise
  themselves like masquers and this night ride down to   90
  Plashy and, in the name of some near adjoining friends,
  offer their sports to make him merry, which he no doubt
  will thankfully accept. Then in the masque we'll have it
  so devised, the dance being done and the room voided,
  then upon some occasion, single the Duke alone, thrust   95
  him in a masquing suit, clap a vizard on his face, and so
  convey him out o'th' house at pleasure.
Scroop. How if he cry and call for help?

---

86. *Greene*] MS *speech prefix* King *is deleted and* Greene *supplied in the margin.*
ha't] *Rossiter;* hate *MS.*   93. have] *Halliwell;* h< *MS.*

---

86. *Greene*] The substitution of Greene as speaker for King Richard in
MS seems appropriate both to Greene's tone of voice and to his enthusiasm
for the plot in contrast with the King's caution.
88–97. *Then . . . pleasure*] Tresilian's masque plot is an invention of the
dramatist.
88. *securely*] without apprehension or suspicion of evil.
94. *voided*] emptied.
95. *single . . . alone*] separate the Duke from the others; an expression from hunting in which an animal was selected from the herd to be
hunted.

Tresilian. What serves your drums but to drown his cries? And
    being in a masque 'twill never be suspected.   100
Greene. Good, i'faith, and to help it, my lord, Lapoole, the
    governor of Calais, is new come over, who, with a troop
    of soldiers closely ambushed in the woods near the house,
    shall shroud themselves till the masque be ended. Then,
    the Duke being attached, he shall be there ready to   105
    receive him, hurry him away to the Thames' side where
    a ship shall be laid ready for his coming; so clap him
    under hatches, hoist sails and secretly convey him out
    o'th' realm to Calais. And so by this means ye shall
    prevent all mischief, for neither of your uncles nor any of   110
    the kingdom shall know what's become of him.
King Richard. I like it well, sweet Greene, and by my crown
    We'll be i'th' masque ourself and so shall you.
    Get horses ready; this night we'll ride to Plashy,
    But see ye carry it close and secretly,   115
    For, whilst this plot's a-working for the Duke,
    I'll set a trap for York and Lancaster.
    Go, Tresilian, let proclamations straight be sent,
    Wherein thou shalt accuse the dukes of treason,
    And then attach, condemn and close imprison them.   120
    Lest the commons should rebel against us,
    We'll send unto the King of France for aid,
    And in requital we'll surrender up
    Our forts of Guynes and Calais to the French.

---

101. Good i'faith] *MS (i'faith deleted).* 112–19.] *Rossiter;* I . . . crown /
We'll . . . ready / This . . . close / And . . . duke / I'll . . . Tresilian / Let . . .
sent / wher . . . Treason *MS.*

---

102. *governor of Calais*] The Governor of Calais at the time of Woodstock's murder was Thomas Mowbray, Duke of Norfolk. The identification
of Lapoole with the post probably derives from the dramatist's conflating the
events of the late 1390s with those of 1388, leading up to Tresilian's fall, when
Michael de Lapoole's brother held the position.
103. *ambushed*] set in ambush.
122–4. *We'll . . . French*] Richard's marriage to the eight-year-old Isabelle
of France in 1396 brought about a truce to seventy years of desultory warfare.
His enemies accused him of courting the French in order to strengthen his
position at home, but this has been disputed by modern historians (see
Hutchison, pp. 159–64). Neither Guynes, 5 miles south of Calais and the site
of the Field of the Cloth of Gold, nor Calais itself, captured by Edward III

Let crown and kingdom waste, yea life and all,   125
Before King Richard see his true friends fall!
Give order our disguises be made ready,
And let Lapoole provide the ship and soldiers.
We will not sleep, by heaven, till we have seized him.
Bushy. [*Aside to Greene*] 'Sfoot, urge our suit again, he will   130
   forget it else.
King Richard. These traitors once surprised, then all is sure:
   Our kingdom quiet and your states secure.
Greene. Most true, sweet king; and then your grace, as you
   promised, farming out the kingdom to us four shall not   135
   need to trouble yourself with any business. This old
   turkey-cock, Tresilian, shall look to the law and we'll
   govern the land most rarely.
King Richard. So, sir, the love of thee and these, my dearest
      Greene,
   Hath won King Richard to consent to that   140
   For which all foreign kings will point at us.
   And of the meanest subject of our land
   We shall be censured strangely when they tell
   How our great father toiled his royal person,
   Spending his blood to purchase towns in France;   145
   And we his son, to ease our wanton youth,

---

125. yea] *Rossiter;* ye *MS.*   130. SD] *Rossiter.*   132. *King Richard*] G *or* C
deleted and King *written in in same hand in MS.*   139–60. So . . . toadstool]
*Marked for omission in the MS with a diagonal line in the same ink as the speech
prefixes above and below the passage but in a different ink from the repeated phrase*
out *in the margin. No speech prefixes are supplied for this passage. Speech prefixes
follow Halliwell.*   143.] out *written in left-hand margin of MS and again at
l. 156.*   strangely] *Rossiter;* strangly *MS.*

---

in 1346, was surrendered. Calais was held until 1558 when Queen Mary lost
it. After so recent a loss audiences would, no doubt, have been particularly
sensitive to Richard's irresponsible proposal. See Holinshed, p. 458.
   125. *waste*] be annihilated.
   137. *turkey-cock*] proverbial image of self-importance (Tilley T612).
   138. *rarely*] splendidly, exceptionally.
   139–60. *So . . . toadstool*] The deletion in the manuscript of this surprisingly frank analysis of kingly irresponsibility and the repeated instruction
'out' in the left-hand margin suggests the players' anxiety to avoid giving
offence or, possibly, the direct intervention of the Master of the Revels; see
'Censorship' section in Introduction.
   144. *toiled*] wearied, exhausted.

Become a landlord to this warlike realm,
Rent out our kingdom like a pelting farm
That erst was held as fair as Babylon,
The maiden conqueress to all the world.   150

Greene. 'Sfoot, what need you care what the world talks? You
still retain the name of king, and if any disturb ye, we four
comes presently from the four parts of the kingdom with
four puissant armies to assist you.

King Richard. You four must be all then, for I think nobody   155
else will follow you, unless it be to hanging.

Greene. Why Richard, King Richard, will ye be as good as
your word and seal the writings? 'Sfoot, and thou dost
not, and I do not join with thine uncles and turn traitor,
would I might be turned to a toadstool!   160

---

148. pelting] *MS (apparently, altered from what appears originally to have been* peltry*)*.

---

147. *landlord*] This appellation occurs five times in the play. Donna B.
Hamilton argues that this description of Richard's status degrades the relationship between monarch and subject to the kind of relationship 'that
existed between a Roman landlord and his slaves' ('The State of the Law in
Richard II', *SQ* (Spring 1983, pp. 5–17), p. 6.

148. *pelting*] paltry, petty. The altered word in the MS is difficult to decipher and is disputed by Rossiter who attributes the reading 'pelting' to
editors' familiarity with Shakespeare (see *R2*, 2.1.60, 'Like to a tenement or
pelting farm').

149–50. *Babylon . . . world*] Whilst Richard recalls the city's imperial
power and splendour, Babylon would also have had negative associations for
contemporary audiences since it was the city in which the Jews endured their
captivity and oppression, the location of the Tower of Babel and, most especially for Protestants, a synonym for Rome where the Pope, the whore of
Babylon, held sway. Thus the King's comments are sharply ironised.

150. *maiden*] unconquered, untaken. Parfitt suggests that 'maiden conqueress' is a compliment to Elizabeth I but this seems unlikely given the
negative associations of Babylon (see note above).

151–4. *You still . . . assist you*] Greene's proposal parallels that in Shake-
peare's *King Lear* (*Tragedy*) where Lear reserves to himself 'the name and all
th'addition to a king' (1.1.136). It is possible that the play's original audience
could have been familiar with the broadly contemporary *The True Chronicle
of King Leir* in which a division of the kingdom occurs.

160. *I might . . . toadstool*] A further irony, perhaps, since toadstools
(poisonous mushrooms) grow from nothing to full stature overnight; cf.
Chapman, *Bussy*, 3.1.117, 'Fortune's proud mushroom shot up in a night',
and Bacon, *Sylva VI*, 546, p. 114, 'Mushromes . . . come up so hastily, as in
a Night, and yet they are Unsown. And therefore such as are Upstarts in
State, they call, in reproach, Mushromes' (see Tilley M1319).

King Richard. Very well, sir; they did well to choose you for
their orator that has King Richard's love and heart in
keeping. Your suit is granted, sir. Let's see the writings.
All. They're here, my lord.
King Richard. View them, Tresilian, then we'll sign and seal   165
them. Look to your bargain, Greene, and be no loser, for
if ye forfeit, or run behind hand with me, I swear I'll both
imprison and punish ye soundly.
Greene. Forfeit, sweet king? 'Sblood, I'll sell their houses ere
I'll forfeit my lease, I warrant thee.   170
King Richard. If they be stubborn, do, and spare not. Rack
them soundly, and we'll maintain it. Remember ye not
the proviso enacted in our last parliament, that no statute,
were it ne'er so profitable for the commonwealth, should
stand in any force 'gainst our proceedings?   175
Greene. 'Tis true, my lord; then what should hinder ye to
accomplish anything that may best please your kingly
spirit to determine?
King Richard. True, Greene, and we will do it in spite of them.
Is't just, Tresilian?   180
Tresilian. Most just, my liege. These gentlemen here, Sir
Henry Greene, Sir Edward Bagot, Sir William Bushy and
Sir Thomas Scroop, all jointly here stand bound to pay
your majesty, or your deputy, wherever you remain,
£7,000 a month for this your kingdom. For which your   185

---

161. very well] *crossed out in MS.* 167. run] rune *MS;* come *Halliwell,
Keller.* 169–274.] *During this section, with some exceptions, speech prefixes are
abbreviated to the first letter only.*

---

166. *be no loser*] i.e. do not fail.
172. *maintain*] back, support.
172–5. *Remember . . . proceedings*] The dramatist is here drawing on
Holinshed's record of the articles against Richard (p. 502): 'Item, the parlement setting and enacting diverse notable statutes, for the profit and
advancement of the commonwealth, he by his privie freends and solicitors
caused to be enacted, that no act then enacted, should be more prejudiciall
to him, than it was to anie of his predecessors: through which proviso he did
often as he listed, and not as the law did meane'.
181–94. *These gentlemen . . . pleasure*] See Holinshed, p. 496. The detailed
dramatisation here of Richard's contract with his flatterers to farm the land
may be referred to by John of Gaunt in *R2*: '[England] is now bound in with
shame, / With inky blots and rotten parchment bonds' (2.1.63–4) and his
further accusation (l. 113): 'Landlord of England art thou now, not king'.

grace, by these writings, surrenders to their hands all your
crown lands, lordships, manors, rents, taxes, subsidies,
fifteens, imposts, foreign customs, staples for wool, tin,
lead and cloth, all forfeitures of goods or lands confiscate,
and all other duties that is, shall, or may appertain to the   190
King or crown's revènues, and for non-payment of the
sum or sums aforesaid, your majesty to seize the lands
and goods of the said gentlemen above named, and their
bodies to be imprisoned at your grace's pleasure.

King Richard. How like you that, Greene? Believe me, if you   195
    fail, I'll not favour ye a day.

Greene. I'll ask no favour at your hands, sir. Ye shall have your
    money at your day, and then do your worst, sir!

King Richard. 'Tis very good. Set to your hands and seals.
    Tresilian, we make you our deputy to receive this money.   200
    Look strictly to them, I charge ye.

Tresilian. If the money come not to my hands at the time
    appointed, I'll make them smoke for't.

Greene. Ay, ay, you're an upright justice, sir, we fear ye not.
    Here, my lord: they're ready, signed and sealed.   205

Tresilian. Deliver them to his majesty all together as your
    special deeds.

All. We do, with humble thanks unto his majesty that makes
    us tenants to so rich a lordship.

---

187. subsidies] *Rossiter;* subsites *MS.* 190. is] Is *MS;* do *Rossiter.*
204–5.] *Parfitt;* I . . . not / heere . . . seald *MS.* 208. *All*] *Halliwell;* Bag:
MS (B superimposed over another letter). 208–9.] *Parfitt;* we . . . matie. / that
. . . lordshipp *MS.*

---

187. *subsidies*] financial grants made by parliament to sovereigns to meet
special needs (*OED* 2).
    188. *fifteens*] a tax of one-fifteenth, formerly imposed on the value of per-
sonal property.
    imposts] customs duties levied on merchandise.
    staples] money accruing from the sale of the right to export goods, thus
the sale of a monopoly.
    199. *hands*] signatures.
    203. *smoke*] suffer.
    205. *Here . . . sealed*] Rossiter points up the ironic parallel with the Dun-
stable oafs signing away their 'trifling crowns'.
    208. All] Halliwell's emendation seems necessary here since Tresil-
ian is asking all four of the favourites formally to acknowledge their
bond.

King Richard. Keep them, Tresilian; now will we sign and seal   210
    to you. Never had English subjects such a landlord.
Greene. Nor never had English king such subjects as we four
    that are able to farm a whole kingdom and pay him rent
    for't.
King Richard. Look that ye do. We shall expect performance   215
    speedily. There's your indenture signed and sealed, which
    as our kingly deed we here deliver.
Greene. Thou never didst a better deed in thy life, sweet bully.
    Thou mayst now live at ease, we'll toil for thee and send
    thy money in tumbling.   220
King Richard. We shall see your care, sir. Reach me the map,
    we may allot their portions and part the realm amongst
    them equally. You four shall here by us divide yourselves
    into the thirty-nine shires and counties of my kingdom,
    parted thus. Come, stand by me and mark those shires   225
    assigned ye: Bagot, thy lot betwixt the Thames and sea
    thus lies: Kent, Surrey, Sussex, Hampshire, Berkshire,
    Wiltshire, Dorsetshire, Somersetshire, Devonshire, Corn-
    wall. Those parts are thine as ample, Bagot, as the crown
    is mine.   230
Bagot. All thanks, love, duty to my princely sovereign.
King Richard. Bushy, from thee shall stretch his government
    over these lands that lie in Wales, together with our coun-

---

219. mayst] <m..s. *Frijlinck; maist conj. Frijlinck; shalt Halliwell, Keller; MS
now obliterated.* 227. Hampshire] ha<mshe *MS.* 229. parts] *Rossiter;
parte MS.* 229–30. Those . . . mine] *as verse in MS with rhyme on* thine /
mine. 231. Bagot] *Bag: MS (Scro: crossed out).* 233. these lands] *Halliwell, Keller;* these< *MS.*

---

217. *kingly deed*] ironical since Richard's action is most unkingly.
218. *bully*] good friend, fine fellow.
221–57. *Reach . . . portion, sir*] This detailed division of the kingdom finds
remarkable reflections in Shakespeare. Richard apportions lands in a manner
which closely resembles the rebels' proposed partition of England in 3.1 of
1H4, and Richard's keeping back the most prosperous portion of the realm
for his most favoured minion, Greene, recalls Lear's desire to reserve the
more 'opulent' third for Cordelia, *Lear (Tragedy)*, 1.1.86. It is hard to believe
that Shakespeare was not familiar with this play.
224. *thirty-nine shires*] Despite Richard's precise claim to disburse thirty-
nine shires, his catalogue lists only thirty-seven shires plus London.
229. *ample*] fully, completely.
232–3. *from . . . over*] Whilst Richard's phrasing is clumsy, the overall
sense is clear from the context, i.e. 'your jurisdiction encompasses'.

ties of Gloucester, Worcester, Hereford, Shropshire,
Staffordshire and Cheshire. There's thy lot.   235
Bushy. Thanks to my king that thus hath honoured me.
King Richard. Sir Thomas Scroop, from Trent to Tweed thy lot
  is parted thus: all Yorkshire, Derbyshire, Lancashire, Cum-
  berland, Westmorland and Northumberland. Receive thy
  lot, thy state and government.   240
Scroop. With faith and duty to your highness' throne.
King Richard. Now, my Greene, what have I left for thee?
Greene. 'Sfoot, and you'll give me nothing, then good night,
  landlord. Since ye have served me last, and I be not the
  last shall pay your rent, ne'er trust me.   245
King Richard. I kept thee last to make thy part the greatest.
  See here, sweet Greene, these shires are thine, even from
  the Thames to Trent thou here shalt lie i'th' middle of my
  land.
Greene. That's best i'th' winter. Is there any pretty wenches   250
  in my government?
King Richard. Guess that by this: thou hast London, Middlesex, Essex, Suffolk, Norfolk, Cambridgeshire, Hertford-
  shire, Bedfordshire, Buckinghamshire, Oxfordshire,
  Northamptonshire, Rutlandshire, Leicestershire, War-   255
  wickshire, Huntingdonshire and Lincolnshire. There's
  your portion, sir.
Greene. 'Slid, I will rule like a king amongst them,
  And thou shalt reign like an emperor over us.
King Richard. Thus have I parted my whole realm amongst
  ye.   260
  Be careful of your charge and government.
  And now to attach our stubborn uncles
  Let warrants be sent down, Tresilian,
  For Gaunt and York, Surrey and Arundel,
  Whiles we this night at Plashy suddenly   265

---

234. Worcester] Wo[rster] *Halliwell, Keller;* w<o *MS.*

237–40. *Trent . . . government*] An appropriate allocation given Scroop's
Yorkshire origins.
  248–9. *lie . . . land*] The sexual connotations are appropriate since
Greene is the king's favourite minion.
  258. *'Slid*] an abbreviation of 'By God's eyelid'.

Surprise plain Woodstock. Being parted thus,
We shall with greater ease arrest and take them.
Your places are not sure while they have breath;
Therefore pursue them hard. Those traitors gone,
The staves are broke the people lean upon,   270
And you may guide and rule then at your pleasures.
Away to Plashy, let our masque be ready.
Beware, Plain Thomas, for King Richard comes
Resolved with blood to wash all former wrongs.
                              Sound [trumpets]. Exeunt omnes.

[4.2]

> *Enter* WOODSTOCK *and his* DUCHESS *with a*
> Gentleman, CHENEY *and others.*

Woodstock. The Queen so sick! Come, come, make haste,
    good wife,
Thou'lt be belated sure, 'tis night already.
On with thy cloak and mask. To horse, to horse.
Duchess of Gloucester. Good troth, my lord, I have no mind
    to ride.
I have been dull and heavy all this day;   5
My sleeps were troubled with sad dreams last night
And I am full of fear and heaviness.
Pray let me ride tomorrow.

268. they] *Rossiter; the* MS.

4.2.7–8.] *Rossiter; one line in* MS.

---

274. *Resolved . . . wrongs*] Whilst at the simplest level this is a statement
of straightforward revenge for Woodstock's past treatment of Richard's
former supporters, at another level the language suggests a striking blas-
phemy in its recollection of the Christian sacrifice.

   4.2.1–3. *The Queen . . . horse*] The visit is the dramatist's invention. Queen
Anne died three years before Woodstock's arrest, which was discreetly
handled in the presence of the Duchess. See Appendix B, Holinshed 1397.

   2. *belated*] overtaken by darkness.

   3. *mask*] Masks were often worn by women to protect the face from the
weather, especially when riding; cf. Barry, 'She's mask'd and in her riding
suit' (2.2.674).

   5. *dull and heavy*] gloomy and sluggish.

   6. *sad*] grave, serious.

Woodstock. What, and the Queen so sick? Away for shame!
Stay for a dream? Thou'st dreamt I'm sure ere this.   10
Duchess of Gloucester. Never so fearful were my dreams till
     now.
Had they concerned myself my fears were past;
But you were made the object of mine eye
And I beheld you murdered cruelly.
Woodstock. Ha, murdered?   15
Alack, good lady, didst thou dream of me?
Take comfort then, all dreams are contrary.
Duchess of Gloucester. Pray God it prove so, for my soul is
     fearful,
The vision did appear so lively to me:
Methoughts as you were ranging through the woods   20
An angry lion with a herd of wolves
Had in an instant round encompassed you;
When to your rescue, 'gainst the course of kind,
A flock of silly sheep made head against them,
Bleating for help; 'gainst whom the forest king   25
Roused up his strength and slew both you and them.
This fear affrights me.
Woodstock. Afore my God, thou'rt foolish; I'll tell thee all
     thy dream:
Thou knowst last night we had some private talk
About the blanks the country's taxed withal,   30
Where I compared the state, as now it stands,
Meaning King Richard and his harmful flatterers,
Unto a savage herd of ravening wolves,
The commons to a flock of silly sheep
Who whilst their slothful shepherd careless stood   35

---

12. they] the *MS.*   15–16.] *Rossiter; one line in MS.*   26–7.] *Rossiter; one line in MS.*   28. Woodstock] *Halliwell, Keller; no speech prefix in MS because edge of page eroded.*   32. harmful flatterers] *MS, written over something smudged out (Frijlinck).*

---

17. *dreams . . . contrary*] dreams have an opposite interpretation; proverbial, 'Dreams go by contraries' (Tilley D588).
23. *'gainst . . . kind*] contrary to their normal nature.
24. *silly sheep*] i.e. the plain and unsophisticated commoners as Woodstock explains at l. 34.
25. *forest king*] i.e. the angry lion, alluding to King Richard.
35. *careless*] uncaring.

Those forest thieves broke in and sucked their blood.
And this thy apprehension took so deep
The form was portrayed lively in thy sleep.
Come, come, 'tis nothing. What, are her horses ready?
Cheney. They are, my lord.   40
Woodstock. Where is the gentleman that brought this message?
Where lies the Queen, sir?
Gentleman. At Sheen, my lord, most sick and so much
     altered
As those about her fears her sudden death.
Woodstock. Forfend it, Heaven. Away, make haste I charge
     ye.   45
What, weeping now? Afore my God, thou'rt fond.
Come, come, I know thou art no augurer of ill.
Dry up thy tears; this kiss, and part; farewell.
Duchess of Gloucester. That farewell from your lips to me
     sounds ill.
Where'er I go my fears will follow still.   50
Woodstock. See her to horseback, Cheney.
          Exeunt DUCHESS *and the rest. Manet* WOODSTOCK.
                              'Fore God, 'tis late,
And but th'important business craves such haste,
She had not gone from Plashy house tonight.
But, woe is me, the good Queen Anne is sick,
And, by my soul, my heart is sad to hear it.   55
So good a lady and so virtuous

---

43. *Gentleman*] *Rossiter; seru: MS (inserted in darker ink).*   51. God] my
deleted before God *in MS.*

43. Gentleman] Rossiter's emendation seems sensible since 'a Gentleman' is designated in the opening entry to the scene.
   Sheen] the old name of Richmond, Surrey. Edward III spent £2,000
on converting a royal manor into the Palace of Sheen, and Richard II
continued the improvements, building a Royal Lodging on La Neyt, an
island in the adjacent Thames. The Lodging was luxurious, with a tiled
bathroom with bronze taps for hot and cold water. Further novelties at
Sheen included personal latrines and fireplaces in small rooms. See Mathew,
pp. 33–4.
   46. *fond*] foolish.
   51. *See . . . Cheney*] Whilst Woodstock's packing his wife off at night may
seem callous, it is made clear later in the scene that he ensures that she is
well accompanied on this journey: '. . . my lady is from home / And most of
my attendance waiting on her' (4.2.130–1).

This realm for many ages could not boast of.
Her charity hath stayed the commons' rage
That would ere this have shaken Richard's chair
Or set all England on a burning fire.   60
And, 'fore my God, I fear when she is gone
This woeful land will all to ruin run.

Enter CHENEY.

How now, Cheney; what, is thy lady gone yet?
Cheney. She is, my lord, with much unwillingness,
And 'tis so dark I cannot blame her grace.   65
The lights of heaven are shut in pitchy clouds
And flakes of fire run tilting through the sky
Like dim ostents to some great tragedy.
Woodstock. God bless good Anne o' Beame! I fear her death
Will be the tragic scene the sky foreshows us.   70
When kingdoms change, the very heavens are troubled.
Pray God, King Richard's wild behaviour
Force not the powers of heaven to frown upon us.
My prayers are still for him. What thinkst thou, Cheney,
May not Plain Thomas live a time to see   75
This state attain her former royalty?
'Fore God, I doubt it not; my heart is merry,
And I am suddenly inspired for mirth.
Ha, what sport shall we have tonight, Cheney?

78–9.] *Rossiter;* And . . . ha: / What . . . Cheney *MS.*

66–8. *The lights . . . tragedy*] The source of these lines may be found in
Holinshed, 1395, p. 484: 'A certeine thing appeared in the likenesse of a fier
in manie parts of the realme of England, now of one fashion, now of another
. . . This fierie apparition oftentimes when any bodie went alone, it would
go with him, and would stand when he stood still. To some it appeared in
the likenesse of a turning wheele burning, to othersome round in the likenesse of a barrell, flashing out flames of fier at the head, to othersome in the
likenesse of a long burning lance . . . In Aprill there was seene a fierie dragon
in manie places in England; which dreadfull sight as it made manie a one
amazed, so it ministred occasion of mistrust to the minds of the marvellors,
that some great mischeefe was imminent, whereof that burning apparition
was a prognostication.'
68. *ostents*] portents, signs. The interpretation of such phenomena as harbingers of disaster is common in the drama of the time; cf. *JC*, 2.2.19–31,
and *Ham.*, Additional Passages, 5–18.

Cheney. I'm glad to hear your grace addicted so,   80
    For I have news of sudden mirth to tell ye
    Which, till I heard ye speak, I durst not utter.
    We shall have a masque tonight, my lord.
Woodstock. Ha, a masque sayest thou? What are they,
    Cheney?
Cheney. It seems, my lord, some country gentlemen,   85
    To show their dear affection to your grace,
    Proffer their sports this night to make you merry.
    Their drums have called for entrance twice already.
Woodstock. Are they so near? I prithee let them enter.
    Tell them we do embrace their loves most kindly.   90
    Give order through the house that all observe them.
                          Exit CHENEY.
    We must accept their loves, although the times
    Are no way suited now for masques and revels.
    What ho, within there!

                Enter Servants.

Servant. My lord.   95
Woodstock. Prepare a banquet. Call for lights and music.
                    [*Exeunt* Servants.]
    They come in love and we'll accept it so.
    Some sports does well, we're all too full of woe.

                Enter CHENEY.

Cheney. They're come, my lord.
Woodstock. They all are welcome, Cheney. Set me a chair: 100
    We will behold their sports in spite of care.

---

95. *Servant*] *ser: deleted in MS and* Toby *inserted in dark ink.*
100–1.] 'Anticke' *in left-hand margin;* fflorish Cornetts: Dance / & musique: cornetts. *in right-hand margin of MS.*

---

80. *addicted*] inclined.
88. *drums . . . entrance*] The beating of drums was used to announce one's
approach.
91. *observe them*] show them respectful attention.
95. Servant] Possibly the bookkeeper's marginal note 'Toby' refers to
Edward Tobye whose name, with others, appears in a licence granted to the
Children of the Revels in 1617.

Sound a flourish of cornets. [*Enter* Masquers *conducted
by* CHENEY *who exits.*] *Antic dance and music; then a
great shout and winding o' horns.* [*Exeunt* Masquers.]
Then enters CYNTHIA.

Cynthia. From the clear orb of our ethereal sphere
Bright Cynthia comes to hunt and revel here.
The groves of Calydon and Arden woods
Of untamed monsters, wild and savage herds,   105

101.1–2. *Enter . . . exits*] *This ed.*

101.1. flourish of cornets] a fanfare played within to herald the entrance
of the masquers. Cornets, which could be played softly or loudly, were wood-
wind instruments related to the modern oboe, not to be confused with the
nineteenth-century cornet, a brass instrument similar to a trumpet. Cornets
were particularly popular in the sixteenth and seventeenth centuries (see
Dessen and Thomson); Henry VIII is recorded as supporting a band of
'cornets and sagbuttes' in 1532. Cornets were frequently used in stage per-
formances, e.g. Marston, (1606), 1.1.182.1, 2.1.103.1 etc.
  Masquers] The manuscript does not indicate who performs the dance, but
it is likely that the actors playing Richard, Greene, Bushy and Bagot who
enter as Diana's knights at l. 124.1–4 also danced as the masquers.
  101.2. Antic dance and music] The manuscript's marginal directions have
been incorporated in the SD here since, although they may relate to a later
revival of the play, they seem to suggest the nature of the staging called for at
this point in the action. Cynthia's reference to 'untamed monsters, wild and
savage herds' (l. 105) endorses the book-keeper's marginal direction
'Anticke', i.e. an initial and vigorous dance before the entrance of Cynthia.
  101.4. CYNTHIA] the moon goddess and also a pseudonym applied to
Elizabeth I; see, for example, Ralegh's *Ocean's Love to Cynthia*. Rossiter,
noting the absence of Scroop from this scene, speculates that he may have
taken the role of Cynthia, but there may be a suggestion that Scroop joins with
Tresilian in the initiative against the other lords at the end of 4.1. Heinemann
(p. 185) suggests that Richard himself plays the part of Cynthia, but the
textual evidence does not support this. The most likely performer of the role
of Cynthia is the boy actor playing Queen Anne, whose role is now completed.
  102–19. *From . . . dancing*] Cynthia's speech works at a number of levels.
Formally a compliment to Woodstock, praised as 'a faithful prince and peer'
both reverend and mild, her narrative also foretells his assassination since
he, from Richard's viewpoint, is the 'cruel tuskèd boar' who is to be hunted
by the disguised King and courtiers. For contemporary audiences, as
Rossiter and Parfitt suggest, the association of Cynthia with Elizabeth I may
have suggested the Tudors' deliverance of England from the curse of Richard
III, formerly Duke of Gloucester, whose emblem was the white boar.
  102. clear . . . sphere] i.e. the moon.
  104. Calydon and Arden woods] Calydon, the ancient city of Aetolia
famous for the hunting of the Cian boar slain by Meleager; Arden, a forest
in Belgium and France between the Sambre and the Moselle made familiar
by Lodge's *Rosalynde* (1590).

We and our knights have freed, and hither come
To hunt these forests where we hear there lies
A cruel tuskèd boar, whose terror flies
Through this large kingdom, and with fear and dread
Strikes her amazèd greatness pale and dead.   110
And, having viewed from far these towers of stone,
We heard the people midst their joy and moan
Extol to heaven a faithful prince and peer
That keeps a court of love and pity here;
Reverend and mild his looks. If such there be   115
This state directs, great prince, that you are he;
And ere our knights to this great hunting go,
Before your grace they would some pastime show
In sprightly dancing. Thus they bade me say
And wait an answer to return or stay.   120
Woodstock. Nay, for Heaven's pity, let them come I prithee.
Pretty device, i'faith. Stand by, make room there.
Stir, stir, good fellows, each man to his task.
We shall have a clear night, the moon directs the masque.

Music. Enter KING RICHARD, GREENE, BUSHY,
BAGOT, *like Diana's knights, led in by four other knights
in green, with horns about their necks and boar-spears in
their hands.*

Woodstock. Ha, country sports, say ye? 'Fore God, 'tis courtly.   125
A general welcome, courteous gentlemen,
And when I see your faces
I'll give it each man more particular.
If your entertainment fail your merit

---

110. amazèd] *Rossiter;* a massed *MS.* 124.1. *Music*] *in left-hand margin at
l. 123 in MS.* 127–8.] *Parfitt; one line in MS.*

116. *state*] Woodstock's status is indicated by his chair of state placed in
a dominant position in the hall.
directs] demonstrates.
124. *moon*] i.e. Cynthia.
124.2. Diana's knights] i.e. followers of Diana, goddess of the moon and
hunting; cf. *1H4,* 1.2.25.
124.3. horns . . . necks] The horns here are probably hunting-horns,
though it is possible that the dancers are carrying stag-horns on their shoulders as in the Abbots Bromley horn dance in Staffordshire (see Chambers,
MS, I, p. 166).
129. *entertainment*] hospitality, reception.

I must ask pardon; my lady is from home   130
And most of my attendance waiting on her,
But we'll do what we can to bid you welcome.
Afore my God, it joys my heart to see
Amidst these days of woe and misery
Ye find a time for harmless mirth and sport;   135
But 'tis your loves and we'll be thankful for't.
Ah, sirrah,
Ye come like knights to hunt the boar indeed;
And heaven he knows we had need of helping hands,
So many wild boars roots and spoils our lands   140
That England almost is destroyed by them;
I care not if King Richard heard me speak it!
I wish his grace all good, high Heaven can tell,
But there's a fault in some, alack the day.
His youth is led by flatterers much astray.   145
But he's our king, and God's great deputy,
And if ye hunt to have me second ye
In any rash attempt against his state,
Afore my God, I'll ne'er consent unto it.
I ever yet was just and true to him   150
And so will still remain: what's now amiss
Our sins have caused, and we must bide Heaven's will.
I speak my heart, I am Plain Thomas still.
Come, come, a hall and music there! Your dance being
    done,
A banquet stands prepared to bid you welcome.   155

Music. They dance. Then enter CHENEY.

136–7.] *Parfitt; one line in MS.*   142. care] *Armstrong;* cared *Rossiter;* card
MS.

146–52.] Woodstock articulates an entirely orthodox and establishment
view of kingship here; cf. *R2*, 1.2, where Gaunt repudiates revenge for
Gloucester's death: 'God's is the quarrel; for God's substitute, / His deputy
anointed in His sight, / Hath caused his death; the which if wrongfully, / Let
heaven revenge' (37–40).

154. *a hall*] a cry to clear the way or make sufficient room; see *R&J*,
1.5.26.

155. *banquet*] a slight repast or 'running banquet'. Woodstock (ll. 129–
32) apologises for the limited entertainment available, his lady being
absent.

How now, Cheney, is this banquet ready?
Cheney. There is no time I fear for banqueting.
   My lord, I wish your grace be provident.
   I fear your person is betrayed, my lord.   *A drum afar off*
   The house is round beset with armèd soldiers!   160
Woodstock. Ha, soldiers? Afore my God, the commons all
      are up then?
   They will rebel against the king I fear me,
   And flock to me to back their bold attempts.
   Go arm the household, Cheney.   *Exit* CHENEY.
                              Hear me, gentlemen—
   'Fore God, I do not like this whispering!   165
   If your intents be honest, show your faces.
King Richard. Guard fast the doors and seize him presently!
   This is the cave that keeps the tuskèd boar
   That roots up England's vineyards uncontrolled.
   Bagot, arrest him. If for help he cry,   170
   Drown all his words with drums confusedly.
Woodstock. Am I betrayed?
Bagot. Ye cannot 'scape, my lord, the toils are pitched
   And all your household fast in hold ere this.
   Thomas of Woodstock, Duke of Gloucester,   175
   Earl of Cambridge and of Buckingham,
   I here arrest thee in King Richard's name
   Of treason to the crown, his state and realm.
Woodstock. I'll put in bail and answer to the law.

---

159. SD] *in left-hand margin at l. 158 in MS.*   171. words with] *Parfitt;*
words: with *MS.*   176–7.] *Rossiter; as prose in MS.*   179–80. I'll . . . law /
Speak . . . here] *Rossiter; one line in MS.*

---

165. *whispering*] It would appear that Richard and his followers are plotting together.
   168. *keeps*] lodges.
   171. *words with*] MS's colon after 'words' may just possibly indicate that
Richard's speech ends here and that the phrase 'with drums confusedly' con-
stitutes a stage direction rather than a continuation of his speech, carrying
out the strategem planned at 4.1.98–9.
   173. *toils are pitched*] snares are set.
   174. *in hold*] in custody.
   175–6. *Duke . . . Buckingham*] The titles given to Woodstock contain a
confusion. He was Earl of Buckingham and Duke of Gloucester, but his
brother Edmund (the York of this play) was Earl of Cambridge.
   179. *put in bail*] provide securities for bail.

Speak, is King Richard here?

All.   No, no, my lord.   180
Away with him.

Woodstock.   Villains, touch me not.
I am descended of the royal blood,
King Richard's uncle,
His grandsire's son, his princely father's brother.
Becomes it princes to be led like slaves?   185

King Richard. Put on a vizard. Stop his cries.

Woodstock. Ha, who bids them so? I know that voice full well.
Afore my God, false men, King Richard's here!
Turn thee, thou headstrong youth, and speak again.
By thy dead father's soul, I charge thee hear me,   190
So Heaven may help me at my greatest need
As I have wished thy good and England's safety.

Bagot. You're still deceived, my lord; the King's not here.

Bushy. On with his masquing suit and bear him hence.
We'll lead ye fairly to King Richard's presence.   195

Woodstock. Nay, from his presence to my death you'll lead
    me,
And I am pleased I shall not live to see
My country's ruin and his misery.
Thou hearst me well, proud King, and well mayst boast
That thou betray'dst me here so suddenly,   200
For had I known thy secret treachery
Nor thou nor these thy flattering minions
With all your strengths had wronged plain Woodstock
    thus.
But use your wills. Your uncles Gaunt and York
Will give you thanks for this, and the poor commons   205
When they shall hear of these your unjust proceedings—

King Richard. Stop's mouth I say! We'll hear no more.

Woodstock. Good Heaven, forgive me. Pray ye forbear a while.

180-1. No . . . him] *Rossiter; one line in MS.* 181-4. Villains . . . brother]
Rossiter; as prose in MS. 203. thus] *Halliwell, Keller;* th< *MS.* 205.
commons] *Halliwell;* como< *MS.* 206. proceedings] *This ed.;* pro-
ceedi[ngs] *Keller;* proceedin< *MS.* 208. while] *Halliwell, Keller;* wh< *MS.*

---

194. *his masquing suit*] presumably something appropriate, perhaps
reflecting the imagery of the boar.

I'll speak but one word more—indeed I will!
Some man commend me to my virtuous wife.   210
Tell her her dreams have ta'en effect indeed:
By wolves and lions now must Woodstock bleed.
King Richard. Deliver him to Lapoole. The ship lies ready;
Convey him o'er to Calais speedily.
There use him as we gave directions.   215
Sound up your drums, our hunting sports are done,
And when you're past the house, cast by your habits
And mount your horses with all swiftest haste.
The boar is taken and our fears are past!
                    Sound [drums and cornets]. Exeunt omnes.

[4.3]

                    Enter CROSBY, FLEMING *and* NIMBLE.

Crosby. Come, sirs, attend; my lord is coming forth.
The high shrieves of Kent and Northumberland
With twenty gentlemen are all arrested
For privy whisperers against the state;
In which I know my lord will find some trick   5
To seize their goods, and then there's work for us.
Nimble. Nay, there will be work for the hangman first; then
we'll rifle the goods, and my lord seizes the lands. If these

---

212. bleed] *Keller;* ble< *MS.*   217. Shrevs Ready *in left-hand margin of MS.*
219.1. SD] *Add. this ed.*

217.] The marginal note 'Shrevs Ready' appears to be the book-keeper's
reminder that the Shrieves will enter shortly, although why this particular
entry should require such attention remains uncertain; see Long, *Few,*
p. 422.
    cast by your habits] throw off your disguises.
    219.1. SD] Cornets may well have accompanied the drums which are
specified by Richard in the text since they sound at the beginning of
the masque intended to represent the hunting of the boar. As Woodstock
is bundled away into captivity the masque-like hunt has been successfully
concluded.

    4.3.2–6. *The high . . . us*] The arrest of the Sheriffs of Northumberland
and Kent appears to be invention, but for the general practice of extortion
see Holinshed, p. 496.

seven hundred whisperers that are taken come off lustily,
he'll have the devil and all shortly.   10

Enter TRESILIAN *with the* Shrieves *of Kent and
Northumberland with* Officers.

Fleming. See, see, they're coming.
Tresilian. Call for a marshal there! Commit the traitors!
Shrieves. We do beseech your honour, hear us speak.
Tresilian. Sir, we'll not hear ye. The proof's too plain against
ye.
Becomes it you, sir, being Shrieve of Kent,   15
To stay the blanks King Richard sent abroad,
Revile our messengers, refuse the charters
And spurn, like traitors, 'gainst the King's decrees?
Shrieve of Kent. My lord, I plead our ancient liberties
Recorded and enrolled in the King's Crown Office,   20
Wherein the Men of Kent are clear discharged
Of fines, fifteens, or any other taxes,
Forever given them by the Conqueror.
Tresilian. You're still deceived. Those charters were not sent
To abrogate your ancient privilege,   25
But for his highness' use they were devised
To gather and collect amongst his subjects
Such sums of money as they well might spare,
And he in their defence must hourly spend.
Is not the subject's wealth at the King's will?   30

4.3.9. lustily] *Rossiter;* lustely *MS;* lusely *Halliwell, Keller;* easily *conj.
Halliwell.*

---

9. *come off lustily*] ambiguous; probably 'pay up handsomely', thus
encouraging Tresilian in his rapacity; or, perhaps, 'happily escape' (for 'come
off' in the sense of 'escape', see *OED* 65 g).
   10. *devil . . . shortly*] Depending on the reading of 'come off lustily' (see
above) Nimble suggests either 'There'll be no stopping him' or 'There'll be
the devil to pay'.
   10.1–2. Kent and Northumberland] An odd pairing, but by combining
these two counties from opposite ends of the kingdom the dramatist suggests the national extent of the repression.
   16. *stay*] stop or resist.
   18. *spurn . . . 'gainst*] oppose contemptuously.
   21. *Men of Kent*] formally men born east of the River Medway in Kent
as against Kentish men born west of the river.
   23. *the Conqueror*] William I, who conquered England in 1066.

What, is he lord of lives and not of lands?
Is not his high displeasure present death?
And dare ye stir his indignation so?
Shrieve of North. We are free born, my lord, yet do confess
 Our lives and goods are at the King's dispose;   35
 But how, my lord?—like to a gentle prince
To take or borrow what we best may spare,
And not like bondslaves, force it from our hands!
Tresilian. Presumptuous traitors, that will we try on you.
 Will you set limits to the King's high pleasure?   40
 Away to prison! Seize their goods and lands.
Shrieve of Kent. Much good may it do ye, my lord. The care
 is ta'en:
As good die there as here abroad be slain.
Shrieve of North. Well, God forgive both you and us, my lord.
 Your hard oppressions have undone the state   45
 And made all England poor and desolate.
Tresilian. Why suffer ye their speech? To prison hie.
 There let them perish, rot, consume and die.
      Exeunt [Officers] *with the* Shrieves.
 Art thou there, Nimble?
Nimble. [*Coming forward*] I am here, my lord, and since your 50
 lordship is now employed to punish traitors, I am come
 to present myself unto you.
Tresilian. What, for a traitor?
Nimble. No, my lord, but for a discoverer of the strangest
 traitor that was ever heard of. For by plain arithmetic of 55

47–62.] *No speech prefixes appear because the edge of MS is clipped. The six speeches
are given to Tresilian and Nimble alternately by Halliwell.* 50. SD] *This ed.*

 35. *dispose*] disposal.
 36–8. *But . . . hands*] The general sense is clear but the syntax is compressed: 'a gentle prince might take or borrow what we can easily spare, but not treat us as bond slaves to force us to pay up'.
 42. *The . . . ta'en*] i.e. 'there's no point in worrying about a situation that cannot be remedied'; cf. the proverbs 'Past cure past care' (Tilley C921) and 'Cure is no care' (Tilley c83).
 43. *abroad*] i.e. out of doors.
 55. *arithmetic*] Rossiter suggests a pun on 'reach' since Tresilian comments that Nimble has a 'reaching head' and posits that MS's 'Aretchmaticke' might be modernised to 'arithmatrick' since at l. 59 Nimble says he has 'a trick for't'. Alternatively, we may see the MS form as a nonsense word divided as *A-[w]retch-maticke*, i.e. Nimble's innate ability to recognise traitors.

my capacity I have found out the very words a traitor
spoke that has whistled treason.

Tresilian. How is that, whistle treason?

Nimble. Most certain, my lord, I have a trick for't. If a carman
do but whistle, I'll find treason in't, I warrant ye.   60

Tresilian. Thou'rt a rare statesman, Nimble; thou'st a reaching head.

Nimble. I'll put treason into any man's head, my lord, let him
answer it as he can. And then, my lord, we have got a
schoolmaster that teaches all the country to sing treason,   65
and like a villain he says, 'God bless your lordship'.

Tresilian. Thou'rt a most strange discoverer. Where are these
traitors?

Nimble. All in prison, my lord. Master Ignorance the Baily of
Dunstable and I have taken great pains about them.   70
Besides, here's a note of seven hundred whisperers,
most on them sleepy knaves, we pulled them out of
Bedfordshire.

Tresilian. Let's see the note. Seven hundred whispering
traitors.

Monstrous villains! We must look to these: 75
Of all the sort these are most dangerous
To stir rebellion 'gainst the King and us.
What are they, Crosby? Are the rebels wealthy?

Crosby. Fat chuffs, my lord, all landed men, rich farmers,
graziers and such fellows that, having been but a little   80
pinched with imprisonment, begin already to offer their
lands for liberty.

Tresilian. We'll not be nice to take their offers, Crosby,
Their lands are better than their lives to us,
And without lands they shall not ransom lives.   85
Go, sirs; to terrify the traitors more
Ye shall have warrants straight to hang them all.
Then if they proffer lands and put in bail

---

88. they] *Rossiter;* the *MS.*

59–60. *carman . . . whistle*] Carmen (carters) were famous for their
whistling.
61–2. *reaching head*] speculative imagination.
72–3. *sleepy . . . Bedfordshire*] A common joke, as in the proverb, 'To go to
Bedfordshire' (Tilley B198).
83. *nice*] scrupulous.

To make a just surrender speedily,
Let them have lives, and after liberty;   90
But those that have nor lands nor goods to pay,
Let them be whipped, then hanged. Make haste away.
Nimble. Well then, I see my whistler must be whipped; he has
but two calves to live on and has lost them too. And for
my schoolmaster I'll have him march about the market-   95
place with ten dozen of rods at's girdle the very day he
goes a-feasting, and every one of his scholars shall have
a jerk at him. Come, sirs.
Tresilian. Away and leave us.
                    Exit NIMBLE *and the rest. Manet* TRESILIAN.

                        Enter BAGOT.

                    Here comes Sir Edward Bagot.
Bagot. Right happily met, my Lord Tresilian.   100
Tresilian. You're well returned to court, Sir Edward,
To this sad house of Sheen made comfortless

98–9.] *Enter Dutches & / a gentleman deleted in left-hand margin of MS.*
99. Away . . . us] *(heere comes the dutches) deleted in MS after this speech.*
99.1. the rest] there< *MS.*   101. Edward] *altered from* 'Thomas' *in MS.*

---

96. *rods at's girdle*] Implying that he is to be whipped. Parfitt compares
Jonson, *Every Man In* (Q), 5.3.340–3 'you, Signior, shall be carried to the
market cross, and be there bound; and so shall you, sir, in a large motley
coat, with a rod at your girdle'.
96–7. *he goes a-feasting*] obscure. Rossiter speculates that perhaps the
schoolmaster is to be doubly tormented by being thrashed on a day he has
confidently mistaken for a holiday. There may also be a reference to Twelfth
Night festivities when roles were reversed, e.g. the cabin boy becomes the
captain or the choirboy the bishop for the day.
97–8. *scholars . . . jerk*] i.e. each one of his scholars will have the chance
to beat him with one of his own rods or canes.
98–9.] The MS deletion of the marginal entry 'Enter Duches & a gentleman' and the speech 'heere comes the dutches' appear to indicate that a
scene or episode in which the Duchess of Gloucester's presence at Sheen
(possibly as witness to the Queen's death) was originally designed for presentation at this or a later point. However in the text as corrected in MS her
arrival is narrated as occurring after Richard has received news of the death
(ll. 119–21). The scribe may have been confused by alterations in the copy
he was following.
102. *Sheen*] The discovery of the location of the action is a surprise so
late in the scene when the audience may well have assumed that the events
witnessed were taking place in the provinces or in London. It is unusual for
a dramatist to surprise his audience in this way and may represent an
awkward transition due to the dramatist's change of direction in deleting an

By the sharp sickness of the good Queen Anne.
Bagot. King Richard's come and gone to visit her.
Sad for her weak estate, he sits and weeps.   105
Her speech is gone. Only at sight of him
She heaved her hands and closed her eyes again
And whether alive or dead is yet uncertain.
Tresilian. Here comes Sir William Bushy.

Enter BUSHY.

What tidings, sir?
Bushy. The King's a widower, sir. Fair Anne o' Beame   110
Hath breathed her last farewell to all the realm.
Tresilian. Peace with her soul, she was a virtuous lady.
How takes King Richard this her sudden death?
Bushy. Fares like a madman, rends his princely hair,
Beats his sad breast, falls grovelling on the earth   115
All careless of his state, wishing to die
And even in death to keep her company;
But that which makes his soul more desperate,
Amidst this heat of passion, weeping comes
His aunt the Duchess, Woodstock's hapless wife,   120
With tender love and comfort;
At sight of whom his grief's again redoubled,
Calling to mind the lady's woeful state,
As yet all ignorant of her own mishap.
He takes her in his arms, weeps on her breast,   125

109.1. SD] *at l. 107 in* MS. 110. Bushy] *Halliwell;* h: MS. 120-1.]
Rossiter; one line in MS. 121. and comfort] and comfo< MS; *omitted in
Halliwell, Keller.*

---

episode in which the Duchess's presence at Sheen is dramatised. She above,
ll. 98–9 n.
    104. *come and gone*] i.e. has arrived at Sheen and is visiting the Queen in
her apartment.
    105. *estate*] condition.
    107. *heaved*] raised.
    114–31. *Fares . . . passions*] Richard's grief at Anne's death is well attested;
this passage seems designed to stimulate a measure of audience sympathy
for the King.
    121. *With . . . comfort*] The line is incomplete, words perhaps being
lost at the page's edge because the MS scribe appears to have attempted to write
two lines of verse in the place of one. Rossiter conjectures that the missing
words, completing the metrical line, might be something like 'for his pain'.

And would have there revealed her husband's fall
Amidst his passions, had not Scroop and Greene
By violence borne him to an inward room,
Where still he cries to get a messenger
To send to Calais to reprieve his uncle.   130
Bagot. I do not like those passions.
    If he reveal the plot we all shall perish.
    Where is the Duchess?
Bushy. With much ado we got her leave the presence
    With an intent in haste to ride to Plashy.   135
Tresilian. She'll find sad comforts there. Would all were well.
    A thousand dangers round enclose our state.
Bagot. And we'll break through, my lord, in spite of fate.
    Come, come, be merry, good Tresilian.

                Enter KING RICHARD *and* SCROOP.

Here comes King Richard; all go comfort him.   140
Scroop. My dearest lord, forsake these sad laments.
    No sorrows can suffice to make her live.
King Richard. Then let sad sorrow kill King Richard too.
    For all my earthly joys with her must die
    And I am killed with cares eternally,   145
    For Anne o' Beame is dead, forever gone.
    She was too virtuous to remain with me,
    And Heaven hath given her higher dignity.
    O God, I fear even here begins our woe!
    Her death's but chorus to some tragic scene   150
    That shortly will confound our state and realm.

139.1. SD] *Greene deleted after* King *in MS.*

___

126–30. *revealed . . . uncle*] The intention here is to emphasise the machi-
avellianism of the flatterers. There is no historical evidence that Richard tried
to prevent Woodstock's murder; on the contrary, Holinshed notes his insistence that the murder be expedited. See Holinshed, p. 489.
    127. *passions*] grief, emotion.
    134. *the presence*] the King's presence or chamber.
    139.1. SD] MS's deletion of Greene's name seems justified since he has
no dialogue in the following action, though his absence from this scene is
odd as he is the favourite whom one would expect to be most prominent in
comforting Richard.
    149–53. *O God . . . end*] Chroniclers and historians have regarded Anne
of Bohemia's death as robbing Richard and his administration of a calming
and rational influence on affairs. See Hutchison, pp. 143–5.

Such sad events black mischief still attend
And bloody acts I fear must crown the end.
Bagot. Presage not so, sweet prince, your state is strong.
Your youthful hopes with expectation crown;   155
Let not one loss so many comforts drown.
King Richard. Despair and madness seize me! O dear
      friends,
What loss can be compared to such a queen?
Down with this house of Sheen! Go ruin all!
Pull down her buildings, let her turrets fall;   160
Forever lay it waste and desolate
That English king may never here keep court,
But to all ages leave a sad report
When men shall see these ruined walls of Sheen
And sighing say, 'Here died King Richard's queen',   165
For which we'll have it wasted, lime and stone,
To keep a monument of Richard's moan.
Oh, torturing grief!
Bushy. Dear liege, all tears for her are vain oblations.
Her quiet soul rests in celestial peace;   170
With joy of that let all your sorrows cease.
King Richard. Send post to Calais and bid Lapoole forbear

---

155. crown] *conj. Rossiter;* crownd *Frijlinck;* crowne *MS.* 156. drown] *conj. Rossiter;* drownd *Frijlinck;* drowne *MS.* 157. O dear] my *deleted before* deere *in MS.* 167–8. To . . . grief] *Rossiter; one line in MS.* 169. Dear liege] oh *deleted before* deere *and* my *before* leidge *in MS.*

---

155. *Your . . . crown*] Bagot, in responding to Richard's depressive vision, reverses the notion of the inevitability of bloody acts crowning the end by urging him to achieve the expectations which his youth promises ('crown' is an imperative here).

159–67. *Down . . . moan*] Anne died of plague at the Palace of Sheen on Whit Sunday, 1394. Richard, in his grief, cursed the place where she died and, in April 1395, ordered John Gedney, Clerk of the Works, to demolish the buildings. Holinshed writes, 'This year on Whit-sundaie being the seaventh of June, queene Anne departed this life, to the great greefe of her husband king Richard, who loved her intirelie. She deceased at Sheen, and was buried at Westminster, upon the south side of saint Edwards shrine. The king tooke such a conceit with the house of Shene, where she departed this life, that he caused the buildings to be throwne down and defaced, whereas the former kings of this land, being wearie of the citie, used customablie thither to resort, as to a place of pleasure, and serving highlie to their recreation' (p. 481).

169. *oblations*] sacrifices, offerings.

On pain of life to act our sad decree.
For heaven's love, go prevent the tragedy.
We have too much provoked the powers divine   175
And here repent thy wrongs, good Uncle Woodstock,
The thought whereof confounds my memory.
If men might die when they would 'point the time,
The time is now King Richard would be gone,
For as a fearful thunderclap doth strike   180
The soundest body of the tallest oak
Yet harmless leaves the outward bark untouched,
So is King Richard struck. Come, come, let's go.
My wounds are inward; inward burn my woe.

Exeunt omnes.

177–8.] A bed / for woodstock *in left-hand margin of MS.*   184. burn] burne *MS;* burns *Rossiter.*

177–8.] The marginal note relates to the requirements for the staging of the next scene; it has been seen as a prompter's reminder to implement an important piece of stage business but it is more likely to be a book-keeper's reminder of the need to provide the prop; see Long, *Bed.*

184. *burn*] Rossiter's emendation weakens the sense of Richard's guilt which is suggested by the subjunctive mood of the MS reading.

Act 5

Enter LAPOOLE *with a light; after him*
the two Murderers.

Lapoole. Come, sirs, be resolute. The time serves well
To act the business you have ta'en in hand.
The Duke is gone to rest; the room is voided;
No ear can hear his cries. Be fearless bold
And win King Richard's love with heaps of gold.   5
Are all your instruments for death made ready?
1 Murderer. All fit to th'purpose. See, my lord, here's first a
towel with which we do intend to strangle him; but if he
strive and this should chance to fail, I'll maul his old
mazzard with this hammer, knock him down like an ox   10
and after cut's throat. How like ye this?
Lapoole. No, wound him not. It must be done so fair and
cunningly
As if he died a common natural death,
For so we must give out to all that ask.
2 Murderer. There is no way then but to smother him.   15
Lapoole. I like that best, yet one thing let me tell ye:
Think not your work contrived so easily
As if you were to match some common man.

5.1. Act 5] 'Actus quint⁹' *in darker ink in left margin.* 3–4. the room . . .
cries] *deleted in MS.* 9. maul] *Parfitt;* malle *MS;* mall *Rossiter.*

5.1.3. *voided*] cleared of people.
3–4. *the room . . . cries*] Lapoole's speeches are cut in several places in this
scene (see also ll. 21, 27, 34–5, 40–3, 279–80, 287–90); the markings in a slightly
darker ink but one associated with the scribe of the MS text. For a discussion
of the significance of these cuts see 'Censorship' section in Introduction.
9. *strive*] struggle.
9–10. *maul his old mazzard*] batter his old skull.
17–23. *Think . . . looks*] Cf. Richard's advice to Clarence's murderers, *R3*,
1.3.344–7.
18. *match*] encounter.

Believe me, sirs, his countenance is such,
So full of dread and lordly majesty,   20
Mixed with such mild and gentle haviour
As will, except you be resolved at full,
Strike you with fear even with his princely looks.
1 Murderer. Not and he looked as grim as Hercules,
As stern and terrible as the devil himself.   25
Lapoole. 'Tis well resolved. Retire yourselves awhile.
Stay in the next withdrawing chamber there,
And when occasion serves I'll call ye forth.
2 Murderer. Do but beckon with your finger, my lord, and like
vultures we come flying and seize him presently.   30
                                        Exeunt two Murderers.
Lapoole. Do so; now by my fairest hopes I swear
The boldness of these villains to this murder
Makes me abhor them and the deed for ever.
Horror of conscience with the King's command
Fights a fell combat in my fearful breast;   35
The King commands his uncle here must die
And my sad conscience bids the contrary
And tells me that his innocent blood thus spilt
Heaven will revenge; murder's a heinous guilt,
A seven times crying sin. Accursèd man,   40
The further that I wade in this foul act
My troubled senses are the more distract,

---

21. Mixed . . . haviour] *deleted in MS.*   27. Stay . . . there] *deleted in MS.*
28. when occasion serves] occasion Serves *is written above the deleted phrase*
I spy the best advantage for ye *in a different ink in MS.*   31. now by my] '&
yett' *deleted before* now; all *deleted after* my *in MS.*   I swear] *Frijlinck (diffi-*
cult to decipher and added in a different ink in MS); of heaven *Halliwell;* I protest
conj. this ed.   34–5. Horror . . . breast] *marked for deletion in MS.*   40–3. A
seven . . . reason] *crossed out in MS.*

---

21. *haviour*] bearing, expression.
24. *and*] even if.
Hercules] mythological Greek hero noted for his strength and courage.
34–46. *Horror . . . least*] The pressures on Lapoole from Richard's insistence on the murder are suggested by Holinshed's account of Mowbray's
delay in carrying out Woodstock's execution. See Appendix B.
35. *fell*] fierce.
40. *seven times*] used rhetorically for emphasis, indicating a large number;
see Onions.
crying] notorious.

Confounded and tormented past my reason.
But there's no lingering: either he must die
Or great King Richard vows my tragedy;   45
Then 'twixt two evils 'tis good to choose the least.
Let danger fright faint fools, I'll save mine own
And let him fall to black destruction.

> *He draws the curtains [and discovers*
> WOODSTOCK *in his bed].*

He sleeps upon his bed. The time serves fitly,
I'll call the murderers in. Sound music there   50
To rock his senses in eternal slumbers.   *Music [sounds].*
Sleep, Woodstock, sleep, thou never more shalt wake.
This town of Calais shall for ever tell
Within her castle walls Plain Thomas fell.

> *Exit* LAPOOLE.

> *Thunder and lightning. Enter the* GHOST *of*
> *the Black Prince.*

1 Ghost. Night, horror and th'eternal shrieks of death   55
Intended to be done this dismal night
Hath shook fair England's great cathedral

48.1–2. SD] *Add. this ed.*

47. *mine own*] i.e. my own life.
48.1. curtains] The text is unclear whether the curtains which Lapoole draws are a curtain or arras across the stage concealing a bed, or the bed-curtains of a four-poster bed which has already been thrust out on to the stage. Both possibilities were familiar to contemporary audiences (see Dessen and Thomson, pp. 24–5) and, whilst both are perfectly feasible here, the disposal of Woodstock's body at ll. 247–56 suggests that the use of a stage curtain is more likely as the murderers appear to carry the body to the bed as if to another room.
51. Music] Besides its function to encourage Woodstock to sleep, the music may have provided an effective and appropriate accompaniment to the ghosts' direful warnings.
54.1. Thunder and lightning] Thunder and lightning became conventional adjuncts to the appearance of ghosts and demons and also as harbingers of tragedy; see Chapman, *Bussy*, 5.3.51.1ff. By the time of *The Revenger's Tragedy* (1606–7) the practice could be parodied as a cliché; see 5.1.41–2.
54.2. the Black Prince] Edward, the Black Prince (1330–76), brother of Thomas of Woodstock and Richard II's father.
55. *eternal*] 'eternal' used here to express extreme abhorence (*OED* 7).

And from my tomb elate at Canterbury
The ghost of Edward the Black Prince is come
To stay King Richard's rage, my wanton son.   60
Thomas of Woodstock, wake! Thy brother calls thee,
Thou royal issue of King Edward's loins,
Thou art beset with murder, rise and fly!
If here thou stay, death comes and thou must die.
Still dost thou sleep? Oh, I am nought but air!   65
Had I the vigour of my former strength
When thou beheldst me fight at Crécy field
Where hand to hand I took King John of France
And his bold sons my captive prisoners,
I'd shake these stiff supporters of thy bed   70
And drag thee from this dull security.
O yet for pity, wake, prevent thy doom!
Thy blood upon my son will surely come;
For which, dear brother Woodstock, haste and fly,
Prevent his ruin and thy tragedy.   *Exit* GHOST.   75

Thunder. Enter Edward the Third's GHOST.

Woodstock. Oh!
2 Ghost. Sleepst thou so soundly and pale death so nigh?
Thomas of Woodstock, wake, my son, and fly!
Thy wrongs have roused thy royal father's ghost
And from his quiet grave King Edward's come   80
To guard thy innocent life. My princely son,
Behold me here, sometimes fair England's lord:

---

76. *Woodstock*] *Frijlinck; direction for Ghost's entry occupies space for speech prefix in MS.*

58. *elate*] raised, lofty; *OED* gives only one citing of this usage dated 1730 (*OED* 1).
60. *stay*] thwart, frustrate.
70. *supporters*] the heraldic figures supporting the arms carved into the bedhead, or, possibly, the bedposts supporting the bed-canopy and curtains which may have been carved in the shapes of heraldic beasts, human or fantastic figures.
71. *dull security*] drowsy slumber, but also with the sense of vulnerable complacency.
75.1. *Edward the Third's* GHOST] Edward III (1313–77), father of the Black Prince and Thomas of Woodstock, grandfather of Richard II.
82. *sometimes*] fomerly.

Seven warlike sons I left, yet being gone
No one succeeded in my kingly throne;
Richard of Bordeaux, my accursèd grandchild,   85
Cut off your titles to the kingly state
And now your lives and all would ruinate,
Murders his grandsire's sons, his father's brothers,
Becomes a landlord to my kingly titles,
Rents out my crown's revènues, racks my subjects   90
That spent their bloods with me in conquering France,
Beheld me ride in state through London streets
And at my stirrup, lowly footing by,
Four captive kings to grace my victory.
Yet that, nor this his riotous youth, can stay   95
Till death hath ta'en his uncles all away.
Thou fifth of Edward's sons, get up and fly,
Haste thee to England, close and speedily.
Thy brothers York and Gaunt are up in arms;
Go join with them, prevent thy further harms.   100
The murderers are at hand—awake, my son!
This hour foretells thy sad destruction.   *Exit* GHOST.
Woodstock. O good angels, guide me—stay, thou blessèd
     spirit!
Thou royal shadow of my kingly father,
Return again; I know thy reverend looks.   105
With thy dear sight once more recomfort me;

---

85. accursèd] *Keller;* accussed *MS.*   103. *Woodstock*] *Halliwell: no speech prefix in MS because margin is eroded.*

83–4. *Seven . . . succeeded*] Of Edward III's seven sons two died in infancy whilst his eldest son, Edward the Black Prince, Richard II's father, died in 1376, a year before Edward III's death.
   86. *cut . . . titles*] Despite the impression which might be created by the Ghost's accusation, Richard gained the throne legitimately, becoming heir on the death of his father, the Black Prince.
   94. *Four . . . victory*] Edward never captured four kings; Rossiter suggests that the Lord Mayor's feasting of four kings in 1357 provided the idea.
   97. *fifth of Edward's sons*] Woodstock was Edward III's seventh son, although the fifth to live to maturity. The fifth son was Edmund Langley, Duke of York.
   98. *close*] secretly.
   99. *Thy . . . arms*] Historically, the ghost's claims are exaggerated; see Appendix B, Holinshed, pp. 489–90.
   106. *recomfort*] console.

Put by the fears my trembling heart foretells,
And here is made apparent to my sight
By dreams and visions of this dreadful night.
Upon my knees I beg it. Ha, protect me Heaven!   110
The doors are all made fast—'twas but my fancy.
All's whist and still, and nothing here appears
But the vast circuit of this empty room.
Thou blessèd hand of mercy, guide my senses!
Afore my God, methoughts as here I slept   115
I did behold in lively form and substance
My father Edward and my warlike brother
Both gliding by my bed, and cried to me
To leave this place, to save my life and fly.
Lighten my fears, dear Lord. I here remain   120
A poor old man thrust from my native country,
Kept and imprisoned in a foreign kingdom.
If I must die, bear record, righteous Heaven,

        Enter LAPOOLE *and the* Murderers.

How I have nightly waked for England's good,
And yet to right her wrongs would spend my blood.   125
Send thy sad doom, King Richard, take my life:
I wish my death might ease my country's grief.
Lapoole. We are prevented; back retire again,
He's risen from his bed.   [*Exit* Murderers.]
                What fate preserves him?
—My lord, how fare you?   130

110–11. *Ha . . . fancy*] Woodstock's response to the Ghosts' warnings
oscillates between dependence and scepticism. Seeking to calm himself, he
takes reassurance from the supposed security of the locked doors of his
chamber and the belief that the Ghosts are figments of his imagination.
112. *whist*] quiet, still.
113. *vast circuit*] perhaps a reference to the entire theatre space which
would hardly have been 'empty'. Such metatheatrical allusions were frequent
in the Renaissance theatre; cf. Tourneur, 3.5.21–2: 'The bastard and the
Duchess have appointed / Their meeting too in this luxurious circle'.
116. *lively*] living.
123.1. SD] MS's entry for Lapoole and the Murderers whilst Woodstock
is still speaking seems intended to show their confusion at seeing (and
hearing) that Woodstock is no longer defencelessly asleep.
125. *yet*] still.
128. *prevented*] forestalled.

Woodstock. Thou canst not kill me, villain!
God's holy angel guards a just man's life
And with his radiant beams as bright as fire
Will guard and keep his righteous innocence.
I am a prince, thou dar'st not murder me.   135
Lapoole. Your grace mistakes, my lord.
Woodstock.   What art thou? Speak.
Lapoole. Lapoole, my lord, this city's governor.
Woodstock. Lapoole, thou art King Richard's flatterer.
O you just gods, record their treachery,
Judge their foul wrongs that under show of friendship   140
Betrayed my simple kind intendiments.
My heart misgave it was no time for revels
When you like masquers came disguised to Plashy,
Joined with that wanton king to trap my life,
For that I know's the end his malice aims at.   145
This castle and my secret sending hither
Imports no less. Therefore I charge ye tell me,
Even by the virtue of nobility,
And partly too on that allegiance
Thou owest the offspring of King Edward's house,   150
If aught thou knowst to prejudice my life
Thou presently reveal and make it known.
Lapoole. Nay, good my lord, forbear that fond suspicion.
Woodstock. I tell thee, Poole, there is no less intended.
Why am I sent thus from my native country,   155
But here at Calais to be murderèd?
And that, Lapoole, confounds my patience.
This town of Calais where I spent my blood
To make it captive to the English king,
Before whose walls great Edward lay encamped   160
With his seven sons almost for fourteen months;

---

141. Betrayed] *Rossiter;* betryd *MS.*

141. *intendiments*] purposes, intentions.
142. *misgave*] suspected.
153. *fond*] foolish.
157. *confounds my patience*] destroys my forbearance.
158–64. *This town . . . won*] The dramatist, in attempting to emphasise
Woodstock's nobility and that of his brothers, allows himself considerable
poetic licence here since Edward III took Calais in 1346, eight years before
Woodstock's birth.

Where the Black Prince my brother, and myself,
The peers of England and our royal father,
Fearless of wounds, ne'er left till it was won;
And was't to make a prison for his son?   165
O righteous Heavens, why do you suffer it?
Lapoole. Disquiet not your thoughts, my gracious lord,
There is no hurt intended, credit me;
Although awhile your freedom be abridged.
I know the King. If you would but submit   170
And write your letters to his majesty,
Your reconcilement might be easily wrought.
Woodstock. For what should I submit or ask his mercy?
Had I offended, with all low submission
I'd lay my neck unto the block before him   175
And willingly endure the stroke of death.
But if not so, why should my fond entreaties
Make my true loyalty appear like treason?
No, no, Lapoole, let guilty men beg pardons,
My mind is clear; and I must tell ye, sir,   180
Princes have hearts like pointed diamonds
That will in sunder burst afore they bend,
And such lives here, though death King Richard send.
Yet fetch me pen and ink, I'll write to him
Not to entreat, but to admonish him   185
That he forsake his foolish ways in time
And learn to govern like a virtuous prince,
Call home his wise and reverend counsellors,
Thrust from his court those cursèd flatterers
That hourly works the realm's confusion.   190
This counsel, if he follow, may in time
Pull down those mischiefs that so fast do climb.
Lapoole. Here's pen and paper, my lord, wilt please ye
          write?
Woodstock. Anon I will. Shut to the doors and leave me.
Goodnight, Lapoole, and pardon me, I prithee,   195

169.] *There is a scribble in the right-hand margin of MS, probably* Wod.
175. unto] *Rossiter;* upon *conj. Keller;* under *MS.*   183. send] *Halliwell,*
Keller; s< *MS.*   184. him] *Halliwell, Keller;* h< *MS.*

180. *clear*] free from guilt.
194. *Anon*] shortly.

That my sad fear made question of thy faith;
My state is fearful and my mind was troubled
Even at thy entrance with most fearful visions,
Which made my passions more extreme and hasty.
Out of my better judgement I repent it   200
And will reward thy love. Once more, goodnight.
Lapoole. Good rest unto your grace—[*Aside*] I mean in
    death.
This dismal night, thou breathst thy latest breath.
He sits to write; I'll call the murderers in
To steal behind and closely strangle him.   205
                              Exit LAPOOLE.
Woodstock. So help me heaven, I know not what to write,
What style to use, nor how I should begin.
My method is too plain to greet a king.
I'll nothing say t'excuse or clear myself
For I have nothing done that needs excuse,   210
But tell him plain, though here I spend my blood,
I wish his safety and all England's good.

                  Enter both the Murderers.

1 Murderer. Creep close to his back, ye rogue; be ready with
    the towel, when I have knocked him down, to strangle
    him.   215
2 Murderer. Do it quickly whilst his back is towards ye, ye
    damned villain; if thou let'st him speak but a word, we
    shall not kill him.
1 Murderer. I'll watch him for that. Down of your knees and
    creep, ye rascal.   220

---

210. done] *Carpenter; doe MS.*   213–15.] *Rossiter; creepe . . . towell / when
. . . hime MS.*

207. *style*] title with which to address the king.
213–46. *be ready . . . murdered now*] Cf. Holinshed, p. 489, 'and there in
the lodging called the princes In, he caused his servants to cast featherbeds
upon him, and so smother him to death, or otherwise to strangle him with
towels (as some write)'. Woodstock's death, performed partly by the use of
a feather bed (see ll. 237–9), has parallels with that of Edward II in Marlowe's
play (4.5); cf also Duke Humphrey's death in the text of *Contention*, 3.2.160ff.
(see below, 252–3 n.).
217–18. *if . . . him*] See above, ll. 17–23 n.

Woodstock. Have mercy, God, my sight o'th' sudden fails
    me;
  I cannot see my paper.
  My trembling fingers will not hold my pen;
  A thick congealèd mist o'erspreads the chamber.
  I'll rise and view the room.   225
1 Murderer. Not too fast for falling.   *Strikes him.*
Woodstock. What villain hand hath done a deed so bad
  To drench his black soul in a prince's blood?
1 Murderer. Do ye prate, sir? Take that and that! 'Zounds, put
  the towel about's throat and strangle him quickly, ye   230
  slave, or by the heart of Hell I'll fell thee too.
2 Murderer. 'Tis done, ye damned slave. Pull, ye dog, and pull
  thy soul to hell in doing it, for thou hast killed the truest
  subject that ever breathed in England.
1 Murderer. Pull, rogue, pull! Think of the gold we shall have   235
  for doing it and then let him and thee go to'th' devil
  together. Bring in the feather bed and roll him up in that
  till he be smothered and stifled, and life and soul pressed
  out together. Quickly, ye hell hound!
2 Murderer. Here, here, ye cannibal. 'Zounds, he kicks and   240
  sprawls; lie on's breast, ye villain.
1 Murderer. Let him sprawl and hang, he's sure enough for
  speaking. Pull off the bed now; smooth down his hair and
  beard; close his eyes and set his neck right. Why so, all
  fine and cleanly. Who can say that this man was murdered   245
  now?

          [*Enter*] LAPOOLE.

222–4.] *Rossiter;* I . . . hold / my . . . chamber *MS.* 226. *1 Murderer*]
Rossiter; 2 m: *MS.* 236. doing] *only* d *clearly visible in MS.*

---

226. 1 Murderer] Despite MS's attribution of this speech to the Second
Murderer, it is clear (see ll. 9–10) that it is the First Murderer who has the
hammer, and that it is he, not the Second Murderer, who strikes Woodstock
with it (see ll. 229–34).
  Not . . . falling] Rossiter explains this as a proverbial expression meaning
'There's no hurry in running into trouble'; he compares Porter's *Two Angry
Women*, l. 875. Cf. also the proverb, 'One may sooner fall than rise' (Tilley F37).
  241. *sprawls*] struggles in a death agony.
  242–3. *sure . . . speaking*] incapable of speaking.
  243. *bed*] i.e. feather bed.

Lapoole. What, is he dead?

2 Murderer. As a door-nail, my lord. What will ye do with his
body?

Lapoole. Take it up gently; lay him in his bed.   250
Then shut the door as if he there had died.

1 Murderer. It cannot be perceived otherwise, my lord. Never
was murder done with such rare skill. At our return we
shall expect reward, my lord.

Lapoole. 'Tis ready told.   255
Bear in the body, then return and take it.

                                Exeunt [Murderers] *with the body.*
Within there, ho!

                        [*Enter* Soldiers.]

Soldiers. My lord?

Lapoole. Be ready with your weapons, guard the room.
There's two false traitors entered the Duke's chamber,   260
Plotting to bear him thence, betray the castle,
Deliver up the town and all our lives
To the French forces that are hard at hand
To second their attempts. Therefore stand close

250–9.] *speech prefixes supplied by Rossiter; left margin of MS cropped.*   252–4.]
Parfitt; It . . . was / murder . . . shall / expect . . . lord *MS;* It . . . lord /
Never . . . skill / At . . . lord *Rossiter.*   255–6. 'Tis . . . it] *Rossiter; one line in
MS.*   256.1. SD] *at ll. 253–4 in MS.*   257.1. SD] *Rossiter.*   258. *Soldiers*]
Rossiter; Souldier Keller; Servant Halliwell.   259. Be . . . weapons] draw all
deleted before be readie *and* soldiers *deleted after* weapons *in MS.*   264. To
. . . attempts] *deleted in MS.*

248. *As a door-nail*] Proverbial, 'As dead (deaf, dumb) as a Doornail'
(Tilley D567).

251. *shut the door*] i.e. close the stage curtain, see 48.1 n. above.

252–3. *Never . . . skill*] For the method of the murder compare the
Quarto text of *The Contention,* 'Then the Curtaines being drawne, Duke
Humphrey is discovered in his bed, and two men lying on his brest and smother-
ing him in his bed'. The secrecy which Lapoole seeks is also paralleled in *The
Contention* by Suffolk's direction, 'Then see cloathes laid smooth about him
still, / That when the King comes, he may percieve / No other, but that he
dide of his owne accord' (sig. E2r). For a parallel use of the feather bed cf.
Marlowe, *Edward,* 5.5.

255. *told*] counted out.

264. *To . . . attempts*] Parfitt suggests that this phrase may have been cut
as being offensive to French sensibilities, but see 'Censorship' section in
Introduction.

And as they enter seize them presently.   265
Our will's your warrant. Use no further words
But hew them straight in pieces with your swords.
1 Soldier. I warrant ye, my lord. And their skins were scaled
   with brass we have swords will pierce them. Come, sirs,
   be ready.   270

                    Enter the Murderers.

1 Murderer. Come, ye miching rascal, the deed's done and all
   things performed rarely. We'll take our reward, steal close
   out o'th' town, buy us fresh geldings, spur, cut and ride
   till we are past all danger, I warrant thee.
Lapoole. Give their reward there. Quick, I say!   275
Soldiers. Down with the traitors. Kill the villains.
Both Murderers. Hell and the devil! 'Zounds, hold, ye
   rascals!

                They kill the Murderers.

Lapoole. Drag hence their bodies; hurl them in the sea.
   The black reward of death's a traitor's pay.
                            Exeunt Soldiers *with their bodies.*
So, this was well performed. Now who but we   280
Can make report of Woodstock's tragedy?
Only he died a natural death at Calais—
So must we give it out, or else King Richard
Through Europe's kingdoms will be hardly censured.
His headstrong uncles, York and Lancaster   285
Are up we hear in open arms against him.
The gentlemen and commons of the realm,
Missing the good old Duke, their plain protector,

278–9. Drag . . . pay] *marked for omission and crossed out in a different ink (dark grey) in MS.* 284. Europe's] *Rossiter;* Europe *MS.* 287–90. The gentlemen . . . sides] *marked for omission in MS in the same or a slightly darker brown ink.*

271. *miching*] sneaking, skulking.
273. *cut*] whip (*OED* 3) or 'run away' (*OED* 19).
278. *Drag . . . sea*] Cf. Marlowe, *Edward*, 5.5.116–17 where the murderer, Lightborn, is killed and his body thrown in the moat.
287–90. *The gentlemen . . . sides*] These lines may have been marked for cutting because of their frank admission of the extent of popular support for the lords' rebellion against their sovereign.

Break their allegiance to their sovereign lord
And all revolt upon the barons' sides.   290
To help which harm, I'll o'er to England straight
And with th'old troops of soldiers ta'en from Calais
I'll back King Richard's power, for should he fail
And his great uncles get the victory,
His friends are sure to die; but if he win   295
They fall, and we shall rise whilst Richard's king.   *Exit.*

[5.2]

> *Drums. March within. Enter* TRESILIAN *and* NIMBLE
> *with armour.*

Tresilian. These proclamations we have sent abroad,
　　Wherein we have accused the dukes of treason,
　　Will daunt their pride and make the people leave them.
　　I hope no less at least. Where art thou, Nimble?
Nimble. So loaden with armour I cannot stir, my lord.   5
Tresilian. Whose drums were those that beat even now?
Nimble. King Richard's drums, my lord. The young lords are
　　pressing soldiers.
Tresilian. Oh, and do they take their press with willingness?
Nimble. As willing as a punk that's pressed on a featherbed.   10
　　They take their pressing apiece with great patience.

296. *Exit*] *Exeunt MS.*

5.2.10. as a punk] as a puncke *MS;* as spuncke *Halliwell.*   11. their press-
ing] *conj. Keller;* ther< *MS;* their shilling *conj. Carpenter.*

　　5.2.0.1. March within] presumably the sound of a march, i.e. the sound
of drums, coming from within the tiring house which establishes the warlike
atmosphere. Whilst the SD 'A march afar off' is common in Renaissance
drama (see *Ham.,* 5.2.301), the unusual feature here is that it is Tresilian and
Nimble who enter rather than the anticipated troops, thus creating a comic
anticlimax which is reinforced by Nimble's exaggerated armour. Cf.
Ambidexter's comic entry in Preston's *Cambyses,* ll. 125.1–3: *'with an old
capcase on his head, an old pale about his hips for harness, a scummer and a potlid
by his side, and a rake on his shoulder'.*
　　3. daunt] humble, subdue.
　　8. pressing] conscripting.
　　10. punk] whore.
　　11. pressing] Parfitt notes that 'shilling' is a possible alternative reading
since Tresilian's reference to 'sovereign' could be held as a pun, albeit uncharacteristic of the character.

Marry, the lords no sooner turn their backs but they run
away like sheep, sir.
Tresilian. They shall be hanged like dogs for't.
What, dares the slaves refuse their sovereign?   15
Nimble. They say the proclamation's false, my lord,
And they'll not fight against the King's friends.
Tresilian. So I feared as much and since 'tis come to this
I must provide betime and seek for safety;
For now the King and our audacious peers   20
Are grown to such a height of burning rage
As nothing now can quench their kindled ire
But open trial by the sword and lance;
And then I fear King Richard's part will fail.
Nimble, our soldiers run thou sayst?   25
Nimble. Ay, by my troth, my lord, and I think 'tis our best
course to run after them, for if they run now, what will
they do when the battle begins? If we tarry here and the
King's uncles catch us, we are sure to be hanged, my lord.
Have ye no trick of law to defend us, no demur or writ   30
of error to remove us?
Tresilian. Nimble, we must be wise.
Nimble. Then let's not stay to have more wit beaten into our
heads. I like not that, my lord.
Tresilian. I am a man for peace and not for war.   35
Nimble. And yet they say you have made more wrangling
i'th' land
Than all the wars has done this seven years.
Tresilian. This battle will revenge their base exclaims.
But hearst thou, Nimble, I'll not be there today.
One man amongst so many is no maim,   40
Therefore I'll keep aloof till all be done.
If good I stay, if bad away I run.
Nimble, it shall be so. I'll neither fight nor die,

---

27. them] *conj. Keller;* th< *MS.* they] the *MS.* 43. it . . . so] I am
resolved *altered in MS to* It shalbe soe *by interlining and deletion.*

---

17. *friends*] i.e. the uncles not the King's minions.
30. *demur*] demurrer, a legal term; a pleading which stops or delays an
action.
38. *exclaims*] protests, outcries.
40. *maim*] loss.

But thus resolved disguise myself and fly.

       Exit TRESILIAN.

Nimble. 'Tis the wisest course, my lord. And I'll go put off 45
mine armour that I may run lustily too. *Exit* NIMBLE.

[5.3]

   Enter with drum and colours, YORK, LANCASTER,
    ARUNDEL, SURREY, *with the* DUCHESS *of*
   GLOUCESTER [*weeping*], *and Soldiers and* CHENEY.

Lancaster. Go to our tents, dear sister, cease your sorrows.
 We will revenge our noble brother's wrongs
 And force that wanton tyrant to reveal
 The death of his dear uncle, harmless Woodstock,
 So traitorously betrayed.
York.   Alack, good man,   5
 It was an easy task to work on him,
 His plainness was too open to their view:
 He feared no wrong because his heart was true.
 Good sister, cease your weeping, there's none here
 But are as full of woe and touched as near.   10
 Conduct and guard her, Cheney, to the tent.
 Expect to hear severest punishment
 On all their heads that have procured his harms,

---

46. lustily] *Rossiter;* t *badly formed in MS;* lasely *Halliwell, Keller;* easely
Carpenter.

5.3.] The dramatist here draws on the events of both 1387 and the
late 1390s. De Vere attempted to challenge the Lords' miltary force by raising an army in the north-west, but on meeting them at Radcot Bridge in
Oxfordshire he fled and the King's forces were dispersed. The deaths of the
King's favourites, i.e. Greene etc., belong to Bolingbroke's *coup d'état* of
1399.

 0.2–3. DUCHESS ... [weeping]] The participation of the Duchess in
the revolt against Richard is the dramatist's invention and is not recorded in
the Chronicles. Her emotional presence here acts as an effective reminder
and emblem of Gloucester's death and of the need for revenge. This treatment may have prompted Shakespeare's presentation of the Duchess
and Gaunt in *R2*, 1.2. Rossiter argues that a knowledge of the Duchess's
part here is assumed by Shakespeare in her single and brief appearance in
R2.

 6. *work on*] deceive, entrap.

Struck from the terror of our threat'ning arms.
Duchess of Gloucester. May all the powers of Heaven assist
　　your hands,   15
　And may their sins sit heavy on their souls
　That they in death this day may perish all
　That traitorously conspired good Woodstock's fall!
　　　　　　　　　　Exeunt CHENEY *and the* DUCHESS.
Lancaster. If he be dead, by good King Edward's soul,
　We'll call King Richard to a strict account   20
　For that and for his realm's misgovernment.
　You peers of England, raised in righteous arms
　Here to re-edify our country's ruin,
　Join all your hearts and hands never to cease
　Till with our swords we work fair England's peace.   25
　　　　　　　　　　　　　　　　　　　　　Drums
Arundel. Most princely Lancaster, our lands and lives
　Are to these just proceedings ever vowed.
Surrey. Those flattering minions that o'erturns the state
　This day in death shall meet their endless fate.
York. Never such vipers were endured so long   30
　To grip and eat the hearts of all the kingdom.   *Drums*
Lancaster. This day shall here determinate all wrongs.
　The meanest man taxed by their foul oppressions
　Shall be permitted freely to accuse,
　And right they shall have to regain their own;   35
　Or all shall sink to dark confusion. *Drums sound within.*
Arundel. How now, what drums are these?

　　　　　　　　　　Enter CHENEY.

5.3.30. *York*] *Rossiter;* >rondell *crossed out,* >rke *on line below in MS.*
32. *Lancaster*] [*La*]*nck Keller;* >ck *MS; Surrye Halliwell.*   35. *own*] *Rossiter;*
one *MS.*   36. SD] [*Dromes*] *sounds* [*wi*]*thin. Halliwell;* >s sounds *in left-hand*
margin at l. 35, >in *on line below in MS;* Drums. Sounds within. *Parfitt.*
37. *Arundel*] *Arondell: Halliwell;York. Rossiter; speaker's name omitted in MS*
where an indeterminate mark has been made.

────────────

23. *re-edify*] rebuild, restore.
32. *determinate*] put an end to.
33. *taxed*] burdened, with an allusion to the blank charters.
34. *accuse*] utter charges, bring an accusation.
37. Arundel] Since Arundel is only partially involved in the passionate
conversation at this point, it would seem appropriate that he alerts the others
to the noise of off-stage drums. Rossiter's preference for York as the speaker

Cheney. To arms, my lords, the minions of the King
    Are swiftly marching on to give ye battle.
Lancaster. They march to death then, Cheney. Dare the
    traitors   40
    Presume to brave the field with English princes?
York. Where is King Richard? He was resolved but lately
    To take some hold of strength and so secure him.
Cheney. Knowing their states were all so desperate
    It seems they have persuaded otherwise,   45
    For now he comes with full resolve to fight.
    Lapoole this morning is arrived at court
    With the Calais soldiers and some French supplies
    To back this now intended enterprise.
Lancaster. Those new supplies have spurred their forward
    hopes   50
    And thrust their resolutions boldly on
    To meet with death and sad destruction.
York. Their drums are near. Just heaven direct this deed
    And as our cause deserves our fortunes speed.

                                          March about.

      Enter with drum and colours the KING [RICHARD],
      GREENE, BUSHY, BAGOT, SCROOP, LAPOOLE *and*
      Soldiers. *They march about all.*

---

38. *Cheney*] *Halliwell; SD for Cheney's entrance fills space of speech prefix in left margin in MS.*

on the grounds that 'only Dukes should interrrupt ducal utterances' is unconvincing.

    41. *brave . . . princes*] i.e. face or encounter English princes on the battle-field. Lancaster's question emphasises the minions' low-born origins.

    42–3. *Where . . . him*] The action appears to be based in the events of 1388; in that year Richard 'kept his Christmas, not at Westminster, but in the Tower; not douting but there to be defended what chance soever should happen' (Holinshed, p. 462).

    43. *hold of strength*] stronghold, fortress.

    45. *persuaded*] i.e. persuaded the King.

    54. *speed*] fare, thrive.

    54.1. *March about*] i.e. about the stage. The dukes' party march about the stage and then take up their position to await the entrance of Richard's forces.

    54.4. SD *They . . . all*] The repeated SD to march about the stage suggests a formal presentation of the armies' manoeuvring before taking up their

King Richard. Although we could have easily surprised,   55
    Dispersed and overthrown your rebel troops
    That draw your swords against our sacred person,
    The highest God's anointed deputy,
    Breaking your holy oaths to Heaven and us;
    Yet of our mild and princely clemency   60
    We have forborne, that by this parliament
    We might be made partaker of the cause
    That moved ye rise in this rebellious sort.
Lancaster. Hast thou, King Richard, made us infamous
    By proclamations false and impudent?   65
    Hast thou condemned us, in our absence too,
    As most notorious traitors to the crown;
    Betrayed our brother Woodstock's harmless life
    And sought base means to put us all to death,
    And dost thou now plead dotish ignorance   70
    Why we are banded thus in our defence?
Greene. Methinks your treasons to his majesty,
    Raising his subjects 'gainst his royal life,
    Should make ye beg for mercy at his feet.
King Richard. You have forgotten, Uncle Lancaster,   75
    How you in prison murdered cruelly
    A friar Carmelite because he was
    To bring in evidence against your grace
    Of most ungracious deeds and practices.

---

65. impudent] *Keller;* Impodent *MS;* impotent *conj. Rossiter.*   71. banded]
conj. Carpenter; landed *MS.*

opposing battle-lines. Cf. the confrontation between the two armies in *JC*,
5.1.20.1.
   61. *parliament*] parley.
   65. *impudent*] Parfitt notes that MS's spelling 'Impodent' unites 'impudent' and 'impotent'.
   70. *dotish*] childish, foolish.
   71. *banded*] Carpenter's conjecture is preferable to MS's 'landed' since
the dukes have joined together rather than invaded the country from abroad.
'Banded' may also carry the sense of taking up position in self-defence (see
note to l. 54.4 above). It is possible though that 'landed' is correct and that
the dramatist had in mind Bolingbroke's return from France, which historically brought about the deaths of Bushy and Green. See *R2*, 3.1.
   75-9. *You . . . practices*] Rossiter traces this incident to Holinshed's
account of 1383 of an Irish friar who accused Lancaster of plotting

Lancaster. And you, my lord, remember not so well   80
    That by that Carmelite at London once,
    When at a supper, you'd have poisoned us.
York. For shame, King Richard, leave this company
    That like dark clouds obscure the sparkling stars
    Of thy great birth and true nobility.   85
Arundel. Yield to your uncles. Who but they should have
    The guidance of your sacred state and council?
Bagot. Yield first your heads and so he shall be sure
    To keep his person and his state secure.
King Richard. And by my crown, if still you thus persist   90
    Your heads and hearts ere long shall answer it.
Arundel. Not till ye send for more supplies from France,
    For England will not yield ye strength to do it.
York. Thou well mayst doubt their loves that lost their hearts.
    Ungracious prince, cannot thy native country   95
    Find men to back this desperate enterprise?
Lancaster. His native country? Why, that is France, my lords!
    At Bordeaux was he born, which place allures
    And ties his deep affections still to France.
    Richard is English blood, not English born.   100
    Thy mother travailed in unhappy hours
    When she at Bordeaux left her heavy load.
    The soil is fat for wines, not fit for men,
    And England now laments that heavy time.
    Her royalties are lost, her state made base,   105
    And thou no king but landlord now become
    To this great state that terrored Christendom.

---

93. strength] ng *altered and* th *added in MS.*   94. York] *MS (altered from*
lanck).   hearts] *Rossiter;* har< *MS.*

against the King and who was tortured to death by Lord John Holland and
Greene.
    81. *That . . . once*] Lancaster refers to the Carmelite who attempted to
poison the magnates at the beginning of the play (see 1.1.21).
    83. *company*] i.e. the company of flatterers.
    98. *Bordeaux*] Richard was born in Bordeaux on 6 January 1367 and spent
the first four years of his life in France. MS's anglicised spelling 'Burdex'
here and at l. 102 may convey Lancaster's dismissive pronunciation of
Richard's Frenchified roots.
    101. *travailed*] suffered the pains of childbirth.
    105. *royalties*] sovereign rule of state (*OED* 1c).
    107. *terrored*] terrified; this usage predates *OED*'s first citing (1635).

King Richard. I cannot brook these braves. Let drums
      sound death
And strike at once to stop this traitor's breath.
Bagot. Stay, my dear lord, and once more hear me, princes. 110
The King was minded ere this brawl began
To come to terms of composition.
Lancaster. Let him revoke the proclamations,
Clear us of all supposèd crimes of treason,
Reveal where our good brother Gloucester keeps, 115
And grant that these pernicious flatterers
May by the law be tried, to quit themselves
Of all such heinous crimes alleged against them,
And we'll lay down our weapons at thy feet.
All Minions. Presumptuous traitors!
All Lords.   Traitors? 120
King Richard. Again we double it, rebellious traitors!
Traitors to Heaven and us. Draw all your swords
And fling defiance to those traitorous lords.
All Minions. Let our drums thunder and begin the fight.
All Lords. Just Heaven protect us and defend the right. 125
                    [*Drums.*] *Exeunt severally.*

110–21. Stay ... rebellious traitors] *lines marked for deletion in MS in a
darker ink.* 120. *All Minions*] *conj. Frijlinck; King's Men Rossiter;* K
deleted in MS, followed by all: my:. *All Lords*] *This ed.; Lords' Men Rossiter;*
All *MS.* 124. *All Minions*] all: *MS,* Enter Bagg: & Cheney *deleted in
left margin.* 125. *All Lords*] all: *MS,* >nter Bushey: & Surry: *deleted in
left margin.* 125.1. SD] *This ed.;* Exeunt severally *Rossiter:* Exeunt omnes
MS.

108. *braves*] defiant insults.
110–21. *Stay ... rebellious traitors*] It seems unlikely that these lines are
marked for deletion for purely dramatic reasons since they bring the confrontation to a head. It is more likely that Lancaster's demand that the King
capitulates and deserts his advisers was thought contentious either by the
acting company or by the censor; cf. 5.1.287–90 and see 'Censorship' section
in Introduction.
112. *terms of composition*] agreement in settling differences.
115. *keeps*] dwells, lodges.
117. *quit*] acquit, clear.
124–5.] The deleted entrances 'Bagg: & Cheney' and 'Bushy: & Surry'
suggest an earlier intention to present alternative combats to the one shown
between Greene and Cheney in 5.4. Possibly the copyist has included these
superseded stage directions from the author's foul papers before realising
their redundancy.

[5.4]

Alarum. Enter GREENE *and* CHENEY:
[*they*] *meet* [*both*] *armed.*

Cheney. Stand, traitor! For thou canst not 'scape my sword.
Greene. What villain fronts me with the name of traitor?
    Was't thou, false Cheney? Now, by King Richard's love,
    I'll tilt thy soul out for that base reproach.
    I would thy master and the late Protector,   5
    With both his treacherous brothers, Gaunt and York,
    Were all opposed, with thee, to try these arms:
    I'd seal't on all your hearts.
Cheney.   This shall suffice
    To free the kingdom from thy villainies.

Alarum. They fight. Enter ARUNDEL.

Arundel. Thou huntst a noble game, right warlike Cheney.   10
    Cut but this ulcer off, thou healst the kingdom.
    Yield thee, false traitor, most detested man,
    That settest King Richard 'gainst his reverend uncles,
    To shed the royal bloods and make the realm
    Weep for their timeless desolation.   15
    Cast down thy weapons, for by this my sword
    We'll bear thee from this place, alive or dead.
Greene. Come both then! I'll stand firm and dare your worst.
    He that flies from it, be his soul accurst!
             [*They fight and* GREENE *is slain.*]
Arundel. So may the foes of England fall in blood,   20

5.4.0.2. SD] *Add. this ed.; meets Armde MS; meets Arund*[*ell*] *Carpenter.*
9.1. *Alarum*] A>larum *in left-hand margin at l. 8 in MS. They fight*] Th y F
gh *largely obliterated in MS.* 18. *Greene*] Ch *deleted before Gree: in MS.* 19.1.
SD] *Halliwell, Keller;* >& >ne *in left-hand margin of MS (on ll. 19 and 20).*

    5.4.0.1 Alarum] frequently used to indicate the off-stage sounds of battle.
Edelman, pp. 52–3, argues not only for the sound of trumpets and drums
but, more impressively, for the sound of cannon, thus establishing a vivid
sense of conflict for the audience.
    2. *fronts me*] confronts me, challenges me.
    4. *tilt . . . out*] i.e. drive your soul from your body.
    8. *I'd . . . hearts*] i.e. 'I'd stamp the seal of traitor on your hearts'.
    15. *timeless*] untimely, ill-timed.
    19.1. GREENE is slain] Historically Greene was executed, with Bushy, by
Bolingbroke at Bristol in 1399; see *R2*, 3.1.

Most desolate traitor. Up with his body, Cheney,
And hale it to the tent of Lancaster.

[*Enter* KIN]G, BAGOT, BUSHY, SCROOP *and* Soldiers.

Cheney. Stand firm, my lord, here's rescue.
Arundel.   Courage then,
We'll bear this body hence in spite of them. *They fight.*

To them enter LANCASTER, YORK *and* SURREY *and
beats them all away.* [*Exeunt fighting.*] *Manet the King
*[*with* GREENE S *corpse*].

King Richard. O princely youth, King Richard's dearest
          friend,   25
What heavy star this day had dominance
To cut off all thy flow'ring youthful hopes!
Prosper, proud rebels, as you dealt by him.
Hard-hearted uncles, unrelenting churls,
That here have murdered all my earthly joys.   30
O my dear Greene, wert thou alive to see
How I'll revenge thy timeless tragedy
On all their heads that did but lift a hand
To hurt this body that I held so dear.
Even by this kiss, and by my crown I swear—   35

Alarum. Enter BAGOT, BUSHY *and* SCROOP
to the King.

21. desolate] *Rossiter;* dessolat *MS;* dissolute *Parfitt.*   22.1. Enter KING]
Halliwell; >g *MS.*   23–4. Courage . . . them] *Rossiter; one line in MS.*   24.
1–3. SD] *This ed.; To them Enter* lancaster, yorke & Surry: & *beats them all
away Manett the King (Enter . . . away crossed out) MS; To them . . . away.
Exeunt fighting, all but the* KING *Rossiter.*   25. friend] friends *(s crossed out)
MS.*

---

21. *desolate*] abandoned, lost. Parfitt's 'dissolute' whilst a plausible reading
in view of the similar spelling in the MS at 1.1.157, is unnecessary here where
'desolate' makes appropriate sense.
    24.3. [*with* GREENE'S corpse]] It is plain that, despite Arundel's inten-
tion to carry off Greene's corpse (ll. 21–2), the body remains on stage since
King Richard addresses and kisses it at l. 35. There is some confusion in the
MS as to what precisely is intended at this point; we have retained the deleted
entry of Lancaster etc. and the subsequent action, since the status of the
deletion is uncertain and the entry, anticipated by Cheney at l. 23, serves to
clear the stage of all but King Richard mourning over Greene's body, thus
allowing a dramatic focus on Richard's grief.

Bagot. Away, my lord. Stand not to wail his death.
  The field is lost; our soldiers shrink and fly;
  Lapoole is taken prisoner by the lords.
  Hie to the Tower; there is no help in swords.
Scroop. Still to continue war were childishness.   40
  Their odds a mountain, ours a molehill is.
Bushy. Let's fly to London and make strong the Tower.
  Loud proclamations post throughout the camp
  With promise of reward to all that take us.
  Get safety for our lives, my princely lord;   45
  If here we stay we shall be all betrayed.
King Richard. O my dear friends, the fearful wrath of
    Heaven
  Sits heavy on our heads for Woodstock's death.
  Blood cries for blood, and that almighty hand
  Permits not murder unrevenged to stand.   50
  Come, come,
  We yet may hide ourselves from worldly strength,
  But Heaven will find us out and strike at length.
                        Alarum
  Each lend a hand to bear this load of woe
  That erst King Richard loved and tendered so.   55
      Exeunt omnes [*bearing the body of* GREENE].

50–1. Permits . . . stand / Come, come] *Parfitt; one line in MS.* 55.1. SD]
*Add. Rossiter; Bush / & lancaster / Enter (spread over three lines in the left-hand
margin of MS) added in a different ink but apparently in the same hand as the text.*

47–53. *the fearful . . . length*] Statements of God's overriding justice are
commonplace in the didactic literature of the period; see, for example,
'Thomas, Duke of Gloucester' in *Mirror*, p. 99: 'Alas king Rycharde sore
mayst thou rewe: / whiche by this facte preparedst the waye, / Of thy harde
destynie to hasten the daye. // For blood axeth blood as guerdon dewe, / And
vengeaunce for vengeaunce is iust rewarde, / O ryghteous God thy iudge-
mentes are true, / For looke what measure we other awarde, / The same for
vs agayne is preparde: / Take heed ye princes by examples past, / Blood wyll
haue blood, eyther fyrst or last.' Richard's recognition of his crimes here may
perhaps prepare the way for the play's resolution in terms of repentance and
uneasy truce between the King and the nobles; but since the text is incomplete this must remain speculative. Rossiter suggests that Shakespeare recalls
these lines in *R2*, 1.1.98–106.
    49. *Blood . . . blood*] Cf. the proverb, 'Blood will have blood' (Tilley B458).
    55.1.] The marginal entry for Bushy and Lancaster seems to have no rel-
evance to this context; Frijlinck speculates that it may be a note for a different scene.

[5.5]

Enter TRESILIAN, *disguised, and* NIMBLE.

Tresilian. Where art thou, Nimble?

Nimble. As light as a feather, my lord. I have put off my
shoes that I might run lustily. The battle's lost and
they're all prisoners. What shall we do, my lord? Yonder's
a ditch, we may run along that and ne'er be seen, I   5
warrant.

Tresilian. I did suspect no less, and so 'tis fall'n;
The day is lost and dashed are all our hopes.
King Richard's taken prisoner by the peers.
O that I were upon some steepy rock   10
Where I might tumble headlong to the sea
Before those cruel lords do seize on me.

Nimble. O that I were transformed into a mouse that I might
creep into any hole i'th' house, and I cared not.

Tresilian. Come, Nimble, 'tis no time to use delay.   15
I'll keep me in this poor disguise awhile
And so unknown prolong my weary life
In hope King Richard shall conclude my peace.
                                                Sound retreat.
Hark, hark, the trumpets call the soldiers back,
Retreat is sounded. Now the time serves fit   20
And we may steal away from hence. Away, good
Nimble.

Nimble. Nay, stay, my lord. 'Slid, and ye go that way, farewell.
But and you'll be ruled by me, I have thought of a trick
that ye shall scape them all most bravely.

5.5.3. shoes] *Halliwell;* shoo<e *MS.*   4. they're all] *Rossiter;* a[ll are] *Halliwell, Keller;* t<h *MS.*   5. a ditch] *Halliwell, Keller;* a< *MS.*   6. warrant]
Halliwell; warra< *MS;* warrant you sir *Rossiter.*   13–14. I might creep]
Rossiter; I [might rune] *Halliwell, Keller;* I< *MS.*   22. Nimble] nim< *MS.*
farewell] *conj. Keller;* way< . *MS.*   23. a trick] *Halliwell, Keller;* a< *MS.*
24. that] *Halliwell, Keller; illegible in MS.*

5.5.0.1. disguised] Cf. Stow: 'This man had disfigured himselfe as if
he had beene a poore weake man, in frize coate, all old and torne, and
had artificially made himself a long beard . . . and had defiled his face,
to the end hee might not be knowen but by his speach.' See Appendix
C.

13. *transformed . . . mouse*] Cf. Marlowe, *Faustus* (A text), 1.4.61–2.

Tresilian. Bethink thyself, good Nimble, quickly man!   25
Nimble. I'll meditate, my lord, and then I'm for ye. [Aside].
    Now, Nimble, show thyself a man of valour. Think of thy
    fortunes: 'tis a hanging matter if thou conceal him;
    besides, there's a thousand marks for him that takes him,
    with the dukes' favours and free pardon. Besides, he's but   30
    a coward, he would ne'er have run from the battle else.
    Saint Tantony assist me, I'll set upon him presently.—My
    lord, I have thought upon this trick: I must take ye
    prisoner.
Tresilian. How, prisoner?   35
Nimble. There's no way to 'scape else. Then must I carry ye
    to the king's uncles, who presently condemns ye for a
    traitor, sends ye away to hanging, and then 'God bless
    my Lord Tresilian'!
Tresilian. Wilt thou betray thy master, villain?   40
Nimble. Ay, if my master be a villain. You think 'tis nothing
    for a man to be hanged for his master? You hear not the
    proclamation?
Tresilian. What proclamation?
Nimble. O, sir, all the country's full of them: that whosoever   45
    sees you, does not presently take ye and bring ye to the
    lords, shall be hanged for his labour. Therefore no more
    words lest I raise the whole camp upon ye. Ye see one of
    your own swords of justice drawn over ye. Therefore go
    quietly lest I cut your head off and save the hangman a   50
    labour.
Tresilian. O villain!
Nimble. No more words, away, sir!   *Exeunt.*

---

26. SD] *Rossiter.*   45. all] alls *MS* (s *crossed out*).

32. *Saint Tantony*] St Antony of Egypt; the saint was pictured with a
pig for his page which followed him everywhere. Nimble presumably calls
upon St Antony in the hope that Tresilian will follow his advice without
demur; cf. the proverb, 'To follow one like a Saint Anthony's pig' (Tilley
S35).
37. *presently*] immediately, at once.
38–9. *God bless . . . Tresilian*] an ironic repetition of the refrain of the
Schoolmaster's song in 3.3.

[5.6]

> *Sound a retreat, then a flourish. Enter with victory*
> LANCASTER, CHENEY, ARUNDEL, SURREY, *and*
> Soldiers [*with drums and colours*] *with* LAPOOLE,
>   BUSHY *and* SCROOP *prisoners.*

Lancaster. Thus princely Edward's sons in tender care
    Of wanton Richard and their father's realm
    Have toiled to purge fair England's pleasant field
    Of all those rancorous weeds that choked the grounds
    And left her pleasant meads like barren hills.   5
    Who is't can tell us which way Bagot fled?
Arundel. Some say to Bristol to make strong the castle.
Lancaster. See that the ports be laid. He'll fly the land,
    For England hath no hold can keep him from us.
    Had we Tresilian hanged, then all were sure.   10
    Where slept our scouts that he escaped the field?
Cheney. He fled, they say, before the fight begun.
Lancaster. Our proclamations soon shall find him forth.
    The root and ground of all these vile abuses.

> *Flourish within. Enter* NIMBLE *with* TRESILIAN,
>   *bound and guarded.*

5.6.0.1–4 SD] *yorke deleted in MS after Lancaster;* Drom Collours *in left-hand margin in different ink.* 7. *Arundel*] Arun: MS; Cheney *Halliwell, Keller.* 14.1. *Flourish within*] '>ithin / >ishe' *in left-hand margin at ll. 12–13 displacing speech prefix for Cheney to the line above.*

5.6.0.1. Enter with victory] The SD appears to suggest that the lords' victory would be visually signified, perhaps by their wearing laurel wreaths.
    0.1–4. SD] Previous editors have found York's absence from what may well be the final scene a puzzle since he, with Lancaster, has the greatest score to settle with the King's minions. Rossiter's speculation that the parts of York and Tresilian were doubled would account for this, although Parfitt notes that that there are difficulties with this theory, particularly in 2.1, where there is no exit for Tresilian before York's entry, though Tresilian has nothing to say and could be absent. A more plausible explanation of York's absence here is that he was to make a later appearance in the scene, in the company of the defeated King, urging reconciliation and a return to responsible government. See Introduction under 'The Ending'.
    1–5. *Thus . . . hills*] See note at 1.3.155–6.
    2. *wanton*] wayward, unrestrained.
    6–7. *Who . . . castle*] Bagot, who fled to Ireland, was subsequently imprisoned by Bolingbroke and later released to die a natural death.
    8. *laid*] watched.
    14.1. Flourish within] The marginal stage direction appears to indi-

Lancaster. How now, what guard is that? What traitor's
          there?   15
Nimble. The traitor now is ta'en.
     I here present the villain,
     And if ye needs will know his name,
     'God bless my Lord Tresilian'.
Cheney. Tresilian, my lord, attached and apprehended by his   20
     man.
Nimble. Yes and it please ye, my lord, 'twas I that took him.
     I was once a trampler in the law after him and I thank
     him he taught me this trick to save myself from hanging.
Lancaster. Thou'rt a good lawyer and hast removed the cause   25
     from thyself fairly.
Nimble. I have removed it with a Habis Corpus, and then I
     took him with a Surssararis, and bound him in this bond
     to answer it. Nay I have studied for my learning, I can
     tell ye, my lord. There was not a stone between West-   30
     minster Hall and Temple Bar but I have told them every
     morning.
Arundel. What moved thee, being his man, to apprehend him?
Nimble. Partly for these causes: first, the fear of the procla-
     mation, for I have plodded in Plowden and can find no   35
     law . . .

     [*The final sheet or sheets of the manuscript are missing.*]

---

15. now . . . there] what guard is that *deleted in MS.*   16–17. The traitor
. . . villain] *Rossiter; one line in MS.*   28. Surssararis] sursseraris, *MS;* Certiorari *Rossiter.*   35. find] f<>nd *MS.*

---

cate an appropriately flamboyant signal for Nimble's entrance with his
captive.
   23. *trampler*] lawyer, attorney; a slang term perhaps deriving from the
view that lawyers 'trampled' on others; the first example of this usage
recorded in *OED* is 1608, Middleton, 1.4.10.
   27–8. *Habis . . . Surssararis*] see note to 1.2.123.
   31. *told*] counted, reckoned; a testament to the drugery of Nimble's
duties at the courts of Westminster Hall and the Inns of Court.
   35. *Plowden*] Edmund Plowden (1518–85), a celebrated lawyer whose
legal commentaries were first published in 1571 and frequently reprinted.
His dictum, 'The case is altered', became proverbial (Tilley c111).

Appendix A

*The Lords oppose the King's intention to seek French assistance
(1386, pp. 349–50)*

To this the king aunswered by these wordes: Well, we do consider
that our people and Commons go about to rise against us: wherefore we thinke we can do no better then to aske ayde of our Cosyn
the French king, and rather submit us unto him, then unto our owne
subjectes.

The Lordes aunswered, Sir that counsaile is not best, but a way
rather to bring you into daunger: For it is well knowen that the
French king is your auncient enemie, and your greatest adversarie.
And if he set foote once within your realme, he will rather dispoyle
you, and invade you, and depose you from your estate royall, then
put any hande to helpe you. You may call to your remembrance, how
your noble progenitors Edward the thirde, and Edward the Prince
your father, toke great laboures upon them, in heat and colde with
great anguishe and troubles, and laboured without rest, to conquere
the realme of Fraunce, the which rightfully did apperteyne unto
them, and nowe unto you. Pleaseth you also to remember how many
Lords noble men, & good commons of both realmes died in
susteynyng of the warres, and what great goodes the realmes
exposed & consumed in those warres. And now great pitie it is to
here, that more burthens be dayly layde upon your subjects neckes,
for mainteynyng of your charges, who are brought unto such
uncredible povertie, that they have not to pay their house rents, nor
to ayde theyr Prince, nor yet to have sufficient for their necessarie
sustenance: For so is your power depoverished, and Lordes and
great men brought to infelicitie, and all your people to great debil-
itie. And as that king can not be poore that hathe riche people: so
can he not be riche that hath poore Commons. And as the King
taketh hurt in this, so doth the Lordes and the Noble men, every
one after his haviour. And all these inconveniences be commonly by

187

evill counsail which are about you. And if you put not the soner your
helpyng hands for the redresse of y^r premisses, this realme of
England shalbe brought to naught and utter ruyne, which cleerley
should be layde unto your default, and in your evill counsail: Seyng
that in the time of your father, this realme throughout all the worlde
was highlye esteemed, and nothing ordered after these wayes:
Wherefore we sent unto you, to exhort you, to sequester all such
persons as might be the occasion of ruyne, eyther of you, or of your
Realme.

The King's attempt to indite the Lords and their response
(1387, pp. 373–4)

Ye have heard before in the beginning of the x yere of this kings
reigne that a great counsayle was holden at Nottyngham, and unto
the same were called the chiefe Justices and Sergeaunts at lawe, and
that there was proponed certaine articles against the Lordes of the
realme that were admitted by Parliament to have the examination
of suche as had beene lewde rulers, and such as had the government
of the kings treasure, and that the same articles, as before may at
large appere, did specially touch the lyves of the sayd honorable per-
sonages, & that by the sentence and judgement of the lawyers they
were all condempned as Traytors. The which when the sayd Lordes
understood, they assembled themselves together and agreed for the
safetie of themselves, and for the better governement of the realme
to gather suche power as they might, and to resort unto the king,
and to admonyshe hym to remove and advoyde from him al such
lewde counsaylors as before had bene complayned upon in Parliament, as aforesayde, and also in all humble maner to beseech his
highnesse to hearken to their complaynts agaynst the sayd evill
counsaylors, which not onely sought the utter destruction of the
realme, but also of his royall person.

The king hering of thys assembly, came to London in November,
being accompanyed with all the aforesayde lewde counsaylors, and
there purposed to have holden a parliament, and to have attaynted
the aforesayd Lordes, which in the last parliament were appointed
and aucthorised to have the examination of suche as had consumed
and made awaye the kings treasure, as aforesayde: But the king
heryng of the Lords approching with a great puyssance, steyed in
such sorte as that parliament went no farther. Notwithstandyng the
king caused to be made, that no Citezene of London should be so

hardie to sell to the Duke of Gloucester, the Erle of Arondell, or anye other the Lords, any harnesse, Bowes, Arrowes, nor any other municien or matter that should tende to the furniture of the warre, upon a great paine.

But this notwithstanding, the Lords with a goodly company well furnished, came to London: and before they approched neere to the Citie, they sent unto the king the Archbishop of Cauntorbury, the Lord John Lovell, the Lord Cobham and the Lord John Everor requiring to have delivered unto them such as were about him, Traytors and seducers both of him and the realme, and troublers both of pore men and riche, and such as sowed discordes and variaunces betwene the king and his nobles: And they farther declared that their comming was for the honour and wealth both of the king and the realme. But the king ruled by his fyve evill counsaylors, was perswaded that the Lordes intended to bring him under: Therefore they gave him cou(n)sayle to make the king of Fraunce sure friend unto him in these great necessities, and for to be more in quiet, to give him the Towne and Marches of Calice, and whatsoever he had else beyond the Seas, and so to call in the french king to chastise his enimies, and those Lordes that never would be tamed.

Tresilian taken and executed (1387, p. 379)

Shortly after this, was founde Robert Tresilian chiefe Justice lurkyng in a Poticaries house at Westmynster, and there founde the meanes to have spyes daylie upon the Lordes what was done in the parliament: for all the dayes of his lyfe he was craftie, but at the last his craft turned to hys destruction: for he was discovered by his awne servant, and so taken and brought to the Duke of Gloucester, and the same daye had to the Towre, and from thence drawen to Tyborne, and there hanged.

The King arrests Warwick, Arundel and Woodstock (1397, pp. 387-9)

All these things considered, even contrary to all mens expectation, sodainely the kinges maiestie bearing in his heart great wrath and displeasure against the true *Lords* of his counsayle as afore sayd, whome he nowe purposed to be revenged of, practised their destructions, which put the realme to great trouble, and in the end it turned to the overthrowe and confusion of the king himselfe, as ye shall here. For the vj daye of Julij next after, the king appointed to keepe a great feast in London, where he purposed to have had the Duke of Gloucester, the Erle of Arondell, the Erle of Warwike and dyvers other, which he hated deadly, purposing there to have trapped and taken all those noble men together without businesse, or further resistance.

[*Both Gloucester and Arundel absented from the feast and only Warwick attended. Richard II, at first, greeted him with warmth and hospitality, but at the end of the dinner Warwick was arrested for treason and delivered into custody.*]

The same night also the king spake unto the Archbishop of Cauntorbury, that he should perswade his brother the Erle of Arondell frankly to submit himselfe, swearing his olde othe by Saint Jhon Baptist, that hurte should he have none thereby, if he would so do. The Archbishop trusting the kings faire promise, moved this matter to the Erle his brother: But he knowing the kings great malice, and that he purposed nothing more then to apprehend and destroye him, would in no wise agree to his brothers counsaile: howbeit the Archbishop would not so leave him, but daylie was importune on him to submit himselfe: Saiying unto him that all which he mistrusted should passe awaye like a clowde. And if he would not submit himselfe when he might, it might fortune to turne to the dishenerityng both of him and his: For it was sayde than, and the same was the opinion of manye, that for none other purpose would he keepe these Lordes under a rest, but for to shewe the Lordes of Almayne that he could rule the greatest of them. And after that he had so holden his Lordes a season, that it was knowne in Almayne and in outward parties, that then his purpose was to restore them againe to their liberties and dignities. So at the last, by these perswasions & other used by the Archbishop of Cauntorburie, hys brother the Erle in an unhappy houre submytted himselfe to the king. And foorthwith he was taken and sent to be kept in the Isle of Wyght. And the same night that he was taken, the king sent secretly to the Maiour of London, commaundyng him that he should make ready as many harnessed men as he could, and that they should be in a readinesse within two or three houres to attend upon the king, whether his pleasure was to go. The king also commaunded the Erles of Rutland, Kent, Huntyngdon and Nottyngham to arme themselves, and to conduct the Londoners. And so they tooke waye to Plasshy in Essex, where then was the Duke of Gloucester in his Castell. Notwithstanding fewe there were that knew, when the king set foorth, whether he would go. And when they came nye the place, the king vewed his people folowyng him, which were numbred by the Heraultes to be xv. thousand. Then the king sayde unto them whatsoever ye see me doe, lykewise studie you to do the same. If I prepare me to fight, doe ye lykewise. If ye see me in peace, rest you also in quyet, doying hurte to no man. The king sent afore the Erle of Rutlande to the Dukes Castel, that they should see what number of defensible men the Duke had within the Castell: for he was afeard both of the valiauntnesse and wisedome of the Duke. But it happened at that time that the most parte of the Dukes household servaunts, by licence were departed to their friendes and wyfes. When the king was certefied that the Duke had so small a number aboute him, he marvelled muche, for it had bene tolde before by such as bare the Duke no good will, that he had fortified and manned his Castell. So then the King approached thereunto, his men of armes goyng before him and behinde him: And albeit that the Duke was somewhat accrased [*i.e. enfeebled*], yet he met him with a solempne procession of the Colledge, and received him with all the reverence and humilitie that he could doe, as it became him best to do, being his sovereigne Lorde. And the King as he sawe the Duke comming unto him, and that he made him lowe curtesie: The King clapped his hande upon his shoulder, and arested him. To whom the Duke aunswered, that he not onely was content to obey his arest, but the arest of the least of his court. And the King sayde unto him, and will you so, good Uncle? And the Duke aunswered, ye surely syr: then the king folowed the procession, and the Duke folowed the King a farre of. And when the king was somewhat set foorth, he looked back, and called the Duke unto him, and sayde, By Saint John Baptist, good Uncle, this that is done, shall be for the best both for you and us; and so entered into the Chapell, where were a great number of reliques and Jewels of great valure: which when the king sawe, he sayde unto his Uncle, I see you are a good husbande: But now go your waye, and take some sustenaunce, and after you have dined, ye shall go to the place that I have appointed, for here you may not tary. Then the Duke prayed the king to shewe him how ma[n]y servauntes he should have to wayte upon him: The king aunswered that he should be advertised thereof before he rose from dyner. The Duke then went to his lodging, which was nigh unto the Chapell. And the king went to his lodging, where was prepared for him and those that came with him, great and honorable fare, both of fishe and flesh, and it was no great marvaile, for the Duke was advertised privily of the kinges comming. After that the king was set at dyner, he sent to the Duke his minde, what number of persons should wayte upon him, and wylled him to make shorte worke and come away.

After dyner the king departed, and left to convey the Duke the Erle of Kent and the Lord Thomas Percye Steward of his house. And when the Duke had dyned, he caused such stuffe to be trussed up, and caryed wyth him, as was necessarie for him. And then bade his wyfe farewell, who was a Lady both honorable, wise and vertuous: and at his departing he desyred her to make humble sute to the king, to have him his good and gracious Lorde, and that she should boldly offer to sweare that he was never Traytor to his person, nor he that willed him any hurt. And when he was a horsback, with a mery cheere, he sayde unto the Lordes that abode for him. Nowe, whether shall we goe? And who shall be our guide? I or one of you? They aunswered with reverence. Nay syr, it becommeth you to leade and we to folow. Then sayde he, let us set forth a Gods name, wheresoever your pleasure is that I shall go, and so was he conveyed to Calice, and thus taken and arested at that time, when he thought that he was most in the kings favour. For not long before the king had geven him so great giftes, honours and Lordships, that every man thought there was no man more acceptable in the kings favour then he.

Now after the taking of these Lordes was blowen abroad, there was made great moane for them throughout all England, as though the Realme had bene delivered into the enemies handes: so great hope had the Commons universally in them, but most specially in the Duke of Gloucester, whome the Realme beleved, that by his prosperitie the same was safe from all inward and outward enemies.

The king perceiving the great affection that the people bare to the duke and the sayd Lordes, and fearing insurrection of the Commons, which were not all clere of their Melancholy, caused to be proclaymed, that this takyng of the Lordes was not done for their offenses committed of olde, but for new matters, wherein they had offended sithens the obteynyng of their pardons, as they should understand plainly at the next Parliament.

Duryng the tyme (sayth mine Aucthour) that these Lordes were in prison, so sory was the people for them, that prayers and

Processions were used throughout all the realme, that it might please God in his goodnes to inspire into the kinges minde, to be good and mercifull unto these Lordes, and to convert his heart from hatred unto love. The king heering of these prayers, forbad streyghtly all Bishoppes and Prelates that such Processions shoulde be no more used.

Woodstock's murder (1397, p. 394)

The king not yet quieted, sent one of his Justices called Wylliam Rykyll, borne in Ireland, to Calice, which was commaunded to enquire of the Duke of Gloucester, whether he had committed any such treasons as before were alleged agaynst the Erle of Arundel, and the Erle of Warwike, and that he should write what he sayde, and what the Duke did confesse: which after the sayde Justice had speedely done, he returned unto the king, and shewed him such things of his awne devise, as he thought would best please the king, affirming that those things the Duke had franckly confessed. The king after the sight thereof, purposed the death of the Duke, and yet not willing to have him brought unto open judgement, for he feared the people, who bare him great love and favour, and therefore he sent the Earle of Nottyngham unto Thomas Mowbray Erle Marshall, which then had the keeping of the Duke in Calice and commaunded him that privily the Duke should be killed. But he fearing to commit such an enorne deede, deferred the matter, though the king would have had it done with all speede. For the which the King was sore mooved agaynst the Erle, and sware that it shoulde coste him his lyfe, if he obeyed not quickly his commaundement. And being thus constreyned, he called out the Duke at midnight, as though he should have taken shypping to go into Englande, and there in his lodgyng with his servaunts, casting on Fetherbeds upon him, he was smothered. And so was this honorable and good man miserable put to death, which for the honor of the king and wealth of the realme had taken great travayles.

Farming out the kingdom (1398, p. 398)

The saiying also was, that before his goyng into Ireland, he had let the realmes to ferme to Sir William Scrope Erle of Wiltshire, and then Treasurer of England, to Sir John Bushe, Sir John Bagot, and syr Henry Grene, knightes, for the term of xiiij yeres: By reason whereof they procured many men to be accused, and such as were accused, there was no remedye to deliver him, or them, but were he poore or riche, he must compounde and make his fine with those Tyrannes, at their will and pleasure.

Appendix B

King Richard and his favourites (1385–6, pp. 447–54)

But the earle of Oxenford being most in favour and credit with the king in those daies, as one that ruled all things at his pleasure, did advise him to the contrarie [*i.e. against pursuing the Scots and French, who had attacked Carlisle, across the border*], by putting him in beleefe (as was said) that his uncles went about to bring him in danger to be lost and surprised of his enimies, whereupon he tooke the next way home, and so brake up his tournie . . . The lord Robert Veer earle of Oxenford, whome the king in the last parlement had made marquesse of Dubline, was now in this parlement created duke of Ireland: the other lords sore envieng so high preferment in a man that so little deserved, as they tooke it. For by reason of the kings great affection which he bare not onelie to this noble man, but also to the lord Michaell de la Poole, whom he had latelie created earle of Suffolke, and after advanced him to the office of lord chancellor (as before ye have heard) not onelie the lords, but also the commons sore grudged at such their high preferrement, in somuch that in this present parlement, the knights & burgesses in the lower house, exhibited a bill against the lord chancellor, of diverse crimes which they laid to his charge, and so used the matter, with the help of the lords, that in the end in some respect they had their willes against him, contrarie to the kings mind as after may appeare . . . Ye have heard what was doone by the states assembled in parlement against the earle of Suffolke, whom the most part of the realme so greatlie hated, but yet neverthelesse, the king had such an affection towards him, that immediatlie after the parlement was dissolved, he undid all that had beene enacted against him, receiving him into more familiaritie than before, and caused him to continue with the duke of Ireland, and Alexander Nevill archbishop of Yorke, which two lords travelled [i.e. *worked*] most earnestlie to moove the king against the other lords, and to disannull all that had beene doone in the last parlement.

There increased therefore in the king an inward hatred, which he conceived against the lords, these men putting into his eare, that he was like no king but rather resembled the shadow of one; saieng, it would come to passe that he should be able to doo nothing of himself, if the lords might injoy the authoritie which they had taken upon them. The king gave credit to these tales, and therefore had the lords in great gelousie, notwitstanding they were thought to be his most true and faithfull subiects, and the other craftie, deceitfull, and untrustie; but such an affection had the king to them, that no informations, nor accusations, though never so manifestlie prooved, could bring them out of his favour, in so much as at the feast of Christmasse next following, he caused the earle of Suffolke to sit with him at his owne table, in robes accustomablie appointed for kings to weare, and not for meaner estates, which was much noted, and no little increased the envie against him.

The King seeks allies against the lords (1388, p. 457)

But now, as concerning the cause whie the shiriffes were called hither, it was cheeflie to understand what power of men they might assure the king of, to serve him against the lords and barons, whome he tooke to be his enimies: and further, that where he meant to call a parlement verie shortlie, they should so use the matter, that no knight might be chosen, but such as the king and his councell should name. But answer was made hereunto by the shiriffes, that the lords were so highlie beloved of the commons, that it laie not in their powers to assemble any great forces against the lords; and as for choosing the knights of the shires, they said that the commons would undoubtedlie use their ancient liberties, and privileges, in choosing such as they thought meetest. But yet, after that the indictments were found, according to the desire of the king and his councellors, and that those which had beene called about this matter, were licenced to depart home; the king and the duke of Ireland sent messengers into everie part of the realme, to reteine men of warre to assist them in the quarrell against the lords, if need were. Manie made answer, that sith they knew the lords to be faithfull and loiall to the king, even from the bottome of their hearts, and were readie to studie, to devise, and to doo all things that might tend to his honor, and wealth of the realme; they might not by anie meanes beare armour against them. But a great number of other, that tooke it that they were reteined for a good and necessarie purpose, promised to be readie, whensoever it should please the king to send for them.

The lords gather their power (1388, p. 458)

The Duke of Glocester considering to what conclusion these things tended, came secretlie to conference with the earles of Arundell, Warwike, and Derbie, who were in like danger, if they provided not more speedilie for their safetie, whereupon he discovered to them the perill wherein they all stood in common, so that when they weied what was the most expedient meane to safe gard their lives, they gathered their power togither, determining to talke with the king with their armour upon their backes, for their more suertie, as well concerning his pretense to bring them to their deaths, as for the favour which he bare to those whom they reputed to be traitors, both to him, and to the whole state of the realme, whereby the same could not avoid speedie ruine, if remedie were not the sooner provided. The king on the other part tooke advise, how he might apprehend these lords (whom he tooke to be plaine traitors) ech one apart, before they might gather their strengths about them; and first, he sent the earle of Northumberland and others, unto the castell of Reigate, to take the earle of Arundell who laie there at that present. But howsoever it fortuned, the earle of Northumberland came backe, and failed to accomplish that which he had in commandement.

After this, a great number were sent by night, to have laid hands on him, and to have brought him to the kings presence; or in case he resisted, to have slaine him, if by any meanes they might: but he being warned by a messenger, that came to him from the duke of Glocester, conveied himselfe awaie, and with such bands as he had got togither, rode all that night, so that in the morning having passed thirtie miles, not without great travell, and all speed possible, he was in the morning advanced to Haringie parke, where he found the duke of Glocester, and the earle of Warwike, with a great power of men about them.

Contrary counsels in the King's party (1388, p. 458)

At the same time the king was about to set forward towards Canturburie, there to performe some vow of pilgrimage, which he had undertaken to make unto the shrine of Thomas Becket. But a brute [rumour] was raised, and a slander (belike) contrived, to bring him in further hatred of his subjects, that he meant to steale over into France, unto the French king, having promised to deliver up into his hands the towne of Calis, with the castell of Guines, and all the fortresses which his predecessors had possessed in those parties, either by right from their ancestors, or by warlike conquest.

Howbeit this his journie to Canturburie was suddenlie staied, upon knowledge had of the gathering togither of the lords in Haringie parke, wherewith the king being sore amazed, called togither such as he trusted, to understand what their opinion was of the matter; and understanding that the purposed intention of the lords, for which they were so assembled, was to this end (as they pretended to bring him into a better trade of life, and more profitable order of governement, he was streight striken with no small feare, demanding of them their advise, what was best for him to doo in such troublesome state of things. Some were of this mind, that it should be best to seeke to appease the lords with faire promises, assuring them, that they should have their desires. Other thought it better to assemble the kings friends, and joining them with the Londoners, to go foorth and trie the hazard of battell with the lords. Among them that were of this mind, the archbishop of Yorke was the chiefest. But other that were thought to understand more of the world than he did, judged it not wisedome so to doo, considering that if the king lost the field, then should great harme and dishonor follow; and if the victorie fell to his side, yet could he gaine naught, but lose a great number of his subjects.

This was in November, at what time the king, upon his returning from Canturburie, meant to have holden a parlement; but through those stirs, neither his journie to Canturburie, nor the parlement went forward: yet he caused order to be given, that no citizen of London should sell to the duke of Glocester, the earl of Arundell, or any other of the lords, any armour, bowes, arrowes, or other munition, or matter that might tend to the furniture of warre, upon a great paine. But notwithstanding, the lords went forward with their businesse: and before they approached the citie of London, they sent to the king the archbishop of Canturburie, the lord John Lovell, the lord Cobham, and the lord John Devere[u]x, requiring to have delivered unto them such as were about him, that were traitors and seducers both of him and the realme, that sought nothing else, but to trouble both poore and rich, and to sow discord and variance betwixt the king and his nobles. And further, they declared that their comming was for the honor and wealth both of the king and the realme.

Rumours of the King's willingness to treat with the French
(1388, p. 458)

But the king being ruled altogither by the duke of Ireland, the earle of Suffolke, and two or three other, was fullie persuaded that the lords intended to bring him under their governement, and therefore he was counselled to make the French king his sure friend in all urgent necessities. And to be assured of him, it was reported, that those councellors advised him to render up into the French kings hands the towne of Calis, and all that he had else in possession, on the further side of the sea.

The Duke of Ireland defeated at Radcot Bridge (1388, p. 461)

But the duke of Ireland having with him Molineue, Vernon, and Ratcliffe, rode forward in statlie and glorious araie, with an armie (as ye have heard) of five thousand men, supposing that none durst come forth to withstand him. Neverthelesse when he came to Ratcote bridge, not past foure miles from Cheping Norton (which bridge if he could have passed, he had beene out of danger of all enimies) he suddenlie spied where the armie of the lords laie, not far distant from him, readie in the midst of a vallie to abide his comming. Some of the earle of Derbies companie had broken the bridge, & so stopped his passage. He therefore perceiving his enimies intention, staied, and caused the kings banner to be spread, and began to set a good countenance of the matter, and to exhort his people to shew themselves valiant; and herewith caused the trumpets to sound. But when it appeared that as some were readie to fight in his quarrel, so there were other that quite forsooke him, and said flatlie they would not fight against so manie noble men, in so unjust a cause: he being thereof advertised, began to wax faint-harted, and to prepare himselfe to escape by flight; and declaring no lesse openlie unto them, said: Before we come to joine, I will seeke to withdraw my selfe out of the waie, and save my selfe if I can; for me they onlie seeke, against you they have no quarrell, so that I being shifted awaie, you shall easilie be preserved. Herewith one of the knights said to him; You have brought us out of our countrie, you have procured us to give you our promise, you have caused us to take this journie in hand: here therefore are we readie to fight & win the victorie with you, if our hap be such; or if fortune will not so favour us, we are readie to spend our lives with you. So said

he, ye shall not do soo, and forthwith striking his horse with spurs
he fled from them for feare which had set wings on his heeles . . .

King Richard's dealings with the French (1388, p. 462)

But now the lords, who after the tournie at Radcote bridge, were
come (as ye have heard) to Oxford; we find that the same time a
brute was raised (whether of truth or not, we have neither to affirme
nor denie) how there was a messenger taken being sent from the
French king with letters, in which was conteined a licence of safe
conduct, for the king of England, the duke of Ireland and others, to
come to Bullongne, with a certeine number limited, where they
should find the French king come downe thither readie to receive
them, to the end that for a certeine summe of monie, which the
French king should give to the king of England, the towne of Calis,
and all the fortresses in those parts, which were in the Englishmens
hands, should be delivered to the Frenchmen; and further that the
king of England should doo his homage to the French king, for the
lands which he held in Gascoigne, and so to have acknowledged
himselfe his liege man.

De Vere, Suffolk and Tresilian attainted; Tresilian apprehended, and hanged by Woodstock (1388, p. 463)

Moreover, in the beginning of this parlement were openlie called
Robert Veer duke of Ireland, Alexander Nevill archbishop of
Yorke, Michael de la Poole earle of Suffolke, Sir Robert Trisilian lord
chiefe justice of England to answer Thomas of Woodstoke duke of
Glocester, Richard earle of Arundell, Henrie earle of Derbie, and
Thomas earle of Notingham, upon certeine articles of high treason,
which these lords did charge them with. And for somuch as none
of these appeared, it was ordeined by the whole assent of the parlement, that they should be banished for ever, and their lands and
goods mooveable and unmooveable to be forfeit and seized into the
kings hands, their lands intailed onelie excepted. Shortlie after was
the lord cheefe justice, Robert Trisilian found in an apothecaries
house at Westminster, lurking there, to understand by spies dailie
what was doone in the parlement: he was descried by one of his
owne men, and so taken and brought to the duke of Glocester, who
caused him forthwith the same daie to be had to the tower, and from
thence drawne to Tiburne, and there hanged.

Richard II dismisses his Council and claims his throne
(1389, pp. 466-7)

This yeare the king by counsell of some that were about him, called the nobles and great men of the realme togither, and as they were set in the councell chamber staieng till he came: at length he entring into the same chamber, and taking his place to sit among them, demanded of them, of what age he was now? Whereto answer was made, that he was full twentie years old. Then (said he) I am of years sufficient to governe mine owne house and familie, and also my kingdome: for it seemeth aginst reason that the state of the meanest person within my kingdome should be better than mine. Everie heire that is once come to the age of twentie yeares, is permitted, if his father be not living, to order his businesse himself: then that thing which is permitted to everie other person of meane degree by law, why is the same denied unto me? These words uttered he with the courage of a prince, not without the instigation and setting on of such as were about him, whose drift was by dis-countenancing others to procure preferment to themselves, abusing the kings tender years and greene wit, with ill counsell for their advantage . . .

When the barons had hard the words of the king, being therewith astonied, they made answer, that there should be no right abridged from him, but that he might take upon him the government as of reason was due. Well said he, yee know that I have beene a long time ruled by tutors, so as it hath not beene lawful to me to doo anie thing, were it of never so small importance, without their consents. Now therefore I will, that they meddle no further with matters perteining to my government, & after the maner of an heire come to lawfull age, I will call to my councell such as pleaseth me, and I will deale in mine owne businesse my selfe. And therefore I will first that the chancellor resigne to me his seale. When the archbishop of Yorke (who in the yeare last past had beene remooved from Elie unto Yorke, and Alexander Nevill displaced) had delivered unto him the seale, the king receiving it of him, put it in his bosome, and suddenlie rising, departed foorth of the chamber, & after a little while returning, sat down againe, and delivered the seale to the bishop of Winchester, William Wickham, and so made him chancel-lor, although sore against the same bishops will. He made also manie other new officers, remooving the old, and used in all things his owne discretion and authoritie. The duke of Glocester, the earle of

Warwike, & other honorable and worthie men, were discharged and put from the councell, and others placed in their roomes, such as pleased the king to appoint. At the same time he made five new justices.

Of this assuming the regiment to himselfe, as diverse diverslie report: so *Henrie Knighton* a man living in those daies, and committing to writing the occurrents of that tumultuous time, saith as followeth. In the moneth of Maie, the king held a councell at Westminster . . . comming personallie to the councell house he remooved all the great officers (contrarie to expectation and thinking) from their offices, and at his pleasure placed in their roomes whome he list . . . The earle of Arundell likewise unto whome the government of the parlement was committed, and the admeraltie of the sea, was remooved, and the earle of Huntington put in his roome. In like sort dealt the king with the residue of his officers, saieing that he ought not to be inferior in degree & of lesse account than an other ordinarie heire whatsoever within the realme of England . . . But now God hath so dealt for us, that we are of full age, so that we are two and twentie yeares old at this present: and we require that we may freelie and at libertie from this time forward rule and governe both ourselves and our inheritance . . . The king having thus spoken, there was not one that went about to breake him of his will, but they all glorified God, who had provided them such a king, as was likelie to proove discreet and wise.

Woodstock's reputation with the people (1391, p. 475)

About the same time the Duke of Glocester went into Prutzen [*Prussian*] land, to the great grief of the people, that made account of his departure as if the sunne had beene taken from the earth, doubting some mishap to follow to the common waelth by his absence, whose presence they thought sufficient to stay all detriments that might chance, for in him the hope of the commons onelie rested.

The King's resentment of Woodstock (1396, p. 488)

The king by waie of complaint, shewed unto him [the Earl of Saint Paul] how stiffe the duke of Glocester was in hindering all such matters as he would have go forward, not onlie seeking to have the peace broken betwixt the realmes of England & France, but also procuring trouble at home, by stirring the people to rebellion. The earle of saint Paule hearing of this stout demeanor of the duke, told the king that it should be best to provide in time against such mischeefs as might insue thereof, and that it was not to be suffered, that a subject should behave himselfe in such sort toward his prince. The king marking his words, thought that he gave him good and faithfull counsell, and thereupon determined to suppresse both the duke and other of his complices, and tooke more diligent regard to the saiengs and dooings of the duke than before he had doone. And as it commeth to passe that those which suspect anie evill, doo ever deeme the worst; so he tooke everie thing in evill part, insomuch that he complained of the duke unto his brethren the dukes of Lancaster and Yorke, in that he should stand against him in all things and seeke his destruction, the death of his counsellors, and overthrow of his realme.

The two dukes of Lancaster and Yorke to deliver the kings mind of suspicion, made answer, that they were not ignorant, how their brother of Glocester, as a man sometime rash in woords, would speake oftentimes more than he could or would bring to effect, and the same proceeded of a faithfull hart, which he bare towards the king, for that it grieved him to understand, that the confines of the English dominions should in anie wise be diminished: therefore his grace ought not to regard his woords, sith he should take no hurt thereby. These persuasions quieted the king for a time, till he was informed of the practise which the duke of Glocester had contrived (as the fame went amongst diverse persons) to imprison the king. For then the duke of Lancaster and Yorke, first reproving the duke of Glocester for his too liberall talking, uttering unadvisedlie woords that became not his person, and which to have concealed had tended more to the opinion of vertue, than to lash out whatsoever his unstaied mind affoorded, which is a great fault . . . and perceiving that he set nothing by their woords, were in doubt least if they should remaine in the court still, he would upon a presumptuous mind, in trust to be borne out by them, attempt some outragious enterprise. Wherefore they thought best to depart for a time into their countries, that by their absence he might the sooner learne to staie himself for doubt of further displeasure. But it came to passe, that their departing from the court was the casting awaie of the duke of Glocester. For after that they were gone, there ceased not such as bare him evill will, to procure the K. to dispatch him out of the way.

Woodstock's response (1396, p. 488)

The duke in deed sore stomached the matter, that his counsell might not be followed in all things, and speciallie for that he saw (as he tooke it) that the king was misled by some persons that were about him, otherwise than stood with his honor: for reformation whereof, he conferred with the abbat of saint Albons, and the prior of Westminster. The abbat was both his coosine and godfather: and having on a daie both the duke and the prior at his house in saint Albons, after dinner he fell in talke with the duke and prior, and amongst other communication required of the prior to tell truth, whether he had anie vision the night before or not. The prior seemed loth to make a direct answer; but at length being earnestlie requested as well by the abbat as the duke; he declared that he had a vision in deed, which was, that the realme of England should be destroied through the misgovernement of king Richard. By the virgine Marie, said the abbat, I had the verie same vision. The duke hereupon disclosed unto them all the secrets of his mind, and by their devises presentlie contrived an assemblie of diverse great lords of the realme at Arundell castell that daie fortnight, at what time he himselfe appointed to be there, with the earles of Derbie, Arundell, Marshall, and Warwike: also the archbishop of Canturburie, the abbat of saint Albons, the prior of Westminster, with diverse others.

These estates being come to Arundell castell at the daie appointed, about the verie beginning of the one and twentith yeare of king Richards reigne, they sware ech to other to be assistant in all such matters as they should determine, and therewith received the sacrament at the hands of the archbishop of Canturburie, who celebrated masse before them the morow after. Which doone, they withdrew into a chamber, and fell in counsell togither, where in the end they light upon this point; to take king Richard, the dukes of Lancaster & Yorke, and commit them to prison, and all the other lords of the kings councell they determined shuld be drawne and hanged. Such was their purpose which they ment to have accomplished in August following. But the earle marshall that was lord deputie of Calis, and had married the earle of Arundels daughter, discovered all their counsell to the king, and the verie daie in which they should begin their enterprise. The king bad the earle marshall take heed what he had said, for if it proved not true, he should repent it: but the earle constantlie hereunto answered, that if the matter might be proved otherwise, he was contented to be drawne and quartered.

The arrest and murder of Woodstock (1397, pp. 488–9)

The king hereupon went to London, where he dined at the house of his brother the earle of Huntington in the street behind All hallowes church upon the banke of the river of Thames, which was a right faire and statelie house. After dinner, he gave his councell to understand all the matter; by whose advise it was agreed, that the king should assemble foorthwith what power he might convenientlie make of men of armes & archers, and streightwaies take horsse, accompanied with his brother the earle of Huntington, & the earle marshall. Hereupon at six of the clocke in the afternoone, the just houre when they used to go to supper, the king mounted on horssebacke, and rode his waie; wherof the Londoners had great marvell. After that the king began to approch the dukes house at Plashie in Essex, where he then laie, he commanded his brother the earle of Huntington to ride afore, to know if the duke were at home, and if he were, then to tell him that the king was comming at hand to speake with him.

The earle with ten persons in his companie amending his pase (for the king had made no great hast all the night before, as should appeare by his journie), came to the house, and entering into the court, asked if the duke were at home, and understanding by a gentlewoman that made him answer, that both the duke and duchesse were yet in bed, he besought hir to go to the duke, and to shew him that the king was comming at hand to speake with him, and foorthwith came the king with a competent number of men of armes, and a great companie of archers, riding into the base court, his trumpets sounding before him. The duke herewith came downe into the base court, where the king was, having none other apparell upon him, but his shirt, and a cloke or a mantell cast about his shoulders, and with humble reverence said that his grace was welcome, asking of the lords how it chanced they came so earlie, and sent him no word of their comming? The king herewith courteouslie requested him to go and make him readie, and appoint his horsse to be sadled, for that he must needs ride with him a little waie, and conferre with him of businesse. The duke went up againe into his chamber to put upon him his clothes, and the king alighting from his horsse, fell in talke with the duchesse and hir ladies. The earle of Huntington and diverse other followed the duke into the hall, and there staied for him, till he had put on his raiment. And within a while they came foorth againe all togither into the base court, where the king was deliting with the duchesse in pleasant talke, whom he willed now to returne to hir lodging againe, for he might staie no longer, and so tooke his horsse againe, and the duke likewise. But shortlie after the king and all his companie were gone foorth of the gate of the base court, he commanded the earle marshall to apprehend the duke, which incontinentlie was doone according to the kings appointment.

Here we find some variance in writers. For as by an old French pamphlet (which I have seene) it should appeare, the king commanded first, that this duke should be conveied unto the tower, where he ment to commen with him [*i.e. visit him*], & not in any other place: but neverthelesse, the king shortlie after appointed, that he should be sent to Calis, as in the same pamphlet is also conteined. Other write, that immediatlie upon his apprehension, the earle marshall conveied him unto the Thames, and there being set aboord in a ship prepared of purpose, he was brought to Calis, where he was at length dispatched out of life either strangled or smoothered with pillowes (as some doo write.) For the king thinking it not good, that the duke of Glocester should stand to his answer openlie, because the people bare him so much good will, sent one of his justices called William Kikill, an Irishman borne, over unto Calis, there to inquire of the duke of Glocester, whether he had committed any such treasons as were alledged against him, and the earles of Arundell and Warwike, as after shall be specified. Justice Kikill hearing what he confessed upon his examination, wrote the same as he was commanded to doo, and therewith speedilie returned to the king, and as it hath beene reported, he informed the king (whether trulie or not, I have not to say) that the duke franklie confessed everie thing, wherewith he was charged. Whereupon the king sent unto Thomas Mowbraie earle marshall and of Notingham, to make the duke secretlie awaie.

The earle prolonged time for the executing of the kings commandement, though the king would have had it doone with all expedition, wherby the king conceived no small displeasure, and sware that it should cost the earle his life if he quickly obeied not his commandement. The earle thus as it seemed in maner inforced, called out the duke at midnight, as if he should have taken ship to passe over into England, and there in the lodging called the princes In, he caused his servants to cast featherbeds upon him, and so smoother him to death, or otherwise to strangle him with towels (as some write.) This was the end of that noble man, fierce of nature, hastie, wilfull, and given more to war than to peace: and in this great lie to be discommended, that he was ever repining against the king in all things, whatsoever he wished to have forward. He was thus made awaie not so soone as the brute ran of his death. But (as it should appeare by some authors) he remained alive till the parlement that next insued, and then about the same time as the earle of Arundell suffered, he was dispatched (as before ye have heard.) His bodie was afterwards with all funerall pompe conveied into England, and buried at his own manor of Plashie within the church there, in a sepulchre which he in his life time had caused to be made, and there erected.

The response to Woodstock's murder (1397, pp. 489–90)

In the meane time, whiles things were thus in broile, before the beginning of the parlement, divers other, beside them of whom we have spoken, were apprehended and put in sundrie prisons. The parlement was summoned to begin at Westminster the 17 of September, and writs thereupon directed to everie of the lords to appeare, and to bring with them a sufficient number of armed men and archers in their best arraie: for it was not knowen how the dukes of Lancaster and Yorke would take the death of their brother, nor how other peeres of the realme would take the apprehension and imprisonment of their kinsemen, the earles of Arundell and Warwike, and of the other prisoners. Suerlie the two dukes when they heard that their brother was so suddenlie made awaie, they wist not what to saie to the matter, and began both to be sorowfull for his death, and doubtfull of their owne states: for sith they saw how the king (abused by the counsell of evill men) absteined not from such an heinous act, they thought he would afterwards attempt greater misorders from time to time. Therefore they assembled in all hast, great numbers of their servants, friends and tenants, and comming to London, were received into the citie. For the Londoners were right sorie for the death of the duke of Glocester, who had ever sought their favour, in somuch that now they would have beene contented to have joined with the dukes in seeking revenge of so noble a mans death, procured and brought to passe without law or reason, as the common brute then walked; although peradventure he was not as yet made awaie.

Here the dukes and other fell in counsell, and manie things were proponed. Some would that they shuld by force revenge the duke of Glocesters death, other thought it meet that the earles Marshall and Huntington, and certeine others, as cheefe authours of all the mischeefe should be pursued and punished for their demerites, having trained up the king in vice and evill customes, even from his youth. But the dukes (after their displeasure was somewhat asswaged) determined to cover the stings of their griefes for a time, and if the king would amend his maners, to forget also the injuries past. In the meane time the king laie at Eltham, and had got about him a great power (namelie of those archers, which he had sent for out of Cheshire, in whome he put a singular trust more than in any other.)

[*Negotiations were entered into, the King denying any responsibility for Gloucester's death and accusing him of attempting to break the truce with France, fomenting rebellion at home and plotting to assassinate the King. Against such accusations the Dukes maintained their brother's innocence and asserted that he was wrongfully put to death.*]

At length, by the intercession and meanes of those noble men that went to and fro betwixt them, they were accorded, & the king promised from thencefoorth to doo nothing but by the assent of the dukes: but he kept small promise in this behalfe, as after well appeared.

The use of blank charters and the farming out of the kingdom
(1398, p. 496)

But yet to content the kings mind manie blanke charters were devised, and brought into the citie, which manie of the substantiall and wealthie citizens were faine to seale, to their great charge, as in the end appeared. And the like charters were sent abroad into all shires within the realme, whereby great grudge and murmuring arose among the people: for when they were so sealed, the kings officers wrote in the same what liked them, as well for charging the parties with paiment of monie, as otherwise . . . The common brute ran, that the king had set to farme the realme of England unto sir William Scroope earle of Wiltshire, and then treasuror of England,

to sir John Bushie, sir John Bagot, and sir Henrie Greene knights
. . . King Richard being destitute of treasure to furnish such a
princelie port as he mainteined, borrowed great summes of monie
of manie of the great lords and peeres of his realme, both spirituall
and temporall, and likewise of other meane persons, promising them
in good earnest, by delivering to them his letters patents for assur-
ance, that he would repaie the monie so borrowed at a daie
appointed: which notwithstanding he never paid. Moreover they
were compelled to put their hands and seales to certaine blankes,
wherof ye have heard before, in the which, when it pleased him he
might write what he thought good. There was also a new oth devised
for the shiriffes of everie countie through the realme to receive: final-
lie, manie of the kings liege people were through spite, envie, and
malice, accused, apprehended, & put in prison, and after brought
before the constable and marshall of England, in the court of chival-
rie, and might not otherwise be delivered, except they could justifie
themselves by combat and fighting in lists against their accusers
hand to hand, although the accusers for the most part were lustie,
yoong and valiant, where the parties accused were perchance old,
impotent, maimed and sicklie. Whereupon not onelie the great
destruction of the realme in generall, but also of everie singular
person in particular, was to be feared and looked for.

Summary of Richard II's character and behaviour (1399, pp. 507–8)

Thus was king Richard deprived of all kinglie honour and princelie
dignitie, by reason he was so given to follow evill counsell, and used
such inconvenient waies and meanes, through insolent misgover-
nance, and youthfull outrage, though otherwise a right noble and
worthie prince. He reigned two and twentie yeares, three monethes
and eight daies . . . He was seemlie of shape and favor, & of nature
good inough, if the wickednesse and naughtie demeanor of such as
were about him had not altered it.

He was prodigal, ambitious, and much given to the pleasure of
the bodie. He kept the greatest port [*i.e. extravagant style of living*]
and mainteined the most plentifull house that ever any king of
England did either before his time or since. For there resorted dailie
to his court above ten thousand persons that had meat and drinke
there allowed them. In his kitchen there were three hundred servi-
tors, and everie other office was furnished after the like rate. Of
ladies, chamberers, and landerers, there were above three hundred

at the least. And in gorgious costlie apparell they exceeded all measure, not one of them that kept within the bounds of his degree. Yeomen and groomes were clothed in silkes, with cloth of graine and skarlet, over sumptuous ye may be sure for their estates. And this vanitie was not onelie used in the court in those daies, but also other people abroad in the towns and countries, had their garments cut far otherwise than had beene accustomed before his daies, with imbroderies, rich furres, and goldsmiths worke, and everie daie there was devising of new fashions, to the great hinderance and decaie of the common-welth.

Appendix C

EXTRACTS FROM STOW'S
THE ANNALES OF ENGLAND (1592)

The lords act against the King's favourites (1388, pp. 474–6)

The Lordes hasted to London, where the king kept his Christmasse in the Tower of London, they having assembled an army of neere hand fortie thousand the morrowe after Christmasse day came to London, and mustered in the fieldes, where they might be seene of them in the Tower: the Londoners were then in great feare, weying divers perilles as the kings displeasure, if they opened their gates to the Lordes, and if they shut them foorth, the indignation of the undiscreete multitude.

The duke of Gloucester with other entred the Tower, and having a little talke with the king, they recited the conspiracie, whereby they had beene indited, and they shewed foorth also the Letters, which hee had sent unto the Duke of Ireland, that he should assemble an army to their destruction, &c. in the end, the king promised on the nexte morrow to come to Westminster, and there to intreate at large for reformation of all matters.

In the morning the king came to Westminster, where, after a little talke, the nobles sayde that for his honour and commodity of his kingdome it was behovefull, that the traitours, whisperers, flatterers, and unprofitable people were remooved out of place, and that others might bee placed in their roomes.

The king, although sore against his mind, when he saw how the Lords were bent, and that hee wanted power to withstand them, condescended to doe what they would have him, and to conclude, the king at the request of the Lords commanded the suspected persons of his court, and family to be awarded to prison, to answere at the next parliament, which persons were sir Simon Burghley, sir William Elmham, sir Nicholas Dagworth, sir John Golefare, which was not yet returned out of France, all these being knights, sir Richard Clifford, and a Priest called Nicholas Slake Dean of the kings Chappell were appointed to Notingham Castell. To the Castell of Dover were

appointed sir John Beauchamp of Holt Steward of the kings house, sir Thomas Trivet, sir John Salisbury, and John Lincoln. To the Castell of Bristow James Berners, and Richard Medford Clearke . . .
To the castle of Glocester were deputed Rob. Trisilian chief justice of England, which was not yet found, & Nicolas Brembar, who found sureties to stand to the lawes of the realme . . .
Moreover, in the beginning of this parliament were openly called, Robert Vere duke of Ireland, Alexander Nevill Archbishop of Yorke, Michael de la Poole Erle of Suffolke, sir Robert Trisilian Lord chiefe justice of England, and Nicholas Brembar, whom the king had oft times made maior of London against the minde of the Citizens, to answere before Thomas of Woodstocke Duke of Gloucester, Richard Earle of Arundell, Thomas Beauchamp Erle of Warwike, Henry earle of Darby, and Thomas earle of Notingham, upon certaine articles of high treason, which these Lords did charge them with: & forasmuch as none of them appeared, it was ordayned by the whole assent of the parliament, that they shoulde bee banished for ever, and their landes and goodes to bee forfeited and seized into the kings handes, their landes entailed excepted, which should descend to their heires . . .

Tresilian's capture and execution (1388–9, p. 476)

The foresaid Lords being fledde as is aforesaid, Robert Trisilian, a Cornishman, Lord chiefe Justice to the king, had hid himselfe in an Apothecaries house in the Sanctuary neere to the gate of Westminster, where hee might see the Lords going to the Parliament, and comming forth thereby to learne what was done, for all his life time he did all things closely, but now his craft being espied was turned to great follie. For on Wednesday the seventeenth of Februarie he was betrayed of his owne servant, and about eleven of the clock before noone, being taken by the Duke of Glocester, and in the Parliament presented, so that the same day in the after noone hee was drawen to Tyborne from the Tower of London through the citie, and there had his throate cut, and his bodie was buried in the gray Friers Church at London. This man had disfigured himselfe, as if he had beene a poore weake man, in a frize coate, all old and torne, and had artificially made himselfe a long beard, such as they called a Paris beard, and had defiled his face, to the end he might not be knowen but by his speach.

King Richard's flatterers and minions (1397, pp. 498-9)

And in the meane season the king assembled together to garde his person, many malefactours of the Countie of Chester which kept watch and ward both day and night about him. Then the king caused a great and generall Parliament to be summoned at Westminst. where he caused a great Hall to be builded in the midst of the pallace betwixt the clock tower, and the doore of the great Hall. This Parliament beganne about the fifteenth of September, at the beginning whereof Edwarde Stafforde Byshoppe of Excester L. Chanceller, made a proposition or sermen, in the which he affirmed that the power of the K. was alone and perfect of it selfe, and those that impeached it were worthy to suffer paine of the law: to this Parliament all the Nobles came with their retinue in armes, for scare of the king: the prolocutors were knights, in whom no goodnesse at al could be found, but a naturall covetousnesse, unsatiable ambition, intollerable pride, and hatred of the trueth, their names were John Bushy, William Bagot, and Thomas Greene. These required chiefly to have the Charters of pardons revoked and disanulled [*cancelled, made null and void*]: and Bushy sayd to the K. because wee are charged to say what they be that have committed any offence against your majestie, and regal authority, we say that Thomas duke of Glocester and Richard Earle of Arundale, in the 18. yere of your raigne, have trayterously compelled you . . . to graunt to them a commission to governe your Realme, and to dispose of the state thereof to the prejudice of your majestie and royaltie. The same day was that commission disannulled with all Articles depending thereupon. Also the generall pardon granted after the great Parliament by them procured, and one speciall pardon for the Earle of Arundale were revoked.

The employment of blank charters (1398, pp. 504-5)

At the feast of S. Michael, the king caused seventeene Counties in East England to bee indited, and layde to their charges, that they had bene against him, with the duke of Glocester, the earles of Arundell and Warwike, wherefore he sent honourable men to induce the Lordes both spiritual and temporal, to make a submission by writing, sealed with their owne handes, acknowledging themselves to be traitors to the king, though they never offended him in word or deede. Moreover, he compelled all the religious gentlemen and commons, to set their seales to blankes, to the ende hee might as he pleased him oppresse them severally, or all at once: some of the commons payd 1000. marks, some 1000. pounds, &c.

King Richard's extravagant character (1399, p. 505)

This yeere the king kept a most royall Christmas, with every day justings and running at the tilt, whereunto resorted such a number of people, that there was every day spent xxviii. or xxvi. oxen, and three hundred sheep, besides fowle without number. Also the king caused a garment for him to be made of golde, silver, and precious stones, to the value of 3000. markes.

Appendix D

Marginal interventions are recorded in bold type. Textual cuts and pencilled crosses and some changes in speech prefixes are not recorded here. As a help to the reader in assessing the nature of the various marginal jottings, they have been organised under separate headings followed by comment and notes. Apart from the manuscript, the Malone Society edition remains the best place to study the occurence of all marginal interventions within their context in the play.

Act divisions

Act: 2ᵈ   Act: 3ᵈ   actus quart⁹   actus quint⁹

Each Act division is written in the same italic hand not found elsewhere in the manuscript, possibly indicating a division of the play into acts for the purposes of musical interludes at a particular revival in the Jacobean or Caroline period.

Relating to matters of casting

G ad	*Lord Mayor.* Your friends are great in London, good my lord. (1.1.124)
George	My fear presageth to my wretched country. (3.2.109)
Toby	*Servant.* My lord. (4.2.95)

These marginalia may relate to the use of particular actors for small parts in revivals of the play. See commentary notes.

Music and sound effects

fflorish	*Trumpets sound Enter* KING RICHARD, GREENE, BAGOT, BUSHY,

215

SCROOP,
TRESILIAN *and others.*
(2.1.0.1-3)

Flourish	Come, sirs, to Westminster attend our state: (2.1.164)
Flourish	For England's honour and King Richard's good. (2.2.24) Stand from the door then. Make way, Cheney.
Flourish	When we are pleased they shall have summons sent And with King Richard hold a parliament. (2.2.216-17)
{**A Flourish**}	Woe to those men that thus incline thy soul To these remorseless acts and deeds so foul. (2.3.104-5)
sound	See it be done. Come, Anne, to our great hall Where Richard keeps his gorgeous festival. (3.1.107-8)
Anticke Dance	They all are welcome, Cheney. Set me a chair: We will behold their sports in spite of care.
Musick	Stir, stir, good fellows, each man to his task. (4.2.123)
A drum afar of	My lord, I wish your grace be provident. (4.2.158)
musique	Sleep, Woodstock, sleep, thou never more shalt wake. (5.1.52)
Drums	Here to re-edify our country's ruin, (5.3.23) To grip and eat the hearts of all the kingdom.

<ff s>he (2.2.27)

fflorish Cornetts: & musique: cornets. (4.2.100-2)

Drums (5.3.31)

Drom   Thus princely Edward's sons in
Collours   tender care (5.6.1)
>ithin   He fled they say before the
>ishe   fight begun
                Lanc. Proclamations soon shall
                find him forth
                The root and ground of all
                these vile abuses
                Enter NIMBLE *with* TRESILIAN,
                bound and guarded.
                    (5.6.12–14.2)

This set of marginal additions serves to emphasise or simply carry
out effects which are called for in the text: providing suitable pomp
for a number of Richard's entries and exits; adding to the musical
and dance effects of the staging of the masque in 4.2, possibly for
a later revival; giving tension and effect to the preparations for war
in Act 5.

                Properties required for staging

                Which in the greatest prince or
                    mightiest peer
Book   That is a subject to your
                    majesty,
                Is nothing less than treason
                    capital,
                And he a traitor that
                    endeavours it. (2.1.35–8)

                Yes, we will meet them, but
                    with such intent
Petitions   As shall dismiss their sudden
                    parliament

[ ]: Mace   Till we be pleased to summon
                    and direct it. (2.1.162–3)

                York. Please you ascend your   **Paper**
                    throne, we'll call them in.   (2.2.60)

Blanks   Let no man enter to disturb our
                    pleasures! (3.1.5)

3: B	take them off and then deliver them as your deeds.	**Seal them** (3.3.134)
Shrevs Ready	And when you're past the house, cast by your habits (4.2.217)	
A bed for woodstock	The thought whereof confounds my memory. If men might die when they would 'point the time, (4.3.177–8)	

All of these marginal notes may refer to the kind of marking up of a manuscript which we may expect of a book-keeper, reminding him of requirements needed for a specific production. 'Shrevs Ready' may sound like a prompter's note but could equally be a book-keeper's reminder to have two supernumary actors ready to fill the roles of the Shreives of Kent and Northumberland.

Deleted entries

~~Enter the Queen Duchess of gloster Ireland~~ {fflorish}	This day shall make you ever fortunate. The third of April. Bushy, note the time Our age accomplished, crown and kingdom's mine (2.1.165–7)
~~Enter Bagg: & Cheney~~	All. Let our drums thunder and begin the fight
~~nter Bushey: & Surrey:~~	All. Just heaven protect us and defend the right. (5.3.124–5)

The first of these deleted entries seems to have been written in erroneously, perhaps at the time at which the speech prefixes were inserted, possibly copying the entry for a scene never written which should have been deleted in the author's foul papers. The second appears to have been copied during the original transcription of the text because very little space has been left for the speech prefixes (in fact there is too little space to discriminate between the minions and the lords here) and again seems to relate to an alternative development of the action which was superseded in the process of composition.

Appendix E

The play would seem to require an absolute minimum of 16 actors for performance, but the addition of two supernumaries would be more comfortable, especially in 5.1, where soldiers from both armies are required onstage at the same time, and would also allow additional presence where the text calls for an indeterminate number of 'Others, Officers, Archers, Soldiers, etc.'. Below is a possible allocation of the parts with the necessary doubling.

Key to chart (in order of appearance)

Lanc	Duke of Lancaster
York	Duke of York
Arun	Duke of Arundell
Surr	Duke of Surrey
Chen	Cheney
Wood	Woodstock
Exto	Exton
DuGl	Duchess of Gloucester
Gree	Greene
Bago	Bagot
Tres	Tresilian
Nimb	Nimble
Rich	King Richard
Anne	Anne of Bohemia
DuIr	Duchess of Ireland
Mess	Messenger
Bush	Bushy
Scro	Scroop
Flem	Fleming
Cros	Crosbie
Arch	Archers
Cour	Courtier
Ser	Servant
Ignor	Master Ignorance

Farm	Farmer
Whis	Whistler
Cowt	Cowtail
Off	Officer
Butc	Butcher
Scho	Schoolmaster
Off	Officers
Ma/O	Man & Other
Kni	Knight
Cynt	Cynthia (in the Masque)
Gent	Gentleman
ShNo	Shrieve of Northumberland
ShKe	Shrieve of Kent
1Mur	First Murderer
2Mur	Second Murderer
Lapo	Lapoole
Sol	Soldiers
1Gho	Ghost of the Black Prince
2Gho	Ghost of Edward III

Abbreviations in square backets relate to a conjectural ending to the play (see Introduction).

Actor	1.1	1.2	1.3	2.1	2.2	2.3	3.1	3.2	3.3	4.1	4.2	4.3	5.1	5.2	5.3	5.4	5.5	5.6
A	Lanc		Lanc		Lanc			Lanc	Ignor		Oth		1Gho		Lanc	Lanc		Lanc
B	York		York	York	York			York	Farm		Oth		2Gho		York	York		[Yor]
C	Arun		Arun		Arun		Cros		Cros		Kni	Cros	Sol		Arun	Arun		Arun
D	Surr		Surr		Surr		Flem		Flem		Kni	Flem	Sol		Surr	Surr		Surr
E	Chen	Chen	Chen		Chen	Chen	Arch	Chen			Chen		1Mur		Chen			Chen
F	Wood	Chen	Wood		Wood	Chen		Wood			Wood		Wood		Sol	Sol		Sol
G	Exto	DuGl		Mess	DuGl	DuGl			Ser	Ma/O	DuGl	Off			DuGl			Sol
H	Gree	Gree	Gree	Gree	Gree		Gree		Whis	Gree	Gree	Off			Gree	Gree		
I	Bago	Bago	Bago	Bago	Bagot		Bago		Cowt	Bago	Bago	Bago			Bago	Bago		Bago
J	Tres	Tres	Tres	Tres	Tres		Tres			Tres	Kni	Tres		Tres	Sol		Tres	Tres
K	Nimb	Nimb		Oth			Nimb		Nimb	Oth		Nimb		Nimb	Sol		Nimb	Nimb
L			Rich	Rich	Rich		Rich			Rich	Rich	Rich			Rich	Rich		[Ric]
M	Oth			Bush	Bush		Bush	Cour	Off	Bush	Bush	Bush	2Mur		Bush	Bush		Bush
N	Oth			Scro	Scro		Scro	Ser	Butc	Scro	Kni	Scro			Scro	Scro		Scro
O	Oth		Anne		Anne	Anne	Anne		Scho		Cynt	ShNo			Sol	Sol		[Sol]
P	Oth		DuIr	Oth		DuIr	Arch		Off		Gent	ShKe	Lapo		Lapo	Lapo		[Sol]

Index

Page numbers refer to the Introduction and DRAMATIS PERSONAE; act-scene-and-line numbers refer to the Commentary. An asterisk (*) preceding an entry indicates that the commentary note in this edition adds materially to the information given in the OED.

223

Lightning Source UK Ltd.
Milton Keynes UK
UKOW03f0332060214

225976UK00002B/81/P

THE
NURTURING INN
POCKETBOOK

C000165091

By Douglas Miller

Drawings by Phil Hailstone

"Current economic conditions are challenging everyone in business to think and act differently and to move on from 'steady state' thinking. These unprecedented conditions offer the perfect environment in which innovation can flourish and Douglas' book provides a rich source of ideas on how to nurture – and benefit from – that innovation."

Jonathan Bond, Director of HR & Learning, Pinsent Masons LLP

Published by:
Management Pocketbooks Ltd
Laurel House, Station Approach, Alresford, Hants SO24 9JH, U.K.
Tel: +44 (0)1962 735573   Fax: +44 (0)1962 733637
E-mail: sales@pocketbook.co.uk
Website: www.pocketbook.co.uk

This edition published 2009.

British Library Cataloguing-in-Publication Data.   A catalogue record for this book is available
from the British Library..

ISBN 978 1 903776 98 8

Design, typesetting and graphics by **efex ltd**. Printed in U.K.

CONTENTS

INTRODUCTION

WHO IS THIS POCKETBOOK FOR?

This pocketbook is for any manager who believes that:

1. Without innovation your organisation won't prosper.

2. An important part of the value of your people comes from the insight they have in their jobs and the ideas that result from that insight.

3. A key responsibility of management per se is to create the right environmental conditions under which idea generation and innovation can thrive.

THE NEED FOR NURTURE

Like the farmer patiently creating the best conditions for growth and then carefully nurturing crops once the first shoots appear, you, as the manager, have a responsibility to create the conditions in which creative ideas are more likely to be generated in your team. Then you need the patience and skill to see them through.

You must have a reasonable expectation that innovation will occur – because of your own positive actions – rather than a naïve hope that it might.

THE CASE FOR INNOVATION

Innovation costs nothing to start
Innovation begins with great ideas. Great ideas are the lifeblood of innovation. And great ideas cost nothing to think up.

Innovation cuts costs
Innovation can mean looking at what you do and asking questions like *'How can we do this....'* with words such as *'quicker, better, cheaper, simpler, differently?'* attached. These innovation catalysing thoughts can save money and/or create income.

You need to be 'sharp-thinking'
Procedure and process are disappearing. Anything that requires little subsequent thought, once it has been devised, is being shipped out to where it can be done cheaper. What's left? How will you survive? Your capacity to be 'clever' – to be 'sharp-thinkers' – is critical. And innovation – the key survival tool – can be a clear manifestation of that 'cleverness'.

INNOVATION MEANS OBSOLESCENCE

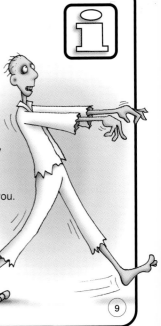

Innovation means cutting out systems, procedures, products or services that are no longer relevant, are a drain on the business, or no longer reflect what the marketplace wants – now or in the near future. It may be essential that your organisation makes its own competitive advantage obsolete, in order to advance and stay ahead of the competition.

So much better that you make these things obsolescent yourself through your own pro-activity than that your competitors do it for you.

Ultimately we need innovation:

- To secure our future – without it we get organisational decay and death

- And because we are human – it's what we do!

It's what makes us different from all other species. Stifle it, and like our organisations we die too. We end up managing the 'walking dead' – present at work but in body only.

GETTING COMPETITIVE ADVANTAGE

So what is innovation anyway? Innovation is often confused in business with the generation of creative ideas. The generation of these creative ideas is essential to innovation – and the more we have the better. But innovation is not just about ideas. Neither is it just the putting of creative ideas into action. It goes one step further:

Innovation is the process by which we create and then act on ideas that have value.

Of course we can never be certain that ideas will have value, but we can do a lot to establish likelihood of success. Foolhardily acting on ideas just because they are 'different' or 'fun' can destroy your business. This doesn't mean that occasionally you shouldn't take a leap into the dark – it might be imperative to do so.

Once upon a time everything you do now, no matter how mundane, was innovative. Without innovation you would not be here now. And without innovation you will not be here in the future.

INNOVATION –
POWERED BY HUMANS

YOUR BELIEFS ABOUT PEOPLE

Where do we start? Innovation thrives when we unchain the creative imaginations of those we manage. To do this we must have a starting point in our beliefs about people – that there is a creative imagination to release in the first place.

A useful starting point is to affirm the following three assumptions:

1. Universal

Creativity is inherent within all human beings, particularly when we are able to widen the arenas in which we can express ourselves creatively.

This means that job variety and enrichment increase the likelihood that someone will be emotionally captured by their job, or at least a part of it, and therefore be more creative within it.

INNOVATION – POWERED BY HUMANS

YOUR BELIEFS ABOUT PEOPLE

2. Developmental
The potential we all have to be creative will become real if people are developed in the right way.

This means that people have developmental goals into which they have input, that the goals are stretching but not straining and that it is acceptable to make mistakes when putting the fruits of their creative labours into practice. This, however, must be nurtured to prevent uncontrolled free-for-all.

3. Environmental
The climate of your team, department or organisation, as a whole, will determine the extent to which people will be creative in their jobs.

As managers, we have the responsibility to create the conditions – the climate – under which people are more likely to engage with their work and generate constructive ideas.

Note: The three 'assumptions' sourced and adapted from *'Creativity and Innovation Management'* Vol 16, No 3, 2007. Tudor Rickards and Fangqi Xu.

HUMAN CONDITIONS

As humans we have a remarkable capacity for creative insight, idea generation and innovation. However, you – in your role as a manager *and in the way you manage* – can either stimulate or stifle this in your people. This chapter suggests four ways to create the right conditions in which your people can innovate best. These are:

1. **Knowing Slowly** – Giving your people time to think rather than forcing them to think.

2. **Time to Play** – Letting ideas flow freely through the encouragement of a more playful work environment.

3. **Brainstorming** – Challenging some of the misconceptions about the conditions in which groups of people generate ideas best.

4. **'I' Sight** – Allowing progression of the three 'I's – Insight, Ideas and therefore Innovation. The start point – insight – will come through your ability to get your people to engage more closely with their jobs.

1. KNOWING SLOWLY: HIGH QUALITY IDEAS HARVEST

A farmer has choices. He or she can choose to add lots of chemicals to the soil or grow crops indoors to accelerate growth. Or the farmer can let the natural elements of rain, sun, soil and aspect work their magic (what the French grape growers refer to as the mystical 'le terroir'). Both methods work.

Acceleration will lead to quantity but natural growth will lead to better quality and flavour, assuming no droughts or floods. Like the farmer, you have those same choices in your own search for a harvest of ideas from your team.

You need to give your people time to think – to engage, play and grapple with the thoughts that enter their heads. Why?

INNOVATION – POWERED BY HUMANS

1. KNOWING SLOWLY

- People rarely think at their best when pressurised to do so – when anxious
- If people perceive mini-crises through the need for hastily conceived ideas and quick decisions they may sense fear and threat – not the best conditions for clear thinking
- Many of us like to incubate ideas. To chew them over in the back of the mind for a while. What can be called 'dimmer switch' thinking: the light is on but turned down low

There are of course exceptions. Some people do think at their best when in a corner. But not that many. Part of your role as a manager is to identify the conditions in which your team members are at their creative best, individually and collectively.

You need to recognise your own personal style. If a team, department or organisation is led by someone who is good at off-the-cuff ideas, that person may not realise that others are not the same. Indeed they may create the mini-crisis environment because that is the environment in which they thrive.

1. KNOWING SLOWLY

You can help your people 'know slowly' by:

- Acknowledging that slowness does not mean stupidity. Slow can mean contemplation, consideration and far more creative connections than the knee-jerk approach of rushed thinking

- Encouraging those who prefer to take their time. In meetings this may mean encouraging the quiet or silent. Ask how they see the problem. Don't always ask for answers. Ask for their perspective – they may be seeing problems or challenges very differently from others. And with more insight

- Avoiding the all-too-frequent feeling that generating ideas is something we do only when the pressure is on

'... innovation is a slow process of accretion, building small insight upon interesting fact upon tried-and-true process. Just as an oyster wraps layer upon layer of nacre atop an offending piece of sand, ultimately yielding a pearl, innovation percolates within hard work over time.'
Janet Rae-Dupree's 'Unboxed' column – New York Times

INNOVATION – POWERED BY HUMANS

1. KNOWING SLOWLY

- Separate the process of encouraging people to have ideas from acting on them. While people must see that ideas do get acted on, they must also understand that ongoing continuous idea generation is a reflection of a healthy working environment
- We should be having ideas all of the time – even if they don't all get taken further
- At times we need quick solutions. That's fine. Get the quick thinkers working. But what we really need are people who are encouraged to think in the way that best suits them. Some people need pressure to think. Some people need time. Value both

The public sector
The public sector can be an environment in which innovation shines. With no shareholders the need for short-termism is not as defined, with the result that people can incubate ideas more – if you the manager encourage this to happen. Managers in the public sector have superb natural conditions for incubating and nurturing innovation.

2. TIME TO PLAY: EXPERIMENTATION

> 'The creation of something new is not accomplished by the intellect, but by the play instinct arising from inner necessity. The creative mind plays with the object it loves.'
> **Carl Jung**

Just imagine what happens to the soil if the farmer grows the same crops in the same soil year after year. The soil becomes exhausted – nutrient free – requiring the vast expense of soil additives (their version of your consultants). Farmers have the option of experimentation – the search for variety – to try different crops to see what grows best.

You have your own version of this too. So, what feeds this experimentation in your team?

Experimentation for your people means giving them time to play when at work – to apply the relaxed, experimental frame of mind we all have when we are at play. Why?

19

2. TIME TO PLAY: REASONS

- Play is low risk and non-threatening – there is no danger in playful experimentation as long as people are aware of how far they can play

- Play means going to non-obvious sources for inspiration. These non-obvious sources may provide the revolutionary breakthroughs needed

- Play is non-stressful. Most of us do not respond well to stress. Our inclination to be creative when stressed diminishes

- Play is remarkably productive. Think about the times you have got 'lost' in something and how amazed you were at what you achieved in that time

- Play is what you do when you are enjoying your job. Work is what you do when you are not enjoying yourself. Those who enjoy their jobs produce more

2. TIME TO PLAY: CONDITIONS

You can help your people play 'safely' by:

- Giving them time. To take a famous example, Google allow their staff 20% of their work time to 'play', that is to say, to experiment creatively in areas outside their job role. It brought them Google Earth, Orkut and gmail

- Setting out the parameters. There should be freedom of thought (OK to think the unthinkable) and 'safe' experimentation. Emphasise the difference between safe experimentation and going live with an idea. Actions should always be agreed between the creator and the manager

- Eliminating fear. There is no success or failure at this stage – just enjoyable exploration

- Not forcing people to play/experiment when they don't want to

- Making it clear that this is not a superficial exercise. If you believe that this approach can work then you must also believe that great ideas of value will be the reward

2. TIME TO PLAY: OTHER ADVANTAGES

- Your people may increase their knowledge outside the business. At its simplest this might mean knowledge of competitors, or it could be practices in industries entirely unrelated to your own but which could be applied to your organisation

- Someone might come up with a completely 'out there' idea which the routine patterns of thinking and working have not unearthed

- Someone might come up with a simple idea that is not earth-shattering but about which people subsequently say, 'why didn't we think of that before?'

- It's cheaper – the cheapest ideas come from inside the business

- Organisations that are 'dying of dead seriousness' are unlikely to be places where people feel comfortable having ideas

3. BRAINSTORMING: 'WE PLOUGH THE FIELDS & SCATTER'

Our farming metaphor continues! Imagine what might happen to the field if the farmer throws all sorts of seeds randomly across it, in the hope that something grows. The farmer might get lucky. Something might 'crop' up. More than likely you will see an incomprehensible mess.

Attempts are often made to generate innovative ideas through group sessions, a collective approach to problem solving or opportunity spotting generally called 'brainstorming'. Traditionally this has meant asking a random, ill-defined question. Research shows it rarely works. Like the farmer, you get the incomprehensible mess – or nothing at all. In order for people to perform at their best in this environment you need to consider a number of factors.

3. BRAINSTORMING: ASK GOOD QUESTIONS

The first element necessary for success is:

● **The parameters for discussion must be clearly defined**. The question for which you want ideas must be focused. A question like: 'How can we improve our product?' is vague and of little value

More focused questions such as: *'How are our customers using our products in ways we hadn't imagined?'* or *'What small, barely noticeable competitors are offering products or services very different from our own and what are they?'* give some definition and purpose to the discussion.

Example
Remember the rise of global aviation phenomena Ryanair and EasyJet? For a long time the traditional European aviation heavyweights ignored/dismissed the new paradigm of flight booking, where the earliest to book get the best deals. Ryanair is now the world's biggest airline in terms of international passenger numbers.

3. BRAINSTORMING: FACTORS FOR SUCCESS

Other necessary factors are:

- Give people warning of brainstorming sessions. Some of us like to chew things over for a while and find, as a consequence, that great ideas come into our heads when we least expect them. We bring more to the party

- Recognise that some very creative people may not thrive in formal brainstorming sessions. They just keep quiet, perhaps intimidated by the voluble 'egos' in the room

- Quietness does not mean lack of engagement, in the same way that volume does not mean insight

'We have found that if you systematically constrain the scope of their thinking (but not too much), people are adept at fully exploring the possibilities, and they can regularly generate lots of good ideas – and occasionally some great ones.'
Kevin Coyne – HBR Dec 2007

3. BRAINSTORMING: FACILITATION TIPS

When overseeing group idea generation or brainstorming:

- Keep your own role to one of co-ordination and facilitation. Others will too readily defer to you as the manager and not express the breadth of their thinking. Don't contaminate the thinking of others by dominating the group

- Where there is a shortage of ideas try to get the group to change their perspective on the problem. Ask, *'how would xyz look at this?'*. A good approach is to ask how a group of schoolchildren might deal with the problem you are grappling with

- If people's ideas get killed off early they become reluctant to offer more. They think *'why bother?'* Save the group critique for later

4. BETTER 'I' SIGHT

'I' sight means the natural progression of **insight** into the job, the **ideas** that come from that insight and consequently **innovation** when we combine those ideas with action.

Insight – We have our best ideas when we are emotionally engaged with the work we are doing. This engagement creates 'insight' into our work. There is little point in asking people who are bored or disconnected with their work to generate ideas.

Ideas – Insight into our work makes us more inclined to ask questions like: *better, quicker, faster, simpler, cheaper*. But we may only proffer suggestions if we feel that those who manage us are interested in what we think. That our ideas have value to them and to our organisation.

Innovation – Without hundreds of ideas we have no innovation. Innovation is the process of generating great ideas and then turning them into something of value. Innovation brings together idea generation and action. People must see that idea generation is not cosmetic. That ideas do get acted on.

4. BETTER 'I' SIGHT

Better 'I' sight in your people is a function of your own management approach:

Insight comes from your capacity to motivate and that person's degree of self-motivation.

Ideas from insight will come if people sense that their ideas are perceived to have value. Is the whole concept of idea generation seen as valuable by the organisation – even if most ideas don't get used? Are your people incentivised to have ideas? Is it written in the job description?

Innovation comes if full management support is given – and is seen to be given (ie chosen ideas get progressed to action).

Recognise that innovation is unlikely to be about the taking of just one great idea and then acting on it.

HARNESSING HUMAN KNOWLEDGE

Innovative ideas come from human knowledge and understanding. Harnessing that knowledge is a key management role. Knowledge comes from five primary sources:

1. **From your institutional memory** – what you have done well in the past. But remember that some (perhaps all) of those things will have to be adapted, revolutionised or abandoned – now or in time.

2. **Masquerading as intuition** – knowledge gained through experience can help to fine-tune intuition. That intuition can help us to sense the time to take a different path or what decision to make. We often instinctively know the time to act but ignore the prompts because we are comfortable with 'the old way'.

HARNESSING HUMAN KNOWLEDGE

3. **From 'naivety'** – intuition can just as easily be sensed by the 'innocent', namely those unencumbered by the traditions and conventions of your organisation or your industry. Their 'knowledge' may be very different from your own. And they may be spectacularly right or spectacularly wrong.

4. **Acquired externally** – all the information available to you in the world beyond your organisation. Are your people curious enough to find it? Do you give them time to do so?

5. **From imagination** – Einstein was quite happy to spend hours gazing through a window as he attempted to stretch the boundaries of his creative imagination – taking his thoughts to places that others had yet to visit. He said: *'The true sign of intelligence is not knowledge but imagination.'* But perhaps the two co-exist.

INNOVATION – POWERED BY HUMANS

HARNESSING HUMAN KNOWLEDGE

What do we do with this 'knowledge'?

A simple sequence runs in three stages:

1 **Knowledge creation**
(from our five primary sources)

2 **Continuous innovation**

3 **Competitive advantage/service responsiveness**
(private sector/public sector)

It is one of your prime responsibilities, as manager, to make the best use of Stage 1 to catalyse Stage 2 and thereby secure Stage 3.

An adaptation of Nonaka and Takeuchi's model (see page 109)

NOTES

PERSONAL BLOCKS TO
<u>INNOVATION</u>

PERSONAL BLOCKS TO INNOVATION

INTRODUCTION

Earlier on, we looked at the beliefs you need to have about people if you are even to begin to create a more innovative environment. You have to believe:

- We are all creative – capable of idea generation
- We can become far more creative if we learn and develop in the right way
- We can be far more creative if the environmental circumstances allow us to be so

In your desire to create a more innovative environment, the resistance – 'the blocks' – is likely to come in two forms. The first will be self-reflective – where people defer to a series of vulnerabilities that will make the generation of ideas personally difficult for them. Overcoming these is the basis of this chapter.

The second form of resistance comes where individuals defer to a series of organisational challenges that make the innovation process seem pointless, as long as these blocks are in place. This is covered in the next chapter.

1. PREMATURE RETIREMENT

'Here I am. And here I will stay.'

The capacity for generating ideas can be diluted over time. The longer your people are around, the more they can fall victim to being present at work in body only. The mind has gone elsewhere – possibly into retirement. And remember, there are as many 25 year olds who have 'retired' from the job as 65 year olds.

Healthy, forward-thinking organisations have a large number of their employees whose thinking is engaged in the future rather than just on present survival.

1. PREMATURE RETIREMENT

SUGGESTIONS

- People often become lethargic because they don't feel centrally involved. Put together small creativity teams that can grapple with existing challenges, and invite them to come up with new ideas – to think the unthinkable. This, however, must be genuine rather than cosmetic

  Example: In 1997 the Prime Minister recruited MP and social policy expert Frank Field to 'think the unthinkable' about the UK's National Health Service. He did and was quickly moved elsewhere as a consequence of his thoughts. Stifle your 'free thinkers' and they will resent you forever.

- Split up the dinosaurs – too many 'in my day' thinkers mean meetings become history lessons and idea-generation sessions become 'idea graveyards'. But one or two 'in my day' thinkers can be good – an effective brake on ill-thought-out innovations

1. PREMATURE RETIREMENT

SUGGESTIONS (CONT'D)

- Put natural high-energy people into lethargic teams – energy is contagious. Or the lethargic can't deal with it and leave

- Your people may be psychologically retired because of your own personal management style. Are you too directive ('do it my way')? Are you forever probing into people's work?

- Change the environment in which people work regularly. Move desks around. Make sure the same people don't always sit next to each other

- Ban emails between people who sit next to each other – innovation and creativity come from conversation

PERSONAL BLOCKS TO INNOVATION

2. NO TIME

> *'Innovation? Nice idea. I just don't have the time though.'*

Some of your people may think that innovation is merely an 'extra' – an irritating addition to an already clogged-up day.

Suggestions:

- Creative thinking is not optional – it is part of what makes us what we are. If people feel they don't or can't think creatively it is because you and/or managerial colleagues have not created the right environment

- No job should ever be 100% one dimensional routine. If the routine cannot be dealt with in 90% of job time, the extra 10% (which could be used for experimentation and 'play') is unlikely to be the answer. The problems are likely to be systemic and institutionalised

- When people are stretched – and generating great ideas – make sure you have a place where those ideas can be lodged for referral later (your intranet, perhaps). They, and hopefully others, can play with and develop the ideas when time allows

3. PROCESS & PROCEDURE & INNOVATION DON'T MIX

'Innovation is for the R&D and marketing departments. My job doesn't need it.'

This is a familiar argument and the reason why, in the past, we often shied away from using the word 'creativity' in wider business practices. Someone working in a finance department traditionally wouldn't have seen the need for creativity in their role; probably in part because his or her manager wouldn't have seen the need either.

Suggestions:

- Get people thinking about those they serve, both internally and externally, and encourage them to ask how they could improve. As soon as customer comments roll in, you can stress that innovation needs to exist anywhere there is a need for improvement. That potentially means everywhere

- Encourage your people to spend time with their (internal or external) customers, to catalyse service improvement ideas

3. PROCESS & PROCEDURE & INNOVATION DON'T MIX

SUGGESTIONS (CONT'D)

- Ask your people to imagine themselves as the 'thing' (the product, the service, the system, etc) they are trying to improve. How could it be better, more attractive, simpler, cost-effective, quicker?

- If they have never seen the need to think differently about what they do, they may need training in how to do so

What's it all for?
While the above suggestions cater for the bigger reasons for innovation, many will want the need brought closer to home.

- Link the need for innovation to overall organisational goals

- Then make the connection between what they do and the achievement of a higher vision and goals – people need to know that what they do makes a contribution

- Many of your people will be tuning into WII FM ('what's in it for me?'). There should be personal reward – monetary or otherwise – for volume of ideas

4. STRESS

'I am under too much pressure – I just can't think straight.'

The relentless pursuit of instant results creates a highly pressurised atmosphere in which the chances of creative insight are reduced. Few of us are at our best creatively when under acute pressure.

- Encourage 'time out' so that creative thoughts can be germinated and incubated. 'Time out' is not an excuse for laziness – it is a time for productive contemplation

- A rhythm in work – when people are challenged but feel in control – is a creative stimulus. Poor planning and continuous knee-jerk reactions to supposed crises do not help create this rhythm. Many crises are figments of managerial imagination

- It is counter-productive to think that the 12 hour day always gets results. Work-life balance is a valuable tool in opening up the imagination

- Subsidise membership of local sports facilities, health clubs etc. A healthy body means a clearer mind

5. PERSONAL PERCEPTION

'I am not creative.'

It is too easy to say that creativity is the preserve of artists, musicians and the marketing department. In fact, everything we do is a creative act that came from a creative thought.

- A key barrier to creative expression is self-censorship. As a manager, emphasise to your people that all their ideas have value. Ideas are often self-censored before expression because the idea generator thinks no one will be interested

- A second key barrier is the fear of looking silly if the idea is too wacky. Encourage all ideas. Dismiss a wacky idea out of hand and its originator will lose the confidence to generate more

- Encourage the silent, eg at meetings. Although the reticent or unconfident may not open up right away, over time they will gain confidence, knowing that they can express their ideas freely and without fear

6. WII FM (WHAT'S IN IT FOR ME?)

'Is it worth my while? I do the work and someone else gets the credit.'

Suggestions:

It can be frustrating when your ideas get taken and 'lost' elsewhere in the organisation. Even more frustrating when your creative thoughts are credited to someone else.

- Don't take credit for individual and team success yourself. When ideas are successful make sure everyone knows where the genesis of the idea lay. Word soon gets round if you are a 'credit thief'

- Use the language of 'we' rather than 'me'

- When things go wrong – and with new innovations they inevitably will – you must take the responsibility yourself. No blaming individual team members – hanging them out to dry. If you do so they will never work for you with any degree of 'heart' again

43

PERSONAL BLOCKS TO INNOVATION

6. WII FM (WHAT'S IN IT FOR ME?)
SUGGESTIONS (CONT'D)

- Reward new ideas – even when they go no further. People need to know that the act of generating ideas is as valuable to the organisation as the ideas that are acted on
- Sometimes all that people need is praise. Praise is a primary but under-utilised motivator
- You yourself must first be fully convinced of the possibility of success and then commit yourself fully to your team's ideas. You cannot back ideas half-heartedly
- There is correlation between innovation and productivity. Give reward for volume of ideas – even if they fail or are not put into practice

ORGANISATIONAL BLOCKS TO INNOVATION

ORGANISATIONAL BLOCKS TO INNOVATION

1. MISTAKES GET PUNISHED HERE

'What happens to me if I try something new and it goes wrong?'

Perhaps one of the biggest fears for employees is that they will be punished if they try things that don't work. This is where your credentials as 'a manager of innovation' come in – it is really about your approach to managing people.

People need to understand the parameters within which they can innovate. Make it clear to your team where they can experiment and where they cannot. (See Mark Brown's 4-box model on page 61 for further guidance.)

Where you allow for initiative and creative experimentation you cannot then 'punish' people when something goes wrong, as it often will. They will stop trying. And make sure that you take responsibility in the eyes of those outside the department. If, however, mistakes are made in areas where you have made it clear that experimentation is off limits – then you can justifiably use sanctions, although you may choose not to do so.

1. MISTAKES GET PUNISHED HERE

SUGGESTIONS

- Feedback and support – in success or failure – are essential parts of an innovation culture. People must know how they are doing. Keep an unobtrusive eye open

- Be open about things that didn't work for you personally – and what you learnt. A little humility does no harm in convincing others that we all experience failure

- Be conscious of people who never seem to fail – they probably aren't trying

- Beware of the people who don't produce much but tell you that when they do it is fantastic. Innovation is usually closely related to proliferation of ideas

- Why not reward sensible failure – people who showed initiative and tried something?

- Remind people that failing to act is a far worse sin than failure: set the standard. Initiative is not a bonus – it is expected

ORGANISATIONAL BLOCKS TO INNOVATION

2. SYSTEM BLINDNESS

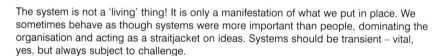

'We have our processes and procedures – innovation won't fit with them.'

The system is not a 'living' thing! It is only a manifestation of what we put in place. We sometimes behave as though systems were more important than people, dominating the organisation and acting as a straitjacket on ideas. Systems should be transient – vital, yes, but always subject to challenge.

- Whenever you add a bureaucratic procedure, ask what you can take away

- Systems and procedures should only exist where they add value for the customer

- Systems should provide an easily applied framework that streamlines our work. They should facilitate speed. Similarly, in innovation, systems should facilitate the progress of ideas – not the reverse

- Encourage creative conflict in the team: *'Are our existing systems and procedures more suited to a bygone age?'*

2. SYSTEM BLINDNESS
SYSTEM CHANGE AT PIZZA EXPRESS

Managing a supply chain might not be an area you associate with innovation – being seen traditionally in terms of systems and processes. And yet the post-millennium resurgence of the UK pizza restaurant chain Pizza Express has in part been put down to the innovative practices of supply chain director, Mark Crawford and his team. Says Crawford:

> *Innovation can come in two forms. It can be in the food itself, but it can also be in terms of cost. We welcome suppliers proactively approaching us and suggesting how we can restructure the packaging of products or order differently to take some of the costs out…We've been successful at, in some instances managing costs, in some instances taking costs out, and in other instances taking costs out and then reinvesting them into higher quality products – it's not always about taking the cost out and buying more cheaply.*

ORGANISATIONAL BLOCKS TO INNOVATION

3. LOCKED IN THE PAST

> *'The old way is the only way – it's always worked before.'*

This particular block is a classic initiative killer, often used with new recruits. You recruited in part for the new person's vitality and initiative (if they didn't show these traits, why did you take them on?) In fact, we all start a new job with great energy. Long-standing employees, too, are subjected to, and demotivated by, that familiar phrase, *'not the way we do it'*.

Brainwashing your new recruit with excessive policy and procedure information as soon as they start, will indicate to them that there is little point in suggesting change. You immediately lose the value of a fresh pair of eyes.

> *'On the first day working in the pub I noticed 40 things wrong with it...cracked windows, ripped carpet etc. On the second day I noticed 39 things wrong with it. On the third day I noticed 38 things wrong with it. On the fortieth day I noticed nothing wrong with it. Even though nothing had changed.'*
> **Oli Barrett – The Daily Networker**

ORGANISATIONAL BLOCKS TO INNOVATION

3. LOCKED IN THE PAST

SUGGESTIONS

- Where the job demands it, emphasise to the new recruit that you are genuinely open to hearing new ideas and approaches

- Don't kill off ideas at meetings with the neutering phrases *'not the way we do it'* or *'it's a good idea, but we can't use it because…'*. People will just stop having them

- Always encourage your people to ask *'Is there a better way of doing this?'* even with long-standing practices and procedures

- Avoid meetings that become history lessons – *'we tried that years ago'*

- Encourage idea generation/brainstorming meetings that you are not part of – participants may be inclined to think more freely, not restricted by the potential straitjacket of management presence

> *'Managers need to learn that it is OK to walk into a meeting and be surprised.'*
> **Ed Catmull – Co-founder of Pixar**

4. GOOD TIMES WILL LAST FOREVER

'We're doing fine. Why change?'

The longer we are exposed to a way of working the more we see that way of working as 'the only way'. Everything, even poor practices, becomes the norm.

Suggestions to break this mindset:

- Be dissatisfied in all things and encourage your people to be the same
- Consciously encourage your team to change the perspective from which they view things – in meetings; as if they were a customer; as if it were their first day in the job
- In job descriptions state that an integral part of the job is to come up with ideas to improve processes, systems, procedures, products or services
- Remind your team that past success guarantees nothing in the future

There is a never-ending list of businesses and indeed entire industries who thought the good times were here forever – the Swiss watch industry, General Motors, Xerox, sub-prime mortgages, public sector 'jobs for life' – only innovation can safeguard your future.

5. SHORT-TERM THINKING

> *'Innovation is important. But let's concentrate on this quarter for now. We can look at this again next quarter, when we've hit the target.'*

This is the classic 'Western' approach to business. It means, of course, that we never get round to rethinking what we do because there is always the next quarter to think of. The short term and the long term can happily co-exist.

- Too much overseeing on your part may lead to the offering of short-term solutions only. Robert Sutton in his book *'Weird Ideas That Work'* talks of the danger of digging the seed up every day to see how much it has grown

- In the initial idea-generation phase, the creative process has to be separated from talk about money. Disconnect creative thinking from business benefits, otherwise you will only get short-term solutions or re-hashes of what you do already

- Bring in outside people, who have no interest in the next quarter, to stimulate long-term thought in your own environment

53

6. LACK OF OUTSIDE INTEREST

'How can I interest them? We barely communicate with that department.'

Ideas from your people may well extend beyond your team out into the far reaches of your organisation. But the silo mentality (teams and departments operating in isolation) may mean that minimal connections are made. How can you get that connectivity?

Suggestions:

- Encourage 'boundary crossing' – team and departmental managers can be highly protective. The fewer 'turf wars' that occur, the more receptive teams and departments are likely to be to innovative interventions

- Empathy – always see things from the point of view of other teams and departments. Asking them for that point of view is a good first step

- Cross-pollinate – different strands of the same organisation are more likely to come together and create something meaningful and actionable for the whole business

6. LACK OF OUTSIDE INTEREST

SUGGESTIONS (CONT'D)

- Invite other teams and departments to meetings that are based around ideas and innovations that will affect them in some way

- Seek invitations – ask other departments if one or two of your people can sit in on their meetings in order to get a clearer idea of how they work. This knowledge can be useful when getting support for your team's ideas in the future

- Get 'ownership' – the earlier you can get others involved, the more they will feel part of the process

- Encourage cross-functional teams – this promotes long-term collaboration and support across the organisation for innovation

- Take advantage of social networking forums favoured by Generation 'Y' employees, the so-called 'Net Gen'. These are often used by this group for peer-to-peer problem solving. Can you encourage this form of networking through your own intranet?

ORGANISATIONAL BLOCKS TO INNOVATION

6. LACK OF OUTSIDE INTEREST
EXAMPLES: SOMETHING OLD, SOMETHING NEW

In his excellent book 'The History of Ideas', Peter Watson suggests that the urbanisation of human beings in the fourth century BC was a prime catalyst in human innovation. Co-habitation on a scale never seen before required collaboration on 'the basic tools for living together'. Out of this closeness and collaboration came law, bureaucracy, education and all the apparatus required of a city state. Those basic tools are just the same for us in our 21st century organisations.

> *'The Geek Squad – who will come to your house and fix your computer – are known to creatively 'problem solve' by communicating across teams through social networks outside their company. The traditional method of referral to the manager has been by-passed. Too slow for quick customer response.'*
> **Sourced from Tapscott and Williams 'Wikinomics'**

7. WHY SHOULD I CARE?

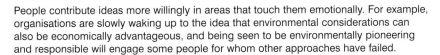

'Only profit matters here – we'd do anything for money.'

People contribute ideas more willingly in areas that touch them emotionally. For example, organisations are slowly waking up to the idea that environmental considerations can also be economically advantageous, and being seen to be environmentally pioneering and responsible will engage some people for whom other approaches have failed.

Suggestions:

- Management should communicate the values it believes in, not just its vision
- To illustrate how seriously the organisation takes special projects such as general environmental impact, carbon footprints or ethical sourcing of supplies, teams working on them should contain representatives from senior management
- Communicate that ethical and environmental issues are being incorporated into the business from choice not necessity. The business benefits are now undeniable

THE FINAL WORD – INNOVATION AT PIXAR

We know Pixar for their innovative film-making, eg *Toy Story* and *Ratatouille*. Ed Catmull, the co-founder of Pixar Animation, has attributed this to a number of factors including the following:

- *Everyone must have the freedom to communicate with anyone*. Catmull recommends the separation of decision-making hierarchies from communication structures

- Creativity is not a solo act. A Pixar film contains thousands of ideas. Similarly, most innovation requires a succession of ideas to bring the original idea to life

- It must be safe to tell the truth. As Catmull says: *'Management's job is not to prevent risk but to build the capability to recover when failures occur'*

- Create don't copy. The more senior you are the greater the temptation to copy previous success. You must accept the uncertainty that the brand new will bring

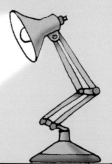

HOW DO YOU
<u>KEEP CONTROL?</u>

INTRODUCTION

It would be unnatural not to have some fears about creating a more innovative environment. You might be asking: *'What are the risks?'* *'Won't it just mean a free-for-all?'* *'How am I supposed to keep control?'* *'How do I know any of this is going to work?'*.

As a manager you have to separate freedom of thought (essential in innovation) from the freedom to act. In other words, you must encourage people to continually generate new and innovative ideas, but they must know where the space exists to act on their own initiative or where they need to seek managerial approval before proceeding.

So how do you let people have greater freedom to experiment in the job without losing control or turning the workplace into a free-for-all? This chapter features a practical tool to help you.

HOW DO YOU KEEP CONTROL?

MARK BROWN'S 4-BOX MODEL

This simple 4-box model was devised by educationist and creativity writer Mark Brown. It enables managers to separate the space in the job for action from the parts where deferment to a manager is necessary, or where it is just not safe to experiment. It starts with two simple steps:

Step one: think of someone in your team and make a list of all of the things that they do in their job. Go well beyond the restriction of the job description. You can do this for yourself too.

Step two: then read the descriptions of the four boxes on the following pages. As you do this, think about the items you have included in the list and place them into the relevant boxes.

MARK BROWN'S 4-BOX MODEL

The 4-box model looks like this:

It says that you can divide the work/tasks people do into four boxes:

Box 1: 'No Go' – where certain tasks have to be done in a controlled, pre-determined manner. *'Do it the way I tell you.'* Some jobs have this as their necessary beating heart – the military, for example – and only those who like this way of working should take on such jobs.

Box 2: 'Yes Then Go' – where management approval needs to be sought before going ahead.

Box 3: 'Go Then Let Know' – areas of the job where you can proceed as you see fit, but should tell your manager afterwards (and good managers will encourage this through regular one-to-ones, feedback, etc).

Box 4: 'Go' – where you are free to do parts of your job in the way you think best.

HOW DO YOU KEEP CONTROL?

MARK BROWN'S 4-BOX MODEL

Box 1: 'No Go' – certain tasks have to be done in a controlled, pre-determined manner.

- There should be no restriction on thought even if restrictions are placed on action – it's OK to 'think the unthinkable'

- Areas of 'No Go' include clearly defined codes of ethical practice, eg: finance; law – which cannot be transgressed; and safety – the breaking of health and safety legislation or short-cutting sensible safety procedures

- It is unreasonable to expect breakthrough thinking from people who have to work in this way for large parts of their time

- Nonetheless, 'No Go' is essential for at least a part of most jobs. People need to know what the No Go areas are (and that they cannot 'experiment' in them) – a breach here justifies admonishment

HOW DO YOU KEEP CONTROL?

MARK BROWN'S 4-BOX MODEL

Box 2: 'Yes Then Go' – management approval is needed before going ahead.

- People should be actively encouraged to have new ideas that can be applied to all aspects of their jobs. But they also need to know that some aspects of their job require approval before acting. There may, for example, be business implications the individual is not or cannot be aware of

- If an individual constantly gets rebutted here, they will slowly lose the capacity and the motivation to generate ideas. They need to see that some ideas do get taken up

- Like the 'No Go' box, too much of the job in Box 2 can be disempowering for the individual and time-consuming for you, if permission is constantly required

These first two boxes of the model are symptomatic of a tighter, controlling management style. They have a key part to play in the repertoire of management approaches. The skill is to know when and when not to apply this approach.

HOW DO YOU KEEP CONTROL?

MARK BROWN'S 4-BOX MODEL

Box 3: 'Go Then Let Know' – areas of the job where you can proceed but should tell your manager afterwards.

- If you have a strong culture of feedback in your organisation then it is likely that most creative experimentation will exist in Box 3. The open discussion flow between managers and managed usually means that 'let know' is a regular, natural occurrence rather than a prescribed one

Box 4: 'Go' – where you are free to do parts of your job in the way you think best.

- Those who have been working in your organisation for a significant period of time should have the majority of their job in Boxes 3 or 4

4-BOX MODEL: FINAL THOUGHTS

- If large parts of employees' jobs reside in Boxes 1 and 2, and you sense that new ideas are not flowing freely, ask if the shackles are being applied too tightly. Are your team members clear that space exists to experiment?

- Give people substantial amounts of time in their jobs to experiment with things that do not require management approval

Your people should be very clear what lies in the first two boxes – the areas of the jobs where they cannot experiment wilfully. In the second two boxes they are allowed more freedom. The quid pro quo is that mistakes will be made in these areas and managers have to accept and live with this – a natural hazard.

Something to think about...
Consider the origins of the credit crisis in 2008: perhaps the problem was the allowance of too much Box 4 action by the regulatory authorities and national governments, when boxes 1 and 2 should have been applied.

SHOULD WE ACT?

INTRODUCTION

The 4-box model will work well for you in a more formal situation, where you are able to sit down with individual team members and talk through the parts of their job where they are either empowered or disempowered to act.

Many ideas will fall into the first two boxes, in particular Box 2, where managerial approval is sought before acting. How do you decide whether to let Box 2 ideas fly?

One of your key criteria will be to assess how deeply the idea or batch of ideas (innovation is rarely about one single idea) will resonate. To do this we need to look at the type of innovation being introduced.

68

INNOVATION TYPES

There are broadly four types of innovation:

 These tinker with your habits – what you do 90% of the time.

 These introduce incremental or evolutionary change – 'thinking inside the box'.

 Type 3 innovations are likely to be dynamic and transformational – what we might describe as 'thinking outside the box but in the box's container'.

 Meta-change – 'What box?'

This chapter looks at the characteristics of these four innovation types. This information is essential in helping managers to assess risk.

SHOULD WE ACT?

 **MODEST CHANGE**

Don't ignore the small innovations for the sake of the grand gesture. Innovation has not been served well by gurus who advise throwing aside everything you have done in the past – almost as though you are in perennial 'start-up' mode. The 1 in 100 times when this is necessary is balanced by the 99 times in 100 when it is not.

For the 99% of the time when you are not throwing everything out, you need to think through what kind of innovation is needed – if any.

The right time to act?
Type 1 innovations are the easiest to act on because they tinker (in the best possible way) with existing practices and procedures. The effect, however, may be significant though probably not revolutionary.

People are more likely to act on innovative ideas they have thought up themselves *and* ones they can personally act on. If the idea is in Box 2 of the 4-box model and is fairly simple to act on – then why not do it?

 MODEST CHANGE

Justifying small actions:

- 90% of what you are doing is superb. Innovation is not about throwing everything you do out of the window. Your existing 'habits' are essential

- Your beautiful routine is part of what has made you successful – once gone it never comes back

- Yesterday's innovation is today's habit

- It is innovative to think through all of your existing practices and develop and gradually improve that which you do already. Innovation does not always mean radical revolution

- Saying 'yes' to small actions encourages people to think that their ideas do get taken seriously and can make a difference

TYPE 2 INCREMENTAL CHANGE

Type 2 innovations are conventional ideas that have a frame of reference most people will identify with.

The right time to act?
Type 2 ideas may have the following characteristics:

- Ideas that are being used in other parts of the business – easier to act on because people are familiar with the concept

- Industry innovations that have been introduced to the market by competitors. If the innovation is becoming the industry norm then you must act, eg MP3 players replacing old style personal stereos. But can you improve on the new standard?

- Old practices, now neglected, that still have relevance to your current situation. In the rush to change we sometimes drop the good stuff as well as the bad. If the rethink sounds sensible – why not?

TYPE ② INCREMENTAL CHANGE
CHARACTERISTICS (CONT'D)

- New recruits bringing suggestions adopted from previous jobs, particularly if they were working for a competitor. New recruits are untainted by your own conventions. What seems obvious to them may seem very different to you. At least some of their suggestions must be acted on. Remind me why you employed them?

- Service improvement suggestions from customers, that seem obvious once suggested but which no one had previously thought of. These could be truly revolutionary. Take customer suggestions very, very seriously

Because they won't be a shock to the system, Type 2 ideas are generally less risky – some of them at least warrant action. Failure will result, however, if the market – internal or external – needs a more radical (Type 3 or 4) shake-up.

73

TRANSFORMATIONAL CHANGE

Type 3 ideas are likely to be different from what your market (internal or external) is used to but not, perhaps, so 'out there' that there is no frame of reference (hence 'in the box's container'). Thus the action, while risky, is not at the extreme end of risk.

The right time to act?
Type 3 innovations are likely to transform what you do. They may, however, be a major and uncomfortable challenge to many in your organisation. You must act if you need to transform what you do now. But, do ask: *'is this the right idea to act on?'* Don't act on an idea because it's the only one you currently have.

There will be a limited frame of reference for those about to be exposed to the new idea – action will mean discomfort for those affected by it so consider the implications seriously.

TYPE TRANSFORMATIONAL CHANGE
LEARNING FROM OTHERS

- Type 3 innovations are often introduced initially by organisations outside your industry, that you can then adapt for your own

- New recruits may bring Type 3 suggestions adopted from their previous places of work – particularly where they come from non-competitors

- They may be ideas adopted from history which have been re-applied

Example
Taking note of the production line techniques used in Detroit's car manufacturing businesses of the 1950s, music entrepreneur Berry Gordy decided to apply them to his fledgling record label. The result was Motown Records, one of the most successful record labels of the 20th century.

SHOULD WE ACT?

 **META-CHANGE**

> *'You can't cross a chasm with two small steps. A big step is needed.'*
> **Lloyd George**

There are times when only the biggest,
boldest innovation will do. The market is
changing; new kids on the block are
changing the way your industry
operates; your products or services are
becoming obsolete; internal practices
are cumbersome and costly. Perhaps
your internal systems are causing
stasis and a revolution is needed.
Or perhaps you are seeking to create an
entirely new market.

If this is you and your situation then you **must** act.

SHOULD WE ACT?

 **META-CHANGE**

Type 4 innovations have the following characteristics:

- Ideas for which people say, *'that's impossible'* but where the step is being taken to make it possible

- Innovative ideas where there are no precedents

- Ideas that present true paradigm shifts in your internal and/or external practices – 'when a paradigm shifts everyone goes back to zero'. That means you *and* your competitors

- Ideas where customers are either 'religiously converted' by the new 'offer' or reject it for its madness

- Sometimes, as with Types 2 and 3, these new innovations can come from competitors or other businesses. The Swiss for example invented the quartz watch but it was the Japanese who developed the watch into a commercial product (and almost finished the Swiss watch industry in the process)

WHEN CONSIDERING ACTION

We know that a lack of innovation means organisational decay and death. Innovation is essential but:

- You must assess when and where to innovate

- You must assess to what extent you need to innovate – tinkering, evolution or revolution?

- When you start again you become the start-up you once were. You go back to zero – is it necessary for everything to go back to zero? Some things? Or just a very few things?

- You must assess and minimise the effects of the risk factors in any innovation

Assessing risk forms the basis for chapter 7.

YOUR ROLE IN ACTION

SPONSORING THE 'INTRAPRISE'

'The best (sponsors) will acquire more intracapital and become, in effect, internal venture capitalists. The result will be a more creative and more innovative free intraprise system.'
Gifford Pinchot – Intrapreneuring in action

Once you have decided to act on an idea or a series of ideas, you then have a primary role in supporting the people who are the principal actors – you are the sponsor of the 'intraprise'.

This chapter examines what your role is as a manager once innovative ideas are out 'in the wild'. Of course, many of these behaviours are just good management practice, but they become accentuated in the action phase of innovation.

GOOD PRACTICE

Share information
Good and bad. Managers who hide the bad lose credibility. Where information indicates success, share and celebrate it. This will win over the sceptics – most people resist change but come on board if success is verifiable. The trickle of support quickly becomes a waterfall.

Be a coach
Act as advisor and/or coach to your innovators – good management practice in any case.

Listen
Take constructive criticism on board. Innovative ideas will be strengthened because of it. In fact this goes further – actively pursue feedback. Don't be defensive when it is given.

Keep open-minded
Ideas that are born and nurtured in your team are easy to fall in love with. They are your team's babies and you may well be blind to their weaknesses and vulnerabilities. Don't be so blind that you cannot accept criticism, improvements or resource limitations.

GOOD PRACTICE

Be democratic

Being open to suggestions creates a harvesting of further thoughts and ideas, particularly from those implementing the innovation. Democracy means applying equal weight to all views. Those on the frontline may know more than the top team, and need to be heard.

Be the first line of defence

Innovators need support. Innovation will breed mistakes, criticism and duplications. You must publicly defend the innovators when these things happen. Gifford Pinchot (the father of intrapreneuring) refers to the need for 'calming the immune system' of those who see innovative change as an attackable foreign body.

Remember the customer

Innovation is meant to benefit others. In the navel-gazing that is often the world of service providers, the customer sometimes gets forgotten. A great question to ask with any innovation is: *'Does this add value in the eyes of the customer?'*

GOOD PRACTICE

Be a resource facilitator
You the manager have the ability to find resources that the innovators themselves may find difficult to access. Finance, of course, being a crucial one.

Keep going
Be persistent – success in innovation rarely comes easily. But don't be pig-headed. Sometimes you will have to admit that you backed the wrong horse and are moving on.

Take a measured approach
If, as a manager, you are not at the top of the hierarchy you may need to adopt a more subtle approach when introducing team-generated innovation. Look first at your own strengths as a team. These will include, at a base level:

- Lots of energy and commitment
- Small and adaptive
- Can choose/change strategy quickly
- Can make small changes that take time to be noticed when stealth is required (it often is in highly political organisations)

DON'T FIGHT THE ORGANISATION

Your organisation doesn't have to do anything. Larger organisations in particular have a type of institutionalised lethargy – often 'driven' by what you may see as highly bureaucratic processes. These processes can make it feel almost impossible to get anything substantial done at all. They give the organisation certain advantages over you, particularly in the following areas:

- Control of resources
- Power and control over staff
- Strength of numbers

As well as these three strengths – which will be common to almost all organisations – you may well be able to identify others that are more specific to your own environment. The point here is that there is nothing to be gained from ignoring these or choosing to have a fight in the areas where you are weakest.

DON'T FIGHT THE ORGANISATION

Do not 'fight' in the realm of organisational strengths. Work in the environments where your own strengths can be best utilised and work with your organisation in areas where it is strong. For example:

- Identify resource holders early and, as suggested elsewhere in this pocketbook, get them involved to secure their commitment

- Identify and work hardest on those who exercise the most power and control. Get into and understand their worlds

- Don't try a miraculous conversion of the workforce to your team's innovative ideas. Identify early champions across your organisation who can be your sales force – your informal networks are essential here

INFORMAL NETWORKS

Informal networks are based on hard-earned emotional bonds rather than hierarchical unnatural ones. This means people give support because they want to rather than because they have to.

Your networks will build up over time if you are able to help others with no expectation of personal gain. The reward comes when those self-same people are willing to support you and your team in the action stage of innovation. You must, long term, invest time in these networks.

Advantages
Informal networks can help you get round the system when you need to get things done quickly. They can:

- Speed up information flow
- Give a more up-to-date photograph of reality
- Provide the internal sales force for your innovation

ASSESSING RISK

ASSESSING RISK

INTRODUCTION

The risks involved in innovating will be based on two overarching criteria. These criteria should be factored into your thinking about the extent to which you might want to innovate. They are:

1. Strategy.
2. Likelihood of success.

These two criteria have a number of factors associated with them which will determine whether the innovative ideas or ideas will have the desired impact. Of course, the two are very closely linked. Tighten your strategy and your likelihood of success will increase. And, if there is a good chance of success it is, in part, probably because you have a good, clear strategy in place.

TWO IMPACT FACTORS

1. STRATEGY

Your strategy – the approach taken to implement the ideas – requires a combination of subjectivity, or most probably 'gut feeling', and a degree of objectivity. Has the strategy been thought through clearly? Factors to consider include:

- Are the objectives clearly stated and clearly communicated?
- What reactions to the changes do you expect and how will you deal with them?
  (Just because you think something is good doesn't mean that anyone else will)
- Are you properly resourced – finance and otherwise?
- Have you got the backing of key internal stakeholders?
- Are you aware of the risks; have you built-in awareness of risk at all stages of action?
- What about external customers – have you tested out these ideas with them?
- Are market conditions changing?

Too often a strategy is weak because the human dimension is ignored. Strategists are often good at process and procedure but can be less good at understanding behaviour.

ASSESSING RISK

TWO IMPACT FACTORS
2. LIKELIHOOD OF SUCCESS

This will be closely linked to the four types of innovation identified earlier. A tweaking of current practice (your habits) is far more likely to succeed than a proposed meta-change. However, a meta-change has more chance if the strategy is sound.

If the risk is a big one – perhaps Innovation Type 4 – don't be put off, if that is the change you need to make. Just be aware that success is much less likely. You will need to work very hard at your strategy to make the innovation happen in the way you want.

Likelihood of success is increased when:

- Your plan is based on tight analysis rather than a more nebulous vision
- The innovation is a Type 1 or 2 rather than a Type 3 or 4
- Has quick rather than big wins
- Doesn't challenge the status quo – causing minimal disruption to the team, department or organisation
- Has fewer people involved so human unpredictability is less of a key variable
- You have a clear and coherent strategy

KEY FACTORS TO INCREASE SUCCESS

YOUR ROLE

Personal factors for success:

- Where you have close personal control of the innovation rather than it being controlled by others
- Where you have the authority to act without having to defer to others
- Where disruption is kept to a minimum
- Where you are able to manage closely the change associated with innovation

Of course, a number of these 'likelihood of success' factors will form a part of your strategy.

KEY FACTORS TO IMPROVE STRATEGY

A great strategy can dramatically increase the likelihood of success and therefore innovation impact. By thinking and re-thinking strategy you tighten up the leaks that may lead to failure. Below are the strategy variables that will point to a greater chance of innovation impact if you get them right.

Great leadership
That's where you come in and really where innovation starts. The innovation has come from your team or department and you are backing it. They need you to lead it as much as you need them to make it work. Your leadership may well include securing the necessary resourcing.

Clear communicated vision
Is everyone clear on the goal? Could you express in one or two sentences where you hope to be with this particular innovative idea in, say, two years' time?

KEY FACTORS TO IMPROVE STRATEGY

COMPLETE HEAD & HEART COMMITMENT

Actions work best when we have emotional (heart) and rational (head) commitment.
Head will include:

- Financial and resourcing considerations
- Necessary systems (that facilitate *not* slow down innovation)
- Clear communication lines
- Risk assessment

Heart commitment comes from vision, leadership, attitude and motivation levels. It also comes from how far individual team or department members have felt involved and consulted – particularly when the original idea was generated by them.

KEY FACTORS TO IMPROVE STRATEGY
LIVING IN THE CUSTOMER'S WORLD

Customers are very good at telling us what they want now or in the very near future but they, like you, may not be able to articulate what they will want in two, three or four years' time. If you need to reflect the market **now**, then talk to the market.

If you need to reflect where the market will be in five years' time then customers may not be the best source of information – your intuition may be all you can rely on. Although some customers will have a clearer idea than you!

Support
Innovation is not best served by ignoring the people who can smooth its path. In business this means finance – you must seek their backing early. Elsewhere it means departments that will be part of the launch and facilitation of the innovative idea.

It may also mean early backing from a select few customers (internal or external) who can be your early champions. It must also be supported at the top.

INNOVATION THROUGH ITERATION
REDUCING RISK

High-risk innovations or innovation with little precedent (also potentially high risk) can be introduced incrementally by following a simple process – thereby reducing the risk:

1. Don't predict what the final outcome will be.
2. Begin with a basic prototype of the initial innovation – radical or otherwise.
3. Introduce the innovation to the client – internal or external – for feedback.
4. Consider the feedback from the client and modify the initial idea as necessary.
5. Present a second version to the client.
6. Listen to further feedback from the client.
7. Continue this process until the client is happy or as far as budgets allow.

Result
8. The client gets what they want with the essential input of expertise from you.

INNOVATION THROUGH ITERATION
EXAMPLE

ICT departments – not always noted for their communication skills – have pioneered the use of methods such as RAD, DSDM and Waterfall to develop new software for users. These methods help to introduce potentially radical innovation in incremental steps – with the full involvement of the client/end user.

The end user gets the IT solution they want rather than one which ICT thinks they should have.

Remember: introduce potentially radical innovation through your clients, not despite them.

SOFT HEART
PLUS HARD HEAD

THE INNOVATION TRIANGLE

Ultimately, even with a well-developed strategy and a good chance of success, implementation will come down to a balance between the 'hard' factors and the 'soft' emotional drivers that exist in all of your people. The soft drivers are:

Motivation: This is what we are going to do

Attitude: This is how we are going to do it

Energy: This is how much we are going to put into doing it

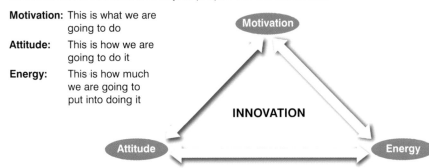

SOFT HEART PLUS HARD HEAD

THE INNOVATION TRIANGLE
MOTIVATION

The extent to which your people will embrace these soft factors will be closely connected to the innovation blocks identified in earlier chapters.

Motivation *(we want to do this)*

- How far do we connect with organisational vision and values?
- How far do we have a say in the setting of innovation goals?
- How much success have we met with already – have previous innovation attempts been successful?
- Is our team/departmental manager a clear and keen supporter of innovation?
- Do we feel that success is realistic?

SOFT HEART PLUS HARD HEAD

THE INNOVATION TRIANGLE

ATTITUDE & ENERGY

Attitude *(this is how we are going to do it)*

- Are we motivated? (see previous page)
- How much control are we allowed to have?
- How much freedom are we allowed to have in ways and means?
- Is our intrinsic attitude a positive one?

Energy *(this is how much we are going to give)*

- Is the individual and collective attitude a good one? (see above)
- Is there some edge – are we stretching ourselves (but not unreasonably)?
- Do we have a realistic attitude to failure? (we don't want to fail but it isn't the end of the world if we do)
- Are new people regularly introduced who provide fresh impetus?

RECRUITING FOR INNOVATION & ACTION

GOOD PRACTICE

This pocketbook has looked at what you can do with your existing team. Now let's look at how you can recruit for a more innovative environment. Recruiting doesn't just mean from outside your organisation. It can also mean recruiting, even temporarily, from within.

Moving beyond the jargon of 'team player'

Those ubiquitous words in recruitment advertising, 'good team player' too often mean: *'fits in with the team'*, *'doesn't rock the boat'*, *'gets on with everyone'* or *'is like me'*. It rarely means: *'constructively challenges'*, *'questions what we do'* or *'brings a different approach'* – which is what you need to be looking for.

Avoiding base level 'competence'

Proven competence is a starting point but too often it is used as an end point when recruiting staff. The competency based interview becomes a tick-box exercise. So what if one or two boxes don't get ticked? Recruiting only for competence may mean missing out on excellence or creative insight or uniqueness. Or passion for the job.

GOOD PRACTICE

Recruiting 'insultants' *('insultants' credited to Ichak Adizes)*
'Insultants' challenge your most fundamentally held beliefs. The longer your team, department or organisation has been around, the more you need insultants to shake you out of any paralysing ruts.

Sourcing the 'contented discontents'
These are the people who have the organisation's best interests at heart – they like working here! But they have in their minds the thought that things could be different – perhaps better.

They may be people working in other parts of your organisation, who are not valued because of their desire to challenge and change. They may exist in your team already but are perhaps not in the right role. Maybe their approach to the job isn't being nurtured or valued at the moment. Perhaps others sense threat when they could be seeing opportunity.

GOOD PRACTICE

Space for the talented?
Creative flair is a precious resource. Can you create a role for someone who is different, energetic and has a lot to offer? Even if they don't fit the pre-assigned role you had imagined?

Don't pigeon-hole
Why recruit an eagle and then stuff him or her in a pigeon-hole? Make use of what attracted you to them in the first place. Making someone do something to which their creative talents are unsuited is a waste.

What can we learn from you?
Recruitment interviewing can be a good source of ideas. People who are unencumbered by the traditions and norms of your industry may offer insights that would not have been generated by the 'contaminated'.

GOOD PRACTICE

Treat HR 'screening' with caution
HR screen out the people *they* wouldn't employ, depriving you of the people you *might* employ. Ask to see CVs early so that you can look for those who might not tick all the boxes but might have something different and interesting to offer.

Recruit for attitude and energy
Great attitude and great energy in the same person are priceless commodities. Great attitude brings engagement with the job (and thus ideas about how to do it better). Great energy brings the drive to put those innovative ideas into action. Often the technical element of the job – which we can over-emphasise in recruitment – can be learnt, but great attitude and energy are far harder to teach.

Employ one or two people you don't like
Recruitment often reverts to the 'mini-me' scenario – employing people with likes and interests similar to one's own. If you want people who challenge convention and the 'groupthink' tendency, recruit people who are less like you.

GOOD PRACTICE

THE JOB DESCRIPTION

Once you have recruited, re-think the job description. Here are some suggestions for inclusion:

- As mentioned elsewhere in this pocketbook, people should know that part of their value to your organisation is that they come up with ideas for improvement in their jobs on a regular basis – related to product, service, administration etc. This should apply equally to administrative departments

- Emphasise the development aspect of the role. That as the applicant's knowledge increases in the job, they should be looking to challenge how that role is performed

- Stress that it really is OK to 'think the unthinkable' (see p.36) and that part of performance evaluation will be based on fresh thinking bought to the job role

Why not think about introducing these suggestions for current employees – and rewarding those who perform?

SUMMARY

- Nurturing innovation means taking a holistic approach to it – what Mark Brown calls TIM or Total Innovation Management

- It means believing that people have unlimited creative capacities

- It means getting people to overcome the blocks that make them believe they cannot create

- Nurturing innovation means creating the right climate conditions for idea generation and action

- Nurturing innovation means balancing the requirement for free idea generation with the avoidance of chaos and free-for-all

RECRUITING FOR INNOVATION & ACTION

SUMMARY

- Nurturing innovation means assessing levels of risk and adapting approaches accordingly
- Nurturing innovation means recognising to what extent you need to be innovative – incremental or transformational?
- It means supporting the ideas of the team (your intraprise) as they are put into action
- It means acknowledging the 'soft' (people and feelings) as well as the 'hard' (process and procedure)
- Nurturing innovation means recruiting for innovators
- Nurturing innovation means recognising that innovation is a perpetual business essential – whether you work in the *for profit* or *not for profit* sector

FURTHER INFORMATION

SOURCE MATERIAL & USEFUL READING

Brilliant Idea by Douglas Miller, Pearson, 2007 (written for 'intrapreneurs') – Chapter 9 'Strategy' is particularly useful

Dinosaur Strain: Survivor's Guide to Personal and Business Success by Mark Brown, ICE Books, 1993

Hare Brain Tortoise Mind: Why Intelligence Increases When You Think Less by Guy Claxton, 4th Estate, 1998

Intrapreneuring in Action by Gifford Pinchot & Ron Pellman, Berrett Koehler, 1999

Make Your Own Good Fortune by Douglas Miller, BBC Active, 2006 (written for opportunity takers)

The Knowledge Creating Company by I. Nonaka and H.Takeuchi, Oxford University Press USA, 1995

The Ten Faces of Innovation: Strategies for Heightening Creativity by Tom Kelley, Profile Books, 2006

Weird Ideas That Work by Robert Sutton, Free Press, 2002

Wikinomics – How Mass Collaboration Changes Everything by D.Tapscott and A. Williams, Atlantic Books, 2007

Harvard Business Review Articles: *Breakthrough thinking from inside the box* by Coyne, Clifford and Dye, HBR, Dec 2007

How Pixar Fosters Collective Creativity, HBR, Sept 2008

RECOMMENDED WEBSITES

Dolphin Index Indicator 'DII' – which is probably the best researched and most comprehensive tool for measuring your organisation's current suitability for innovation against a series of 'climate factors'. **www.dolphinindex.com**

www.headscratchers.com

www.iceurope.com – Mark Brown's personal website

www.m1creativity.co.uk – a good summarising website of the different research projects available on innovation 'climate' factors

www.ted.com – I particularly recommend a speech on this site by Sir Ken Robinson, 'The Case for Creativity'

Oli Barrett's blog: **www.dailynetworker.co.uk**. Oli – perhaps Britain's leading networking entrepreneur – has a particular interest in creativity and innovation and is a good source of contemporary thinking.